Managing Maturing
Businesses

Managing Maturing Businesses

Restructuring Declining Industries and
Revitalizing Troubled Operations

Kathryn Rudie Harrigan
Columbia University

Lexington Books
D.C. Heath and Company/Lexington, Massachusetts/Toronto

Library of Congress Cataloging-in-Publication Data

Harrigan, Kathryn Rudie.
    Managing maturing businesses.

    Bibliography: p.
    Includes index.
    1. Organizational change—Management. 2. Corporate reorganizations—Management.
3. Corporate turnarounds—Management. I. Title.
HD58.8.H365   1988   658   87-45966
ISBN 0-669-17082-8 (alk. paper)

Published simultaneously in Canada
Printed in the United States of America
International Standard Book Number: 0-669-17082-8
Library of Congress Catalog Card Number: 87-45966

The paper used in this publication meets the minimum requirements of American National
Standard for Information Sciences—Permanence of Paper for Printed Library Materials,
ANSI Z39.48-1984. ∞™

88 89 90 91 92 8 7 6 5 4 3 2 1

Contents

Figures

Tables

Foreword

I t is always a pleasure to welcome a book that serves the needs of both practitioners and scholars in the realm of strategic management. Here is a volume that achieves the dual mission of improving management practice as well as adding to the knowledge base of the field. And it does much more than that. It tackles a subject of crucial importance that has been thoughtlessly neglected, largely for reasons of misconception or mythology.

The past few years have witnessed much public agonizing over the declining competitiveness of the United States in global markets. American management has been roundly criticized for sins of commission and omission. Some of the rebukes are valid and justified; others are rooted in popular misconceptions about managerial roles and priorities. Unfortunately, in many cases, managers themselves have accepted the myths for the reality and thus diminished the effectiveness of their contribution. This book not only deals with the realities, but its very title also provides a convenient framework for examining the mythologies I find most disturbing. Let me take up each of the title's three words: *Managing, Maturing, Businesses,* in turn.

Managing and the measurement of its effectiveness have always been closely associated with financial performance and the "bottom line"—and rightly so. Dollar figures are a convenient common unit in which diverse operations can be summarized, consolidated, and compared. They are also the units in which stockholder values are recorded. Financial analysis is indeed one of the primary tools of competent management. It is not, by any means, the *only* one.

It is true that some of management's canniest and most energetic efforts have been directed at minimizing cost of capital, maximizing returns on "floats," and generally manipulating the financial structure for optimal impact on reported net income. But financial management is not synonymous with, nor does it subsume, the full gamut of general management. Must we be reminded that a single financial figure—the net present value (discounted at some appropriate rate)—does *not* provide us with a valid comparison of two different businesses, in two widely diverse industries, and with dramatically different market shares? Yet it is just this kind of thinking that has given rise to the oft-repeated criticism that our executives think their job is to make money, rather than make automobiles, or shoes, or bulldozers.

In reality it is, of course, the invention, production, marketing, and distribution of goods and services that creates added value and thus generates sales and profits. The formulation of effective business strategies and the intricate operations of their implementation determine the achievement of corporate competitiveness and performance.

This book deals with the *realities*, rather than the myths, of managing. It examines strategic options, operational and structural alternatives, and their relevance to specific market and competitive environments. It focuses attention on that particular category of business identified by the second word in its title: *maturing*.

Maturing happens to be a heavily symbolic word that raises many long-standing, emotional reactions in American managers. Almost no one seems to love a mature business, and very few even admit entering that stage of the life cycle. The American dream of perpetual youth and the conviction that bigger is better (especially if it is also faster) have combined to malign the perfectly natural and unavoidable phenomenon of maturity.

For the typical American executive, maturity (alternately described as slow-growth or no-growth) is synonymous with stagnation, which is equated to decline, and which in turn is simply a euphemism for death. Clearly it is not a theme with which an ambitious manager should be associated.

This negative connotation is reinforced in the glib jargon of Cash Cows and Dogs and the mistaken, but popular, notion that all Dogs should be put to sleep at the earliest possible opportunity. No wonder that high-potential managers will eagerly grasp for the Stars, may grudgingly accept a sleek Cash Cow, but will resolutely shy away from any connection with a Dog. I might add, in passing, that the term *endgame* (used in this book and in other works dealing with maturity) does little to dispel the negative image, even if it conveys a useful concept to the sophisticated chess player.

Reality is, of course, quite different from the myth. A substantial majority—as many as two-thirds, according to this author—of all businesses in the industrialized world are "maturing." They employ the mass of every developed nation's work force, as well as the preponderance of its managers and executives. Neither are they a drag on their national economies, nor are their days numbered. As the author rightly points out, many an enterprise's half-life can span decades and will often yield remarkably impressive cash flows, earnings, and profitability.

This book is aimed directly at this large and crucially important segment of the economy. It examines the basic decision of whether to fight or flee and then proceeds to lay out a number of alternate survival strategies. It assesses the potential profitability of mature businesses and the need for restructuring the industries to which they belong. A number of intriguing examples provide empirical illustrations for the concepts and frameworks discussed earlier. A final chapter deals with the bigger picture: the implications for governments, public policy, and a new perspective on corporate strategies. It is this last topic, the corporate strategy, that gives shape to the "business" that managers manage. It also involves the last of the three mythologies evoked by this book's title.

Business is ostensibly the activity in which profit-making corporations are engaged. It is the corporation that has, historically, served as the mighty engine of economic progress in a growing American economy. Yet in recent years, and spurred by Wall Street insights, there has emerged a new vision of the corporation and its primary purpose. Viewed from the perspective of today's typical stockholder, a corporation is perceived as a "Trading Chip" whose value is determined largely by the anticipated short-term fluctuations in its share price. The flood of mergers and acquisitions of recent years and the frenzy of speculation and arbitrage in their wake have served only to reinforce a highly nonproductive view of the corporation.

In this climate, the market for corporate common stock has developed such novel concepts as the "break-up value" of a corporation; the "premium for control" it can command in a takeover; the extent to which it is "undervalued" by the market; and the relative ease with which it can be dismembered. In this kind of market a desirable corporation, that is, a "good" Trading Chip, is one that has an extremely narrow product line, invests only in quick-return assets, and is leveraged to the hilt.

It is obvious that the criteria for success as a Trading Chip have little to do with a corporation's competence in the production of goods and services. Yet managers may be all too readily tempted to apply such criteria to their own businesses, for defensive purposes if for no other reason.

When that is done, almost every hard-learned lesson in business strategy is forgotten or ignored. The efforts and progress achieved over years of hard work are dissipated, and long-term effectiveness is sacrificed for immediate gains. This is the severe penalty paid when myth substitutes for reality.

In a world in which the mythologies I have explored have gained so much popularity it is essential to remind managers of the realities in which they operate. This book is just such a powerful and competent reminder. In contrast to these myths, it focuses on *managing* operations and activities, not financial statements. It deals with the critically important *mature* segment of the economy, and it takes a *business* view of the corporation as a producer of goods and services, rather than as a vehicle for short-term capital gains. In this sense it is undoubtedly a book whose time has come.

Managers and scholars alike will find it timely, clearly focused, and solidly documented. Its author, my friend and valued colleague Kathryn Harrigan, is clearly in full command of her materials. She is traveling familiar territory—territory that she had helped explore and map as one of its early pioneers.

Like many other explorers, I suspect, I have always found my travels most rewarding when conducted by a first-rate, professional guide, closely familiar with every aspect of the landscape.

Boris Yavitz
Paul Garrett Professor and former dean
Graduate School of Business
Columbia University

Preface

This book extends my earlier work concerning the second half of a business's life. It illustrates how industry structures change when demand growth plateaus (and declines) and what managers can do to improve the profitability of operating in such environments. The first chapters help managers to confront the most difficult part of making restructuring investments: assessing whether sick businesses can be saved. Subsequent chapters help managers to confront the second most difficult part of restructuring mature industries: justifying revitalization projects to impatient providers of capital.

Avoiding Difficult Decisions

Too many managers refuse to admit that the transition has begun. Even more managers refuse to undertake the fundamental changes in working methods needed to thrive in maturing businesses. Instead, they try to hide the truth from top management by disguising the facts—presenting data about unit shipments of no-growth products in aggregation with those of growth products; showing only revenue growth (not trends in terms of industrywide unit shipments); attributing slowing growth to extraordinary (and nonroutine) events; or making other excuses. Because it is extremely difficult for managers to admit that industry growth has plateaued and sweeping industry downsizings are needed, they drag their feet and plead for "just one more year" to turn around the troubled business unit. Meanwhile they fail to make fundamental operating changes in their businesses. Too few managers will bite the bullet by thinning out product lines, abandoning costly customers, closing redundant plants, and making other hard decisions. They delay the inevitable need to restructure sick industries and revitalize troubled businesses, or (worse yet) divest problem businesses instead of working to improve operations therein either because they do not know how to improve operations or do not believe that providers of capital would fund programs of revitalization.

Few managers (or providers of capital) see much promise in maturing industries because competition is often so bitter there. Investing in maturing industries can be riskier than investing in growing ones because abrupt changes in industry attractiveness entraps invested capital. Technological progress and global competition shortens the half-lives of product and/or process innovations and prevents firms from recovering their outlays before the assets they develop become obsolete. Because a new slate of competitors often dominates competition in mature industries, aggressive global firms are raising the competitive stakes. At a time when capacity-rationalization is needed in industries like automobiles and steel, cash-rich global firms are playing a game of "chicken" in which they force local competitors' plants to close by building their own new, world-scale plants in overseas markets that they once served by exporting.

In Europe, aggressive global competitors are investing to get around tariff barriers and position themselves for 1992 when tariffs are harmonized and trade barriers are lowered among members of the European Economic Community. Then lower-cost European firms can displace inefficient local producers (unless governments reward complacency by subsidizing local firms). To accelerate this restructuring process, global firms are expanding their toehold investments aggressively to squeeze out complacent local producers. As aggressive global competitors further compress the benefits of investing in mature industries, high uncertainty about future demand and evolving competitive conditions spurs weak firms to respond with knee-jerk responses that ultimately undermine the viability of their entire industries. Like loose cannons aboard ships, the actions of unsuccessful firms ultimately discourage capital formation and harm other firms' abilities to lower their respective production costs.

Confronting Obstacles to Restructuring and Revitalization

Although many of these problems could be remedied through astute restructuring investments, some mature businesses are beyond saving. Managers must assess whether mature industries with seemingly unattractive structures can be revitalized. If they can be improved through divestitures or plant closings, changes in vertical integration, acquisitions to build up a critical mass, or other strategic investments, restructuring expenditures can be justified. If industries are so sick that they show little hope of yielding fair returns after restructuring investments have been made (or if governments obstruct the inevitable restructuring process), managers should not waste their firms' efforts and resources in fighting for pyrrhic victories.

After assessing whether a sick business can be saved, managers must confront why capacity adjustments do not occur and why working practices are not changed. If industries are not downsized, competition is volatile and head-to-head competitors dissipate their strengths in futile attempts to stave off the inevitable need to close redundant plants. Continued excess capacity sours investors' willingness to commit additional funds to facility moderniza-tions. Obsolete facilities sap worker morale, and uncertainty about future viability lowers productivity. Ultimately, consumers suffer when weakened suppliers can no longer afford to serve them as efficiently as before. Customers' delight with short-term, kamikaze-like price wars to fill empty plants gives way to dismay when it later becomes evident that domestic firms have destroyed their longer-term abilities to remain competitive against worldwide rivals and eroded their economy's manufacturing base. Too late they realize that eating one's seed corn in the autumn results in starvation in subsequent years, and failing to rationalize excess productive capacity in mature industries discourages healthy and well-managed firms from making further investments therein.

Managers must confront government policies that destroy shareholder value—by ruining the attractiveness of mature industries by preserving struc-tural conditions that entrap resources that managers had hoped to recover and by discouraging further expenditures. Surviving firms forgo the benefits of scale, scope, experience-curve, and vertical-integration economies when they are prevented from acquiring and rationalizing the assets of marginal competitors. Customers are penalized when they forgo the efficiencies of large-scale pro-duction, hence lower operating costs, because their vendors cannot afford to commercialize risky innovations or share the higher profits that accrue from greater operating efficiencies with employees in the form of higher wages. Customers are penalized when vendors are prevented from reducing waste by using vertically integrated arrangements to forecast demand for perishable prod-ucts and cooperative alliances to operate fully utilized plants of larger minimum-efficient scales.

Finally, managers must confront internal operating systems that prevent their firms from changing the working practices that create excessive costs, distort market intelligence, and impede strategic flexibility. Change is seldom comfortable, especially where firms have grown complacent. Yet change becomes inevitable when industries mature because (to use a cowboy metaphor), "there ain't room enough in town for the two of us!" Only the most efficient, most flexible, and most alert firms can hope to survive as their industries are invaded by hungry global competitors. Survival may mean sacrificing long-held beliefs about class distinctions, job descriptions, and comparable worth as work-ing practices are changed. The social fiber of inflexible firms may crack under the stress and strain of trying to adapt if managers have not laid the ground-work for modifying their operating systems in time. For many firms, time is running out.

I have been very lucky that conscientious and creative managers have been willing to share with me their ideas for adjusting to industry maturity. The managers whose successes (and failures) in running mature businesses are recounted herein provide the real excitement in this topic. They should be the role models for others to emulate because they bring home the bacon for fledgling businesses to consume. The real heroes of the 1980s are the managers who worked with competitors to strengthen their mature industries and retain their manufacturing skills by improving their firms' working practices. They deserve greater recognition for bringing honor to the task of solving problems and serving customers well.

Acknowledgments

T his study of mature and declining industries was made possible through funding from the Strategy Research Center, Columbia Business School. Having recently become its director, I am especially grateful to the corporations that support the research centers of the Management Institute. These funds greatly facilitate our scholarly investigations of strategic-management issues by covering expenses for travel, telephone interviews, research assistants, typing, and other necessary support.

I am grateful for the many ideas provoked by students at Columbia and for the support of my research assistants at Columbia Business School: Amy Zinsser, M.B.A. 1986 (of McKinsey & Company), and Brian Flynn, M.B.A. 1987 (of Bain & Company). I was especially glad to have the assistance of Rocki-Lee DeWitt (Ph.D. candidate), who helped with bibliographic and library assistance. Rocki collected the concentration ratios and Herfindahl-Hirschman indices for chapter 7. Jack Willoughby (former Bagehot fellow and currently senior writer at Forbes) immortalized my stories about endgame in Forbes' seventieth anniversary issue (July 13, 1987). Renata Karlin (Shell Oil, formerly of *Business Week* Executive Programs) encouraged me to create the seminar on endgame strategies, and Mary Anne Devanna (Columbia Executive Programs) sponsored and marketed the Arden House seminar on managing maturing businesses. I thank Mary Anne and the seminar's original faculty for their enthusiastic suggestions. Thanks also to David Lewin, E. Kirby Warren, and Bill Brandt for designing the topic into their executive programs at Arden House. Maureen Quinn-Bowen (Frost & Sullivan), Jules Dewaele (Top Management Center), and Shafiq Naz (Management Centre Europe) were also enthusiastic sponsors of my programs on industry restructuring.

This book is a product of my first sabbatical at Columbia University; I thank the university president and provost for granting me teaching relief. Thanks to Dean John C. Burton for his support and to his vice deans—to Paul McNulty for providing the research assistance needed to devote time to writing and to E. Kirby Warren for providing teaching relief needed for the Strategic Management Society. Thanks to W. Edwards Deming for his seminars and for his spirited assertion that only managers can improve their firms' working practices.

A decade later, I am quite pleased that Caroline McCarley (my original editor at Lexington Books) voted to take a chance on an unknown author in publishing *Strategies for Declining Businesses* when many publishers had rejected the manuscript. I am grateful to Bob Bovenschulte, general manager of Lexington Books (and an accomplished flipper of my overhead transparencies), for allowing me extra writing time so I could rest in the South Pacific.

Joy Glazener reassembled and typed the manuscript's many iterations after I had sliced and diced each draft into slivers of paper. As always, Joy kept her sense of humor while working under harrowing time pressures. With this book, Joy progresses from beatification to canonization. Flaws in this manuscript are mine alone; excellence is due to the generous support of Columbia University and its people.

1
The Problem—Widespread Industry Maturity

Over two-thirds of the industries within mature economies—in Western Europe, Japan, and the United States—are experiencing slow growth, no growth, or negative growth in demand for their products. Many managers responsible for these mature businesses fail to notice that demand is stagnant because they keep score in revenues, rather than unit volumes. These managers also do not compare their firms' unit shipments against industry patterns. Consequently, they fail to foresee the coming of the endgame—the last half of a product's life cycle or an industry's evolution—and the impending death struggles that often accompany endgame.

The Endgame

The endgame is the second half of a business's life.[1] As figure 1–1 indicates, it begins when industrywide sales plateau and continues indefinitely—sometimes for decades (or longer). The pressures of excess productive capacity can squeeze profit margins during endgame. But slowing (or declining) sales growth does not have to result in declining profits if remedial steps are taken. More than one-third of the companies I surveyed in a sample of declining industries were averaging pretax returns on capital deployed in excess of 35 percent because they learned to cope with the special challenges of endgame competition.[2]

Need for a New Competitive Approach

The onset of endgame means that more than half of all businesses have to run hard today just to stay in place in terms of return on investment, profit margins, and market share. Endgame means that there are now a great many managers who must find ways to run a troubled business successfully. For some, the problem is short run—the result of a tough and lingering recession that has increased competition and slowed sales. For many other companies, however, recession only heightens a long-term fact of life for their businesses: there will be slow

The Endgame

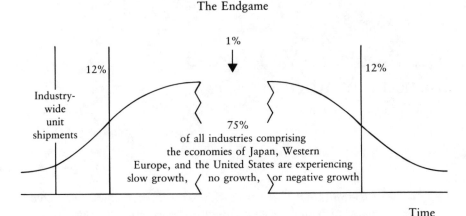

Figure 1–1. **Life-cycle of Industrywide Unit Shipments**

(or no) growth because of foreign competition, technological changes, or resource scarcities. Demand for the products of these firms will never revitalize, a competitive fact that too few managers are willing to acknowledge. Indeed, for many managers, even talking about the problems of flat or declining demand is taboo—like talking about growing old and dying in polite company. Reward systems in these managers' firms are skewed toward glamour businesses rather than cash-generating businesses, and the erosion of their firms' competitiveness reflects their unwillingness to bite the bullet by helping to restructure the troubled industries where they participate. Because the ability to adjust strategy and operations to changing market conditions is crucial to sustaining hard-won competitive successes, these firms are less likely to be among the "last icemen"—the firms that always make money in the endgame.

Managers must decide how their firms can cope with the adverse and inevitable competitive environment of endgame—a setting where stagnant growth and poor prospects for revitalized demand make excess capacity a competitive fact. Few firms can afford the grit of Dow Chemical, which shut in its newly completed Oyster Bay (Louisiana) refinery in 1982 to avoid the price wars it would have created by bringing excess capacity onstream. Yet many firms need a new strategic approach to face this competitive challenge.

The Competitive Environment of Endgame

Competition is more challenging in the endgame because sales growth is slowing, price wars are incited by overhanging excess capacity, and global competitors enter the industry even as overwhelmed domestic firms are exiting. Not only do government policies of income maintenance prevent inefficient plants from being shut down in some endgames, but they may also keep such plants running full tilt because it is cheaper to subsidize a money-losing plant than to support unemployed workers.

Slowing sales growth. Industrywide sales plateau in the endgame due to (1) demographics, like the end of the baby boom, or (2) technological change, like transistors replacing electronic receiving tubes. But occasionally the slow demand growth of endgame is due to (3) import competition that is created as the economies of newly industrializing countries vend their products in the global marketplace. Demand growth slows also due to (4) lifestyle changes, (5) conservation policies, (6) cheaper raw materials that use alternative technological and processing routes, (7) technological and styling obsolescence, (8) more attractive substitute products, or other reasons.

Being in the endgame does not mean that demand will be gone in five years. In the case of baby foods, the number of babies born per thousand fertile women peaked in the United States in 1957. It took firms ten years to recognize the problem of declining demand and another ten years to act. By the 1980s, these same firms were enjoying a temporary baby boom and hoping that babies would remain in fashion. Demand for cigars has been declining for decades, yet cigar manufacturers prosper. (Ownership of cigar firms has changed, but consumers continue to smoke.) Endgame looms now over the internal-combustion engine and mainframe-computer industries, yet firms continue to invest in them. Investing in endgame industries is riskier now, but many firms regard doing so to be well worth the added risk. Although there is no guarantee that a hundred-year-old business that has plateaued in industrywide sales growth will have another hundred years for its endgame, competition in many mature industries goes on and on.

Overhanging excess capacity. Regardless of the reasons for slowing shipments, when industries enter the endgame, the problem of excess capacity (and threat of bitter price wars) looms over them. Table 1–1 lists United States industries that have been experiencing declining demand growth. In many of these industries, otherwise well-managed firms have not been phasing out their no-longer-profitable product lines and closing redundant plants—a sure recipe for a disastrous endgame. The problem of excess capacity is inevitable in mature industries because of the long lead times associated with firms' commitments to new generations of costly and durable assets. (These are often investments made in anticipation of market growth that is forecast but never materializes.) Disbelief in (or failure to recognize) the endgame retards firms from making the necessary, subsequent reductions in productive capacity—especially among

Table 1–1
Industries Where Unit Shipments Have Plateaued or Declined[a]

Acetylene and acetylene-route plastics	Mainframe computers
Adding machines	Manual typewriters
All-wool carpeting	Metal crowns for home canning
Aluminum extraction	Metal gears (where plastic will suffice)
Appliance-control thermostats	Milk carton cardboard
Awnings	Millinery and millinery blocks
Baby foods and baby products	Oiled, waxed, and wax-laminated paper
Barbed-wire fencing	Oilpatch services
Basic petrochemicals	Old-style packinghouses
Beer	Paper mills
Belted nonradial tires	Passenger-liner service
Boilers for fossil-fuel plants	Percolator coffeemakers
Buggy whips	Permanent-wave machines
Buttons and hooks	Petroleum refining
Canned peas, other vegetables	Phonograph records and players
Carbon black	Pocket watches
Chemical reagents for quality-control tests	Power circuit breakers
	Power-transmission cable
Cigars, cigarettes, pipe tobacco	Prefabricated housing
Commercial-passenger airplane propellers	Rayon and acetate fiber (and fabric)
Copper extraction	Red meat
Cork products	Residential oil burners
Corsets, girdles, and brassieres	Sewing machines
Creamery butter, cheese, whole milk	Silk stockings
Diapers and rubber panties	Slide rules
Domestic-heating stoves	Soft-drink bottles
Electronic receiving tubes	Steam locomotives and passenger train cars
Evaporated milk	
Farming machinery	Steam radiators
Fountain pens	Steel
Gas-lighting fixtures	Straight razors
Germanium-based semiconductors	Sugar
Hand-held irons and ironing boards	Swiss watches, mechanical watches
Hard-eyewear lenses	Synthetic soda ash
Hardwood flooring	Tetraethyl lead
Harpoons	Tinplate cans
Horse shoes	Toys
Hospitals	Trolley-car services
Hot breakfast cereals	"Vanilla" computer time-sharing services
Ising-glass used in cars and stoves	Venetian blinds
Kerosene lamps	Vinyl phonograph records
Lace and net goods	Washboards
Lead pencils and crayons	Whiskey distilling
Leather belting for machines	Windmill water pumps
Leather shoes	Wiring accessories for construction
Leather-tanning services	Wooden containers
Linoleum	Wooden furniture
Low-greige cotton yarns	Wringer washing machines

[a]Declining demand in some industries (such as whiskey distilling and petroleum refining) may be temporary. In other industries (such as electronic receiving tubes), declining demand is not expected to resuscitate.

the smaller, inefficient producers that are most likely to pursue "maverick"[a] strategies to the detriment of other firms. A variety of other forces ("exit barriers," discussed in chapter 4) prevent larger, efficient producers from closing old facilities.

As demand shrinks during the endgame, only a few competitors' plants are needed to satisfy remaining demand. Higher profits could be enjoyed by all survivors if firms could make orderly changes in working practices early. Through preemptive investments, committed firms can prevent competitors from occupying the most desirable market niches—the niches where firms intend to fight bitterly to retain their competitive advantage. Through unambiguous signaling of their commitments, firms can even avert bloodshed—if industrywide consensus recognizes the importance of mutual profitability to remaining participants. Too often, however, endgame competition is not that rational.

Some firms hang on stubbornly because they expect others to exit first. Firms with deep pockets (or a long-term commitment to their industry) find ways to survive and become the last icemen. Unfortunately, as I explain in chapter 2, this cannot be a strategy option for every firm. There can be but one last iceman.

Global endgame. The difficulties of managing the endgame successfully are exacerbated by the fact that demand for some products is slowing simultaneously in several industrialized regions.[b] Managers in Japan, Western Europe, and the United States are all seeking new markets for their products simultaneously because their respective domestic demand has plateaued. Many

---

[a]"Maverick" competitors are firms that behave in unorthodox ways. Most frequently, mavericks are undiversified, or single business, firms that have no other activities to engage in. Mavericks are often also family-owned firms. For such firms, endgame strategies are stark choices between (1) attaining the technical efficiencies necessary to compete effectively in mature industries (see chapter 7) or (2) exiting. Maverick competitors are most likely to engage in short-term, self-destructive behaviors for the sake of filling their underutilized plants and keeping employees occupied. When they have thus depleted all sources of competitive advantage, maverick firms are more likely to plunge into bankruptcy (thereby harming their creditors and employees, while they "poison the well" for other firms seeking funding). As they thrash about in their death throes, maverick firms are also more likely to take desperate actions that destroy the value of assets owned by their competitors.

[b]The origins of worldwide excess capacity can be traced to the emergency capacity buildup during World War II and the return to the private sector of facilities built by federal authorities under wartime authority, as in the petrochemicals industry. Overcapacity was still a worldwide problem in 1988 because firms were investing as if the world economy were still growing at 4 percent rather than the actual rate of 2 percent. Easy availability of raw materials (and boundless optimism concerning demand growth) encouraged firms in mature economies to continue investing in capital assets and plant capacity without making corresponding retirements of older assets. Firms in newly industrializing nations were building world-scale facilities to foster economic development, create jobs, and earn foreign currency for trade. Their rapidly expanding and increasingly well-educated populations were rushing to urban centers and seeking jobs in factories. Meanwhile, local firms were expanding capacity to create those jobs.

managers have concluded that the only markets that can afford their firms' products are those in the other industrialized regions, and this realization has sent managers on buying sprees to acquire market access in regions that their firms did not serve previously. Overseas competitors enter the endgame as national boundaries become meaningless to their marketing campaigns. Where assets cannot be purchased outright, overseas firms are scrambling to forge strategic alliances. They are using joint ventures as well as a variety of other types of co-production and cross-marketing agreements to enter new sales territories.

Although local interests make the task of global capacity rationalization difficult in some markets, aggressive firms know that investments in reindustrialization that result from playing the endgame well place market-share leadership in the hands of stronger, surviving firms. In some mature industries, these last icemen are neither the pioneering firms nor those that were dominant during the growth years. Instead, a new slate of competitors often dominates endgame competition. Realizing this, aggressive international firms are raising the competitive stakes. At a time when capacity rationalization is needed in industries like automobiles and steel, cash-rich international firms are playing a game of "chicken" in which they force local competitors' plans to close by building their own new, world-scale plants in overseas markets that they once served by exporting.[3]

The Need for Preemptive Action

Many managers refuse to acknowledge that these changes are occurring. They refuse to face the ugly reality that theirs are sick businesses or that their firms' strategic postures are simply wrong. Yet there is an urgent need for managers to distinguish between industries where their firms are merely uncompetitive and those that are entering the endgame. Perceptive managers can help strong firms to reposition themselves to serve the most attractive market niches in endgame, once managers have identified how demand will grow (or decline) and how competitors will react to slowing growth. The difference between running out a doggy business and finding new opportunities in endgame is largely a difference in attitude and infrastructure. Once managers have selected appropriate endgame strategies, they must strive to execute those strategies successfully while reducing the pain associated with the process of adjusting to flat industrywide growth.

A Theoretical "Black Hole"

Until I studied the endgame, very little attention had been given to the problems of industries facing declining demand and to the responses appropriate for firms within them. The existing literature could be divided into four categories: literature concerning declining brands (or models) of a product,[4] literature concerning divestitures,[5] life-cycle literature,[6] and strategic-portfolio literature.[7] None of these literatures made any attempt to sort out the factors that influence the strategic choices managers will face during prolonged industrywide sales declines. Most of these writings looked at only one pattern of declining product or industry demand and espoused only one strategy alternative for coping with this problem. Unfortunately, such a simplified view of the strategies appropriate for mature industries is *inadequate* for the needs of managers running businesses that are entering the endgame. Differences in industry structures, in the reasons for plateaued sales, in expectations regarding future demand, in the strengths of different competitors, and so on, may substantially alter particular firms' performances in the endgame. Managers need to understand how these forces affect their mature industries and what they can do about it (see chapter 3).

Always Winners

There were winning firms in each of the industries I studied.[8] Frequently, leading firms were not among those winners because they had grown complacent and allowed more nimble firms to overtake them. Sometimes the losers were simply not cost competitive. Frequently, they had invested in capital assets instead of the noncapital systems needed to serve laggard customers effectively. Occasionally, the losers embraced customers that were too costly to serve well. But in every industry examined, good cash flows and returns on invested capital were attained in businesses facing slowing demand through skillful management. "Skillful" management meant changing how things were done in terms of (1) reading what customers wanted, (2) relaying this information through the organization, and (3) delivering consistent value to customers. It also meant using tactics that were consistent with the endgame strategies and paying close attention to the details of implementation.

Winning firms recognized that cash-generating businesses require a different set of management skills than those required when industries are young. Their managers used a special set of endgame strategies to cope with the problems of stagnant growth that differed significantly from the strategies embraced by businesses operating in growth environments (see chapter 2). They followed through with tactics that enabled their firms to change working practices to suit their strategies (see chapter 5).

New Industry Relationships

Once managers have confronted the bitter reality that their businesses are entering the endgame, difficult decisions must be made. Make-or-buy relationships that were once assumed to be critical to competitive success must be reevaluated as competitive conditions change. Vertical integration strategies must be fine-tuned to suit new competitive realities. It may be necessary to adopt unorthodox forms of business relationship with outsiders—especially if no ready buyers for firms' assets are available. Joint ventures may become preludes to divestiture if competition in the endgame sours.

An awareness of how to make resource allocation choices among mature businesses improves a firm's performance. Managers can determine whether to stay and fight—or retreat—in mature businesses only by assessing whether industries warrant further investments, whether firms' competitive strengths suggest they will be survivors, and whether competitors' strategic commitments to industries will make implementation of firms' transformations messy.

Timing

Firms' key strategy problems as their businesses confront endgame are those of timing. Managers' analyses of this problem must suggest not only which strategies are feasible, but also when to implement decisions to buy competitors' assets, drop part of firms' product lines, or exit completely. All the tactics described in the chapters that follow were executed with varying degrees of success by some of the firms that I studied. Other firms' assets were trapped within businesses facing declining demand. The differences in these firms' performances were largely differences in timing and in judgment, but the problems that confronted them were similar across industry boundaries.

Some of the strategy alternatives sketched in chapter 2 necessitate early execution if they are to succeed. Notably, where reinvestments or repositioning will be required in order to remain in mature industries, managers must commit their firms' resources before competitors can maneuver into more advantageous positions. Similarly, exits should be executed before asset resale markets sour. Although it may seem desirable for firms to wait for situations to become less uncertain, waiting could be detrimental. Firms cut off their strategy options (and their respective promises of profitable performance) by waiting.

Notes

1. Although the endgame in chess is the final phase of play and is associated with a serious reduction of forces, *Endgame* is also the title of Samuel Beckett's existential drama where players are not driven out. Instead, status quo returns with the final curtain. Similarly in business, successful endgame strategies may reduce productive capacity to match flagging demand, but such frictionless rationalizations are not guaranteed. They must be consciously managed or no advantage is gained, despite the competitive energies expended.

2. In the 1980 sample (which was comprised of sixty-one businesses facing industrywide declining demand), 9 percent of the firms enjoyed average returns on

invested capital of 60 percent (the highest return was 180 percent), 5 percent enjoyed average returns of 55 percent, and 25 percent enjoyed average returns of 35 percent. Losses were incurred by 8 percent of the sample, and 13 percent of the firms merely broke even. The remaining 38 percent of the sample earned a lackluster average return on invested capital of 15 percent.

3. Identities of surviving firms sometimes change in endgame because overseas competitors with differing expectations about performance requirements and payback horizons find markets that domestic firms disdain to be attractive. For example, according to the U.S. Department of Commerce, the book value of U.S. chemical-firm assets owned by non-U.S. firms reached $26.5 billion by June 1987. These owners included Britain's ICI, Anglo-Dutch Shell Chemicals, Switzerland's Ciba-Geigy, and West Germany's Hoechst, Bayer, and BASF. Non-U.S. firms owned $22.7 billion in U.S. property, $15.4 billion in U.S. insurance firms, $11.6 billion in U.S. banks, and $10.4 billion in U.S. retailing firms. Non-U.S. oil companies owned $29.8 billion in U.S. assets (including refining and petrochemical operations).

4. R.S. Alexander, 1964, "The Death and Burial of Sick Products," *Journal of Marketing*, April:1–7; P. Kotler, 1965, "Phasing Out Weak Products," *Harvard Business Review*, vol. 43, no. 2, March–April:107–118; A.C. Hutchinson, 1971, "Planned Euthanasia for Old Products," *Long Range Planning*, December; R.T. Hise and M.A. McGinnis, 1975, "Product Elimination: Practice, Policies and Ethics," *Business Horizons*, June:25–32.

5. A. Bettauer, 1967, "Strategy for Divestments," *Harvard Business Review*, vol. 45, no. 2, March–April:116–124; R.H. Hayes, 1972, "New Emphasis on Divestment Opportunities," *Harvard Business Review*, vol. 50, no. 4, July–August:55–64; J.W. Davis, 1974, "The Strategic Divestment Decision," *Long Range Planning*, February:00–00.

6. R.D. Buzzell, 1966, "Competitive Behavior and Product Life Cycles," in J.S. Wright and J.L. Goldstucker (eds.), *New Ideas for Successful Marketing*, Chicago: American Marketing Association, 46–68; C.R. Wasson, 1974, *Dynamic Competitive Strategy and Product Life Cycles*, St. Charles, Ill.: Challenge Books; D.K. Clifford, Jr., 1976, "Managing the Product Life Cycle," in R.R. Rothberg (ed.), *Corporate Strategy and Product Innovation*, New York: Free Press, 21–30.

7. S. Tilles, 1966, "Strategies for Allocating Funds," *Harvard Business Review*, vol. 44, no. 1, January–February:72–80; Boston Consulting Group, 1972, *Perspectives on Experience*, Boston: Boston Consulting Group; E.E. Carter and K.J. Cohen, 1972, Portfolio Aspects of Strategic Planning, *Journal of Business Policy*, vol. 4, summer:8–30.

8. In *Strategies for Declining Businesses* (Lexington, Mass.: Lexington Books, 1980), Harrigan used field studies and a delphi interview methodology to track how sixty-one firms in eight U.S. industries coped with declining demand and excess capacity during the years 1960 to 1978. Sample industries included electronic receiving tubes, baby foods, cigars, leather tanning, percolator coffee makers, synthetic soda ash, acetylene, and rayon fiber. In *Strategies for Vertical Integration* (Lexington, Mass.: Lexington Books, 1983), Harrigan added the experiences of whiskey distillers and petroleum refiners to her sample of endgame strategies. Sample industries were chosen from seven-digit SIC classifications using U.S. Department of Commerce *Census of Manufactures* data concerning *unit* shipments and were investigated using field studies.

In *Strategies for Joint Ventures* (Lexington, Mass.: Lexington Books, 1985), Harrigan added the experiences of firms in the automobile, computer, electronic component, farm and industrial equipment, metal processing and fabrication, petrochemical, pharmaceutical, and steel industries to her sample of industries that were entering the endgame. Sample industries were chosen from announcements in *Mergers and Acquisitions* and *Predicasts' Index of Corporate Change*. Data were gathered through field studies and survey questionnaires.

2
Strategy Options—Flee or Fight?

T his chapter introduces the endgame strategies and the tactics needed to implement them.[1] Although divestiture is among the strategy alternatives I discuss, my remarks focus primarily on strategies for navigating mature businesses through endgame competition. Most of chapter 2 is directed to managers who realize that strong firms possess the ability to reposition themselves in mature and declining businesses to serve the most attractive market niches once they have identified (1) how demand will decline and (2) what competitors are likely to do in response to stagnant demand. Smart managers have been making money in declining industries ranging from acetylene-route plastics to wringer washing machines (see table 1–1), but endgame competition is not an activity that every firm is well suited to engage in. The "last iceman" cannot afford to be complacent. Even when it dominates an endgame market, managers within the surviving firm must strive for continual improvements in operations. Unfortunately, some managers do not know what is needed to improve their firms' value-adding capabilities.

Knowing when to exit and when to remain (and invest aggressively) is a subtle skill that involves knowing what customers value, anticipating what they will find desirable, foreseeing how demand will deteriorate, and reading what competitors will do about it. The first mental barrier to overcome in formulating endgame strategy is seeing that there will be excess capacity as demand plateaus. The second barrier is choosing what to do about it. Part of the endgame battle can be won through psychological warfare, but many large and diversified firms are complacent. Their managers believe that slumping businesses absorb too much managerial attention to salvage and use too many resources that might be better deployed elsewhere.

Such attitudes would be justified if firms truly had attractive, alternative uses for their capital and human assets. Too often their managers simply seek to run businesses where it is easy to succeed and plead for government protection from stronger competitors where it becomes difficult to succeed because they lack the wherewithal to bring their own operations abreast with those of rivals. As I explain below, these are the very firms that should *quickly* divest themselves of businesses facing stagnant demand because their employees do not know how to manage in the endgame effectively. Unfortunately, some of these firms are slow to exit. They are more likely to respond to declining demand by favoring their historical tactics rather than by adjusting their activities to suit the strategy they hope to pursue. Successful firms, by contrast, are flexible in their tactics.

Strategy Alternatives

A number of different types of strategies have proved to be successful in mature industries. Some firms, such as E.I. du Pont de Nemours in rayon, exited quickly after recognizing that demand for their products was deteriorating. Other firms milked their endgame businesses, as PPG Industries did in synthetic soda ash, and exited later when they had recovered enough cash. Still other firms, such as Regal Ware, Inc., in percolator coffee makers, stuck it out through the bitter part of the endgame until most competitors had discontinued their products, and reaped the benefits of doing so.

In any particular endgame environment, some strategy alternatives were more appropriate than others, and some firms enjoyed a greater range of alternatives by virtue of how well they had prepared themselves (through their past use of asset deployment) for the problems of slow demand growth and excess capacity. Some management teams were better prepared for industry maturity than others. As long as their industries' long-term outlooks were favorable, these managers renovated plants and machinery, acquired the assets of competitors, or otherwise increased their firms' commitments to mature businesses, even while aggregate demand was falling as a result of obsolescence, demographics, or cultural changes. They accurately diagnosed the outlook for the various market segments of their firms' lines of business and analyzed where enduring demand might exist. While managers in other firms were wringing their hands over the industry's misfortunes, these managers saw opportunities that made them increase their firms' investments in declining businesses. Most important, these managers adjusted their firms' tactics with respect to (1) pricing, (2) asset deployment, (3) cost-effectiveness measures, and (4) timing of implementation to suit the endgame strategies their firms pursued.

From the many industry histories I examined, patterns suggesting five strategic responses to demand maturity or decline can be identified. These include (1) divesting businesses quickly by disposing of their assets as advantageously as possible, (2) milking firms' investments in the troubled business to recover cash quickly, regardless of their resulting competitive postures therein, (3) increasing firms' investments in troubled businesses (to dominate or gain better competitive positions), (4) holding firms' investment levels until uncertainties about the future of troubled industries can be resolved, and (5) shrinking firms' investments selectively by sloughing off unpromising products or market segments while simultaneously strengthening their positions within lucrative niches of enduring customer demand with better-focused lines of products.

Exit Strategies

Two of these strategy alternatives—divest now and milk the investment—are tantamount to concluding that there is little promise of acceptable profitability in the forthcoming endgame competition. The three other strategies— increase the investment, the holding pattern, and shrink selectively—suggest that the structures of endgame industries are favorable and firms are well enough positioned to exploit the opportunities of endgame.

Sometimes businesses are well positioned to survive and prosper in endgame competition if their managers are freed from the constraints that large, multibusiness corporations impose. Opportunities that seem immaterial to businesses that are part of large firms may look quite attractive when those same businesses are independent. Remaining pockets of demand are often smaller than the markets that big firms are accustomed to serving. For that reason, most large firms will embrace one of the exit strategies—divestiture or milking—as competition within the endgame progresses. The firms best suited to compete when demand declines are often medium-sized firms with managers that are willing to devote greater attention to the details of improving endgame businesses than managers within larger, diversified firms are. Many endgame survivors were spun off from larger firms when competition grew too volatile for them to tolerate.

Divest Now!

Approach. The objective of early exit is prudent timing. If managers hope to recover much of the value of their firms' assets, this could mean a quick sale or their abandonment. Managers may even sell their firms' assets to competitors, if necessary, or junk them (as Diamond Shamrock did in acetylene) to avoid sustaining chronic losses and release working capital to other uses that managers believe will yield better returns. Firms that cannot manage effectively in beleaguered environments should exit from them quickly to give other firms the chance to earn the high returns that are available from well-managed endgames. Firms that cannot capture a secure customer foothold should sell out as soon as possible, as did Raytheon (a defense contractor and former manufacturer of television receivers), which stopped making vacuum tubes back in 1963 by selling its designs and equipment to Toshiba. Firms that must be especially attentive to the demands of pension fund managers or other providers of capital that seek short-term payoffs should exit quickly from endgames that they cannot hope to win. Venture capitalists may become preferred investors for these businesses after they have been spun off.

Firms may wish to divest quickly if competitors are cutting their prices severely or otherwise impairing industrywide profitability. Moreover, if their analysis of industry traits suggests that their business environment is evolving to one that will not be hospitable for other types of strategies (and if competitors' behaviors reduce the likelihood that later exits will yield returns as high as immediate divestitures), it may be advantageous to cash in on declining businesses *early*, before other firms reach the same conclusion. This is what Ashland Oil did in petroleum-exploration and -production activities, what Raytheon did in electronic receiving tubes, and what du Pont did in rayon acetate. By contrast, although most U.S. whisky distillers stopped making their own barrels by 1988, only the first distillers who discontinued their cooperage operations were able to sell their barrel-making assets satisfactorily.

Timing. Timing is crucial in implementing all of the endgame strategies, but none more so than the early divestiture strategy. Exit requires early execution if it is to succeed because outsiders (sometimes called the "bigger fools") will buy a finite number of plants from firms that wish to exit. Firms that exit early are less concerned with how much longer demand will endure than with how much value can be retrieved by leaving an endgame setting immediately. (Some endgames last a century or longer—as in the example of declining demand for cigars—while others are short-lived, as was demand for red dye number 2, a carcinogenic food additive.) Expectations concerning future demand affect the value that departing firms can hope to recover from their endgame businesses, and the highest salvage values are recovered early in the endgame— before other firms (and potential buyers of their endgame assets) recognize that the endgame has begun.

Milk the Investment

Approach. Most mature businesses generate more cash than they can consume. The proportion of cash extracted from mature businesses when the milking strategy is pursued makes this alternative far more drastic than harvesting strategies. Managers milk businesses to increase their firms' immediate return on investment (by surrendering market share) or to funnel as much cash as possible to other projects quickly. The most effective milking strategies are executed without regard for subsequent market position, and the greatest risk in pursuing milking strategies within mature businesses is that uncontrollable, adverse events may force firms to shut down early before managers can extract all of the value invested in their businesses. Milking strategies are "second best" alternatives because if early exit had been available at an attractive price, managers would have divested their firms' interests rather than milk them.

Examples of firms that milked their businesses before finally exiting include Spencer Products in its leather-tanning venture and General Electric in percolator coffee makers.

When to milk. Milking strategies are used when immediate exit is impossible (as a result of exit barriers). They are inherently risky because they represent managers' assessments that further investments in that business are unwarranted and the best solution is precluded. Moreover, the competitive environments in industries where milking strategies have been selected are frequently so risky that panic-stricken competitors may be pricing their products below cost just to keep their facilities utilized, or other adverse structural traits may be eroding industry profit margins (see chapter 3).

Pricing. If managers are milking endgame businesses, they use price discrimination to extract as much cash from their sales as possible. Loss of customers is not a concern because managers know that their firms will be able to retain the patronage of some customers even as they raise their firms' prices, due to those customers' short-term, switching-cost barriers. If endgames are expected to collapse into price warfare soon, price increases should be substantial and be posted quickly—before it is too late.

Asset deployment. Milking strategies are most effective where managers consolidate functions within the skeletal organizations they create while transferring resources to other product lines. Because managers make no reinvestments in endgame businesses when they are milking them—not even for maintenance—they do not increase their firms' exit barriers for the sake of short-term gains in market share. Because the milking strategy's objective is most like that of outright divestiture, managers must avoid increasing their firms' asset bases while they strive to cut operating costs.

Toothpaste. In an extreme example of milking, two young entrepreneurs lived well for years off the heavy advertising campaign that established the brand name "Ipana" for toothpaste. Bristol-Myers developed Ipana and paid for the advertising campaign in the 1950s, but dropped the toothpaste later. It sold the use of Ipana's brand name to L'Amore. All the entrepreneurs at L'Amore had to do was put dentifrice in tubes and place the tubes in stores. Customer loyalties made it easy to distribute the product because the old advertising campaign was so memorable.

Cost effectiveness. Managers drive their firms to cost effectiveness while pursuing the milking strategy by cutting sales and administrative costs. Managers learn to operate in endgames with a significantly reduced sales force (or use manufacturers' representatives instead of firms' own employees) while they milk their businesses. Instead of making expenditures for promotional advertising, they rely on company image (and cumulative goodwill from past advertising expenditures) for sales momentum while they run out trapped assets. Managers who are milking their firms' investments in mature businesses terminate long-term contracts and seek outsiders to handle selling, distribution, and servicing tasks for them. Freight consolidators replace firms' own truck fleets as shipments decline to less-than-carload quantities. Simultaneously, managers build alternative distribution systems, perhaps by de-integrating and using outsiders to service difficult market segments, when they are milking their firms' investments.

Timing. Although firms that pursue milking strategies do not intend to stay long in the market, they must move quickly to capture the best prices for their products in order to enjoy abundant cash flows for the longest time period. Preemption to reach the most lucrative customers is important in milking strategies because competitors may also be trying to position themselves to milk their respective endgame businesses.

Survival Strategies

All of the survival strategy alternatives discussed herein assume that mature businesses generate funds that firms use elsewhere. Unlike the exit strategies discussed above, however, implementation of the survival strategies will require cash. Indeed, the most aggressive strategies for endgame competition may require resource allocations in excess of the amounts firms readily designate for businesses that face stagnant demand and the threat of volatile competition.

Although more than half of the industries in Western Europe, Japan, and the United States face slow growth, no growth, or negative growth in unit shipments, only a few firms see tremendous opportunities in the endgame. Because these firms are prepared to invest aggressively to survive endgame competition, their managers can take the longer-term perspective necessary to make major changes in firms' systems of operation. They can enter into the long-term supply contracts necessary to improve quality control while reducing costs and undertake other aggressive improvements in how their firms anticipate customers' needs.

If they are done well, the three survival strategies—increase the investment, the holding pattern, and shrink selectively—are tantamount to accelerating a steamroller as it speeds downhill, ripping off the vehicle's steering wheel, and waving it aloft. By choosing these strategies, managers are signaling unambiguously to competitors that their firms intend to remain in mature industries—and possibly will make the struggle difficult for adversaries that might copy their decisions. Survival strategies are backed up by organizational restructurings (for greater flexibility) and ardent selling campaigns directed at the lucrative pockets of demand on which firms will focus. Even if these efforts do not make firms become their industries' last icemen, it may be possible to become preferred vendors to more attractive customers by improving their management systems and working practices.

Becoming the "Last Iceman"—Increase Investment Level

Approach. The last iceman always makes money because customers will pay $20 for the replacement stem of a 1927 shower faucet when their alternative is a $600 replumbing job. Similarly, the price of replacement receiving tubes needed to control a building's elevator system would have to be very high before the entire bank of elevators was replaced. Surviving firms can serve last bits of demand very comfortably when competitors drop away—provided that the excess capacity that clutters industries is destroyed. Managers must assess whether it is worthwhile to take steps to make their firms become last icemen.

Increasing investments in mature (or declining) industries are strong signals to customers (and to capital markets) that managers believe that their firms will attain long-term advantages by investing aggressively. Firms reinforce their commitments to mature businesses by purchasing the assets of competitors who wish to exit or by taking other precautions to ensure that endgames do not degenerate into bloodthirsty price cutting when rivals experience excess capacity. (The short-term tactics that reinforce the long-term objectives of increased investment strategy may call for temporary price reductions to force marginal competitors out of the industry, as I explain below. In general, price wars are to be avoided during endgame.)

Automobiles. In the 1980s, the worldwide automotive industry suffered from vast excess capacity of 10 to 15 million cars per year due to the many plants built by new entrants to make small cars and trucks as well as the reluctance of established automotive firms to close redundant plants. For several years, the U.S. automotive firms hoped to be bailed out of their excess capacity problems by the next surge in demand or by persuading competitors to shut down their excess capacity. Meanwhile aggressive firms (like Honda) built plants in the United States with manufacturing capacities to make 220,000 cars. Honda further signaled its commitment to survive by creating a separate U.S. dealer network to market its upscale product line of Legend and Integra luxury cars.

Tires. As the automotive industry became global and auto makers forged international linkages, tire makers followed. The result was a major wave of restructurings. Under siege by Sir James Goldsmith, Goodyear Tire & Rubber was forced to divest its non-tire businesses. In 1987, Continental A.G. (of West Germany) acquired GenCorp's General Tire & Rubber Co. General Tire subsequently announced joint ventures with two Japanese tire makers. Sumitomo Rubber Industries Ltd. purchased Dunlop Tire Co.'s North American and European operations.

In December 1987, B.F. Goodrich decided to sell its interest in a tire joint venture, Uniroyal Goodrich Tire, to an investor group, Clayton & Dubilier. Under new ownership, the tire company planned to drop its old niche-marketing strategy to become a broad-based producer.

In February 1988, Pirelli bid to acquire Firestone Tire & Rubber Co., but Bridgestone Corp. of Japan was victorious instead. Firestone gave Bridgestone distribution access in the United States and manufacturing plants in Europe and would guarantee that Firestone tire-retailing stores would be supplied with Firestone-brand tires while also expanding the product line breadth handled by its independent dealers. Bridgestone also bought an instant 4 percent market share in Europe where Bridgestone had little market presence in 1987.

When to increase investment. Firms pursue last iceman strategies in mature industries when they believe that there are long-term advantages in doing so. Increased investment strategies are pursued where (1) firms see large and enduring pockets of demand for the product experiencing declining demand growth, (2) the cost of repositioning to serve these customers most advantageously seems likely to be recovered rapidly or is not substantial, and (3) few other competitors are capable of or positioned to serve the attractive customer niches advantageously. Increased investment strategies are easiest to implement within industries that have relatively low exit barriers, few maverick competitors, high switching costs for customers, and other favorable traits (detailed in chapter 3). Firms that pursue last iceman strategies are often cost efficient in manufacturing troubled products or sell patented (or branded) products to loyal customers. They are constantly improving their operations by improving their working practices.

Pricing. When firms pursue last iceman strategies, they avoid price wars. It may be necessary for them to shade prices downward—if any price changes are made—to maintain sufficient sales volumes to fill their plants. Aggressive pricing may also be used to edge less committed firms out of mature industries.

Asset deployment. The last iceman in mature industries strives to reduce competitors' exit barriers by acquiring their assets and serving their customers. Declining industries are made more attractive for firms that choose to remain through their willingness to (1) help competitors to exit, (2) act as suppliers to rivals who have discontinued manufacturing operations but continue to merchandise declining products, and (3) produce for private-brand resellers to utilize excess capacity. While last icemen are helping adversaries to exit through horizontal integration strategies, they are simultaneously increasing their commitments to endgame businesses by upgrading their products through investments for innovation, applications engineering, and quality control. Last icemen offer wider product lines than other competitors because they pick up the designs of rivals that have exited. Investments in promotional campaigns are made to communicate these product additions and improvements to customers and competitors—by reassuring customers that their vendors are dependable and warning competitors that winning in endgame will be more difficult than many of them had assumed it to be. It is important for last icemen to signal these intentions with great fanfare.

Receiving tubes and barbed wire. Aggressive last iceman strategies require a strong stomach and large bankroll to buy up the capacity of competitors and destroy it. In 1975, Sylvania (now owned by North American Philips) retrieved Westinghouse Electric's equipment for making electronic receiving tubes from a Taiwanese firm, Union Electric. Sylvania loaded the equipment on a barge, towed it into the Bashi Channel, and sank it to ensure that it did not face import competition from assets that Westinghouse Electric had trashed. Similarly, Broken Hill Proprietary Ltd. (of Australia) purchased and smashed the assets of twenty barbed-wire manufacturers to reduce industry capacity, and after purchasing fertilizer plants worldwide, Norsk Hydro restructured itself by shutting down 40 to 50 percent of its newly expanded fertilizer capacity.

Textile looms, fertilizer, and rayon. Whenever firms acquire their competitors in mature industries, opportunities exist to retire obsolete assets while revitalizing surviving plants. Last icemen avoid selling equipment from closed plants to scrap merchants, who may allow those assets to fall into the hands of competitors. Textile firms, like J. P. Stevens and Burlington Industries, smash redundant looms rather than see them sold to Third World countries that can dump outputs back into the global marketplace. Cargill, a family-owned grain trader and agribusiness firm, bought a bankrupt Florida phosphate-fertilizer company to keep the assets out of the hands of competitors. They learned from the adverse experience of rayon manufacturer, Beaunit Corporation, who sold its Childersburg, Alabama, equipment for scrap to a junk dealer only to have it resold to Spanish competitor, SNIACE. (The equipment was shipped to Torrelavega, where it was reassembled, operated, and used to compete against Beaunit's own fibers.)

Cost effectiveness. Managers that favor increased investment strategies can ensure that their firms will be survivors by investing in cost-effectiveness improvements. Their campaigns for doing so could include replacing obsolete manufacturing processes with investments in process innovations (to develop superior manufacturing technologies and other necessary skills). They could include selective vertical integration—investing in upstream players for cost-effective sourcing and investing in downstream players to reduce distribution expenses. They could also include cost sharing, by jointly using the nearby facilities of competitors and integrating ongoing activities.

Receiving tubes. An important part of attaining cost effectiveness is translating into action any knowledge concerning which products face price-insensitive demand and which products must be priced competitively in the use of redundant plants. During the electronic receiving-tube endgame, Sylvania rationalized the use of its Pennsylvania plants according to products' sales volumes and price elasticities. Sylvania manufactured the receiving-tube designs of competitors to give customers a second source of electronic components and acquired other firms' assets when they exited. In 1977 Sylvania rationalized its manufacturing system by weeding out the low-volume receiving-tube designs and transferring their production to its plant in Emporium. (The automated Altoona receiving-tube plant was kept fully loaded with longer production runs, making products that used general-purpose equipment and interchangeable tooling.)

For most of the year, the Emporium receiving-tube plant ran at only 10 percent of its engineered capacity. Once or twice a year, the Emporium plant made sole-source products, using specialized equipment and special production techniques. The low-volume, high-cost, and difficult-to-make receiving tubes were also made there. Because demand for the products made in the Emporium plant was price insensitive, customers bore the fully allocated cost of making those receiving tubes. Because Sylvania's Altoona receiving-tube plant was fully utilized in long production runs, Sylvania was able to retain the lowest industry-wide costs for its receiving-tube outputs until demand for the general-purpose receiving-tube products dwindled to volumes that made their costs too high to stave off product substitution.

Timing. Long-term planning is needed to make firms capable of implementing increased investment strategies, and this strategy is less likely to succeed if more than one firm tries to implement it. For that reason, last iceman strategies are risky and it is important for firms pursuing them to move preemptively into the market segments they intend to serve with *broad* signals to ward off copy-cats.

Crude oil. As demand for crude oil fell, OPEC members sought guaranteed outlets for their crude oil by purchasing refineries and retailing networks in their major markets—Western Europe and the United States. Direct-market access had become an overriding necessity for leading oil producers by 1988. When oil supplies outstripped demand in early 1987, Saudi Arabia tried to hold up prices by cutting its production of crude oil. Venezuelan and Kuwaiti output did not flag, however, because both nations were selling refined oil products through their own marketing outlets.

In January 1988, Petroleos de Venezuela, the Venezuelan national oil company, negotiated to buy a 50 percent interest in Texaco's Swedish and West German refining operations and was seeking equal partnerships with several other West European and U.S. oil firms. In 1987, Petroleos de Venezuela formed joint refining ventures with Southland Corp. and Union Pacific in the United States, with Veba A.G. in West Germany, and with a Swedish partner. It was negotiating in 1988 with Societe Nationale Elf Aquitaine to acquire its excess refineries and marketing outlets.

Other oil-rich nations joined the flurry to integrate vertically. Tamoil Italia (70 percent owned by Libya) bought the refinery and service station assets of Amoco Italia in 1983 and the marketing network of Fintermica, an Italian energy group, in 1987. In February 1988, Saudi Arabia negotiated to buy a 50 percent interest in Texaco refineries along the East and Gulf coasts of the United States, and some 45 other oil companies with refineries contacted the kingdom about joint venture possibilities. Nigeria was discussing the purchase of minority interests in Sun Company, Hill Petroleum, Mapco Inc., and Crown Central Petroleum Corp. of the United States, and in Petromed of Spain.

Kuwait Petroleum Corp. had discussed joint-venture possibilities with other vertically integrated oil companies but preferred outright ownership of its refining and marketing facilities, such as the 4,800 "Q8" brand gasoline stations in Europe that it acquired from Gulf Oil in 1983, from Hays Petroleum Services in 1986, and from other European firms. By February 1988, the Kuwaiti Investment Office had acquired 20 percent of British Petroleum, a firm that refined and sold more oil than it produced in 1987, and 47 percent of Spain's biggest private chemicals group, Union Explosivos Rio Tinto.

Hold the Investment Level

Approach. Holding strategies are pursued when managers conclude that their firms are already in the best strategic postures to compete within mature industries, but execution of more dramatic actions must wait until key uncertainties are resolved. In strategies of defensive reinvestment, firms match competitors' price changes and marketing expenditures and make maintenance investments in their plants to compensate for losses of operating efficiency, like Mobil's bottlenecking investments that enabled their oil refineries to run at lower throughputs.

Petroleum refining. Mobil Oil delayed the shutdown of a petroleum refinery for several years by intentionally fitting it with smaller-gauged valves. This artificially created "bottleneck" enabled the refinery to run at lower throughput volumes while incurring fewer of the cost penalties that would have been incurred by running the refinery at its most efficient, engineered capacity. In this manner, Mobil "bought time" until it could determine whether demand for oil was declining to levels that made the refinery's shutdown necessary.

When to wait. Managers put their firms into short-term holding patterns when their overall assessment of the endgame's potential is favorable, but uncertainty concerning a major contingency must be resolved—for example, exits of major competitors must occur, the viability of lower-cost, perfect-substitute products must be proven, favorable legislation must be enacted, and so on. When the predetermined "trigger point" is reached, managers switch their firms' endgame orientations to the more aggressive survival strategies—increase the investment or shrink selectively—if a favorable, foreseeable event occurs. They embrace one of the exit strategies—divest now or milk the investment—if unfavorable, foreseeable events occur instead. Because managers can be preempted from executing the more rewarding endgame strategies by waiting too long, holding strategies are viable only for a short time—no more than two or three years.

Construction machinery. Demand for construction equipment plunged by 70 percent from 1980 to 1983 as demand for coal fell and worldwide construction activity slowed. By 1987, demand in the construction equipment industry was still below 60 percent of capacity while manufacturing capacity continued to rise. Every newly industrializing nation appeared to want its own bulldozer manufacturer, and firms in some countries—notably in South Korea, Taiwan, and Italy—made aggressive efforts to serve the worldwide construction equipment market. Severe price discounting had plagued the construction machinery industry in 1986, and 1987 demand for construction machinery was expected to be flat or drop 5 to 10 percent from 1986 volumes.

Rather than wait any longer, Caterpillar Inc. took a $109 million pretax charge in 1986 for planned closings of a lift truck plant in Dallas, Oregon, and D6H track-type tractor plants in Davenport, Iowa, and Glasgow, Scotland. Caterpillar had planned to make the closings in 1988 to improve its capacity utilization after completing a significant modernization program. By not waiting when shrinking demand for tractors triggered suicidal discounting by machinery makers who battled to preserve their market shares and reduce inventories, Caterpillar alone was able to enjoy the benefits of lower break-even volumes.

Pricing. While managers are pursuing hold investment strategies, they try to match competitors' price moves rather than instigate them—with one exception. If prices fall, firms in holding patterns may step out from the pack to signal their price-preserving intentions by raising prices temporarily. Even when they do so, their purpose is to signal cautiously that they do not desire price wars.

Asset deployment. While managers are waiting for uncertainty to be resolved, they do not immediately thin their firms' product lines, close their plants, or consolidate their assets under holding strategies because they may need productive capacity if demand revives or they wish to strengthen their position in declining industries later. No downsizing is undertaken because sacrificed market share would be difficult to recover later (should industry conditions improve). Courtaulds, for example, held its position in rayon because it expected to gain customers when other firms' plants were forced to close. Firms in holding patterns do not increase their asset base. If more capacity is needed while they are treading water, firms in holding patterns use outsourcing arrangements (or even offshore suppliers) as stopgap measures. Firms pursuing holding strategies match competitors' marketing expenditures and may even utilize excess capacity by manufacturing on a private-brand basis for competitors until trigger points are reached.

Cost effectiveness. Until managers have resolved the uncertainties that placed their firms into holding strategies, they invest only to maintain their firms' cost effectiveness. Their objective is to use existing assets and resources more wisely instead of buying new ones. Even when managers oversee holding patterns, they must strive to attain continual improvements in operations by improving working practices.

Timing. In order to pursue effective holding strategies, managers must heighten the level of their firms' competitor and market intelligence. Their objective is to develop contingency plans to exploit opportunities that may be created by competitors' plant closings or exits, changes in growth rates, customer preferences, and so on.

Industrial rayon filament. During the 1960s, E.I. du Pont de Nemours was a leading producer of the heavy-denier, high-tenacity rayon filament used for tire cord even though product demand had peaked in 1949. Great uncertainty existed concerning when tire manufacturers would stop using rayon filament in tire carcasses for original-equipment applications. The rate of deteriorating demand for rayon filament use in tires sold in replacement markets was heavily dependent on the year when the switchover occurred, but until it did occur almost all existing rayon filament-making capacity was needed to serve tire manufacturers.

Although their requests for operating improvements were funded, du Pont's managers in charge of rayon filament were also directed to evaluate *how* the firm would exit from this line of business, if the firm ever decided to exit. In 1968, seven years after du Pont first asked the managers of its rayon filament business to consider how to exit, the Chevrolet automobile division of General Motors used nylon-reinforced tires on its new models instead of rayon-reinforced tires. Du Pont decided to begin divesting its rayon filament operations. Because its managers had studied the problem for so long and had identified so many of the problems associated with exit that would disrupt du Pont's relationships with suppliers, customers, and employees, most of these difficulties were avoided when its exit strategy was implemented.

Shrink Selectively

Approach. The objective of shrink-selectively strategies is to capture promising customers before competitors can identify them, as Mead Johnson did with infant formula while it abandoned Pablum infant cereal and Bibb baby juices. In shrink-selectively strategies, firms pursuing wide product-line postures *reposition* themselves to concentrate on serving customer groups where demand is expected to endure the longest and be most lucrative. They fund their restructuring process by retrieving the value of investments used formerly to serve less attractive customers within mature industries, in market segments where demand is slumping.

Shrink selectively strategies require astute market segmentation skills in order to identify which pockets of demand will live on and be price insensitive (and which groups of customers will become unattractive to serve). They are successful only if there are enough lucrative customers to serve and if managers can turn market segments into defensible market *niches*. Most firms that pursue survival strategies in endgame will choose to shrink some aspects of their mature businesses while they divert resources into other, more promising activities and customers. The biggest risk to successful implementation of selective shrinking strategies is self-delusion. Many managers underestimate the difficulty of repositioning their firms to serve customers that they have previously neglected. Other managers are reluctant to drop any customers— regardless of how costly they are to service. Harley-Davidson survived by not trying to be everything to everybody. It left the low end of the motorcycle market to Japanese invaders while it sold high-horsepower "hogs."

Hospitals. Too many hospitals and insurance plans were competing for too few patients as admissions fell in 1988, while the already fierce marketing wars among health maintenance organizations (HMOs) intensified. Overcapacity (40 percent empty beds in 1986, compared with 25 percent one year earlier) undermined hospital profits as costs rose while patient volume declined. The profit squeeze from overcapacity was intensified by two sources of pressures for quality control: the reimbursement gap from third-party payment systems and malpractice suits. Pressures to contain costs were reinforced when corporate clients abandoned insurers who could not keep their prices low.

To cope with falling demand, hospital chains dumped their in-house health care insurance plans, scaled back on high-cost, acute-care facilities (by converting them into higher profit services, such as drug rehabilitation and psychiatric clinics). Some hospitals created drug overdose trauma centers to fill empty beds.

When to shrink selectively. Managers embrace shrink-selectively strategies where demand within some mature market segments seems to be both enduring and large enough to sustain their firms. If managers believe their firms could reach attractive customers by rethinking the uses of their products, shrinking strategies are an appropriate way to move from old markets to new ones. Shrink-selectively strategies are apt whenever firms can compete in endgames by rolling over the components of their product lines, swapping out facilities and locations, or making other adjustments to upgrade productive resources.

Automobiles. General Motors Corporation announced in January 1987 that it would close five assembly complexes (with more shutdowns likely in 1988) for a total of nine plant closings, partial closings of two more plants, and production cutbacks at other remaining plants. In November 1986, General Motors had announced its plan to sell a Fisher-Guide division parts plant in Elyria, Ohio, to an outside supplier, and buy back the parts it needed. In January 1987, General Motors announced its intention to move another 10 percent of its parts production to lower-cost, outside suppliers. (The outsourced parts were never competitive while made in-house.) Meanwhile, since 1983, General Motors has pursued joint ventures to make small cars; in 1987, its joint venture with Toyota announced a capacity expansion to make 50,000 cars per year.

In March 1987, Chrysler Corporation announced a phaseout by 1989 of production at its thirty-six-year-old Indianapolis, Indiana, electrical plant, which produced alternators, starters, voltage regulators, power-steering units, distributors, and front-windshield-wiper motors. The plant was utilizing less than 50 percent of its capacity at that time, and Chrysler planned to discontinue all in-house manufacturing of some of these parts. At the same time, Chrysler acquired American Motors Corporation (AMC) from Renault, thereby adding AMC's 1,600-dealer network to its own 4,300-dealer network, adding four assembly plants to Chrysler's nine plants, and boosting total car and truck capacity by one-third, to 2.9 million vehicles per year. Chrysler also obtained access to AMC's four-wheel-drive Jeep product line and larger Renault cars.

Pricing. When managers pursue selective shrinking strategies, they raise prices in unattractive customer segments—even to the point of pricing their firms out of those markets. Meanwhile, they maintain historic price levels in the market segments they prefer to serve—the lucrative and enduring customer niches. Although it may be necessary to shade prices downward slightly in order to hold desired customers, price wars are deadly in mature markets because they sap investments in cost-cutting technology, product improvements, and other necessary activities.

Successful implementation of the survival strategies assumes that firms' repositioning efforts will be justified by healthy future cash flows. Abandoning customers that managers find less attractive should ease competitors' pressures to cut prices. But if détente with competitors is not possible—if other firms are determined to serve the same customers that the firm has identified as being most attractive and are willing to use price cutting to attain their objectives—managers must assess which firms could best survive a price war and how difficult it would be to raise prices again later to provide adequate profits. Retreat may be prudent if other firms possess true cost advantages or are intent on acting irrationally.

Asset deployment. Successful implementation of shrinking strategies requires managers to redeploy all of their firms' assets toward serving favorable customer segments. Firms must pamper the most attractive customers by exploiting their advantageous geographical locations or selling products that price-insensitive customers value—leather boots for the military, expensive Cuban cigars, or quick delivery of extra tin cans to pack an especially bountiful seasonal harvest. More assets may be devoted to serving the lucrative after-market where, for example, radio- and television-broadcast stations, the defense industry, and fanatics for high-fidelity audio entertainment still pay premium prices for replacement tubes in 1988 even though the last television receiver equipped with receiving tubes was produced in the 1970s. Redeploying assets to serve such customers in selective shrinking strategies is wise if managers can preempt rivals from doing so first and prevent them from copying their moves later. As part of the rationalization process, managers must restructure their firm's organization, as Apple Computer did in 1986 when it eliminated the rival Lisa and Apple II divisions and hunkered down to fight for a first-tier position in the stagnant market for personal computers. As managers reorganize their operations around key value-adding opportunities, outsourcing of some activities may be necessary. Facilities may be added in attractive neighborhoods while operations are scaled back in unpromising locations.

Pharmaceuticals. Competitors may even cooperate by sharing facilities, as Sandoz and Ciba-Geigy have done with a plant in Tom's River, New Jersey, which is used for short runs of low-volume drugs. Under the commonplace "man-in-plant" convention in the pharmaceutical industry, different competitors incurred legal responsibility for the drugs produced in a shared plant on different days of the month. Although one drug company may have owned and operated the assets in the pharmaceutical plant under typical contracts for the "tableting and labeling" of off-patent substances, the physical presence of the customer drug firm's manager in the subcontractor's plant made the plant theirs for that day.

Acetylene. Demand for acetylene feedstocks deteriorated abruptly in 1966 when most customers switched to ethylene. Tenneco Chemical was forced to operate its huge, new Houston, Texas, plant at an uneconomic 34 percent of capacity to fulfill its obligations to du Pont. Tenneco cut its losses in 1978 by closing its 100 million pound-per-year acetylene cracking plant and leasing a 35 million pound-per-year cracking plant and workforce from Rohm & Haas to satisfy du Pont.

Cost effectiveness. If firms must battle to win the most attractive customers when they pursue shrink-selectively strategies, their managers must reduce expenses incurred in serving unattractive customers. Managers strive for cost effectiveness by consolidating their firms' product offerings and centralizing activities that were previously disparate.

Steel. In 1987, Inland Steel Industries (in Chicago) planned to build a continuous-process cold-rolling mill to upgrade the quality of its sheet products. It also planned to drop out of phases where it was not expert (like coking) by not rebuilding its coke ovens. Instead, Inland Steel planned to buy coke from an outside supplier—as Carnegie bought coke from Frick in the late nineteenth century.

In 1982, Bethlehem Steel had cut research spending when it began to incur losses, followed with further cuts in 1983 and 1984. Bethlehem Steel sold its research center, reduced the number of researchers to 450 from the nearly 1,000 researchers employed during the 1960s, and moved many of the remaining employees out of central research laboratories and into the plants. In 1987, Bethlehem Steel announced plans to invest at least $150 million in 1987 and up to $250 million in 1988 in new plants and equipment to make a more suitable product line.

Timing. Where reinvestments and repositionings are needed to remain viable, firms must commit their resources to new targets before competitors can maneuver into more advantageous positions. Advanced planning is necessary if managers hope to select the best market segments to serve when they use shrink-selectively strategies. Only then can they hope to preempt competitors from reaching those customers.

Bulk chemicals. Excess capacity was created in the chemical industry when nation after newly industrializing nation built world-scale facilities during the mid-1970s when demand for bulk chemicals was growing by 15 percent per year. Established firms also invested heavily in new plants to meet demand that they thought would continue to rise. State-owned chemical firms poured money into capacity to make products that found fewer and fewer buyers. When demand slowed abruptly, producers of bulk chemicals cut prices in a fierce attempt to fill their large, new plants and protect their market shares. To cope with overcapacity, chemical firms scrapped plants and reduced total productive capacity to improve the utilization of surviving plants from 66 percent in 1981 to 82.3 percent in 1987. Chemical manufacturers changed their product focus, as well. In 1977, bulk chemicals—plastics and petrochemicals—were favored; in 1987, the chemical industry emphasized specialty chemicals.

Dow Chemical won the timing advantage in its restructuring. In 1978, when Dow's top management team began thinking about how the profitability of their industry would evolve, Dow Chemical decided to cut back on bulk chemicals and develop a leading position in specialty chemicals, instead. Since 1981, when Dow began following this plan, it has sold bulk chemical plants worth $1.8 billion and ended several petrochemical joint ventures (in Japan, Saudi Arabia, South Korea, and Yugoslavia). An early retirement program and asset-related writedowns were a part of Dow's downsizing campaign. Dow's selling prices were higher than competitors that tried to copy its strategy—because Dow did it first. Under this plan, only 46 percent of Dow's profits came from bulk chemicals by 1986. The other 54 percent came from specialized products—engineering plastics, agricultural chemicals, drugs, and biotechnology.

No Single Success Pattern

As these strategy alternative examples indicate, there is no single recipe for success when firms are confronted with slow demand growth, stagnant growth, or declining demand. My research findings suggest that there are many different types of industrywide sales-growth declines. Some types of declines are better than others because they represent superior opportunities to prosper during the endgame or exit successfully. A number of different strategies can be used during the sales-growth decline. There is no single road to success. Many innovative ways of retrieving the value of firms' assets have been found, and a variety of tactics for executing these different strategies proved effective, as these examples suggest.

Example of Unexpected Endgame

About fifteen years ago, eight large U.S. firms committed an average of $10 million each to the construction of new plants that used an experimental technology to manufacture products for several customers who held long-term contracts. However, bugs in this technology cut these plants' maximum output to levels far below their engineered capacity. High manufacturing costs were incurred. Two years later, a rival technology relying on different raw materials was commercialized, and the firms' own raw materials prices quadrupled. As a result of these events, industrywide consumption of the product dwindled.

Seeing this change, one firm wrote off its plant immediately and contracted for the supplies of these products that it consumed internally from a competitor. It broke even. Another firm was locked into production because its customers would not renegotiate their contracts. It did nothing and suffered losses. A third firm managed to satisfy its contractual obligations by retiring its own plant and leasing a competitor's plant that was of smaller, more appropriate capacity for its customers' needs, as Tenneco did with its acetylene plant. It prospered.

An Example of Predictable Endgame

Several very large companies were heavily invested in making a basic product when a major technological breakthrough that could spawn several subsequent generations of product improvements was announced. All of these firms had been planning to erect highly automated plants for their existing basic products to lower the cost of their domestic labor forces. The new technology had not yet been commercialized. It was quite expensive, but everyone agreed that it definitely made their basic product obsolete.

One firm immediately sold its patents and ideas to a foreign producer who began to import the product less expensively than it could be produced domestically. It prospered. A second firm that used the basic product internally made investments in automated plants and helped its competitors to exit. It prospered, too.

Even with no trade barriers, competition from imported versions of the product did not take away the market from domestic vendors overnight because customers were reluctant to purchase their basic products from vendors with whom they had no track records. Their needs for attentive after-sale service gave local firms the necessary breathing space for rationalizing their own operations and fighting imports that hoped to penetrate their markets.

Summary

There are always winners in the endgame. Gerber Products and Dow Chemical increased their investments in the declining baby food and chemical businesses, respectively—in markets where each firm faced excellent opportunities for profitability. On the other hand, Courtaulds and Havatampa Cigar held their respective investment postures in the declining rayon and cigar businesses, where they were appropriately situated for the markets they served. Mead-Johnson and Sunbeam Appliance shrank and restructured their investment postures in the declining baby foods and percolator coffee-maker businesses, respectively, when they could not compete profitably across all segments of the market. PPG Industries and du Pont milked their investments in the declining synthetic soda ash and acetate businesses, respectively, when analyses suggested that there would be little to be gained by staying in these businesses. Finally, Raytheon and du Pont divested their declining electronic receiving tube and acetylene businesses, respectively, when they saw an opportunity to cut their losses and recover a portion of their investments quickly.

As managers prepare to maneuver through the endgame, they analyze the causes of depressed demand in order to identify whether niches of enduring customers exist. Next, they evaluate which firms are best suited to serve the most attractive customers and estimate whether their firm can justify repositioning investments to serve those niches. If analysis suggests that their firms are not the strongest or that no niches exist, managers should divest troubled businesses immediately (assuming that a ready market exists for their firms' assets) or begin milking their firms' asset bases if outright sale is impossible.

Firms' relative successes during decline were affected by their relative competitive strengths as well as by the structure of the industries they were in. Appropriate strategies for coping with decline varied according to firms' strengths and whether their industry environments were favorable for prolonged participation and easy exit. There were a few exceptions to the general patterns observed because some firms discovered unique ways to beat the laws of the marketplace. Firms could not always adopt the most advantageous strategies because competitors' actions sometimes shifted the balance in industries that seemed to be favorable or unfavorable. Managers sometimes misread the signals that would have suggested an alternative action plan, or they were willing to live with lower profit levels due to the central importance of the businesses involved to their overall corporate portfolios.

Endgame strategies are used for businesses that have products in the second half of their life expectancy. Good cash flows and returns on invested capital can be attained in such mature business environments through skillful management of tactics in ways that differ from how businesses in growth environments are managed. Choosing which endgame strategy to pursue is a matter of understanding the factors that determine mature industries' attractiveness and firms' relative competitive strengths. These factors (and their effects on endgame competition) are analyzed in chapter 3.

Note

1. Many examples of endgame strategies and tactics have previously been cited in an interview with J. Willoughby. See "Endgame Strategy," *Forbes,* vol. 140, no. 1, July 13, 1987:181–182; J. Willoughby, "Buggywhips, Inc.," *op. cit.,* 183–207; J. Willoughby, "Profile: Gordon Cain," *op. cit.,* 208–210.

3
Assessing Profitability Potential
(to Avoid Pyrrhic Victories)

T his chapter explains how to choose whether firms should strive for
leadership in a particular mature industry. Such analysis is needed
when formulating endgame strategies because some industry structures
are more conducive to high profits than others or are more malleable to restructuring than other industry structures. Knowing the difference between favorable
endgame environments (and unfavorable ones) can save managers years of
fruitless efforts devoted to restructuring competitive situations where profit
margins will never justify such efforts.

Early endgame analysis is better than late recognition of the problems that
accompany maturing demand because of the "early mover" advantages firms
enjoy when preempting competitors. To keep open all of the endgame strategy
alternatives described in chapter 2, managers should perform endgame strategy
audits well in advance—when industrywide demand first begins to slow. If
analysis suggests that funding cutbacks may be necessary, the discipline of including *pro forma* exit plans ("horizon budgeting") in regular strategic-planning
cycles of maturing business as will help to uncover problems that could later
reduce firms' strategic flexibility (see chapter 4).

The Endgame Strategy Matrix

Figure 3–1 depicts the endgame strategy matrix that matches the five strategy
alternatives presented in chapter 2 with an assessment of industry conditions
and competitive strengths that is developed in this chapter. The endgame
strategy matrix is sometimes depicted with nine cells, as in figure 3–2, but in
either form it represents a basic "go" versus "no-go" decision regarding future
funding of the mature business. (To clarify this bipolar decision, draw a diagonal
line from the northeast corner of either version of the matrix to the southwest
corner. Businesses above the diagonal are candidates for further funding;
businesses below the diagonal are not.)

Chapter 3 explains how firms' endgame successes are determined by anticipating how sluggish demand will grow (or decline), having favorable industry structures, building positions of competitive strength for serving chosen

	Great strengths relative to competitors for attractive niches	No strengths relative to competitors for attractive niches
Favorable industry structure and demand outlook	"Increase investment" or "Hold investment level"	"Shrink selectively" or "Milk the investment"
Unfavorable industry structure and demand outlook	"Shrink selectively" or "Milk the investment"	"Divest now"

Figure 3–1. Endgame Strategy Matrix

	Great strengths relative to competitors for attractive niches	Some strengths relative to competitors for attractive niches	No strengths relative to competitors for attractive niches
Favorable industry structure and demand outlook	"Increase investment" or "Hold investment level"	"Hold investment level" or "Shrink selectively"	"Shrink selectively" or "Milk the investment"
Medium industry structure and demand outlook	"Hold investment level" or "Shrink selectively"	"Shrink selectively" or "Milk the investment"	"Milk the investment" or "Divest now"
Unfavorable industry structure and demand outlook	"Shrink selectively" or "Milk the investment"	"Milk the investment" or "Divest now"	"Divest now"

Figure 3–2. Expanded Endgame Strategy Matrix

customers, and other factors (which are developed in later chapters). As figures 3–1 and 3–2 imply, firms should not consider undertaking aggressive endgame strategy alternatives if industry structures suggest that recovery of past investments will be difficult. In such risky environments, exit strategies are more suitable.

Assessing Endgame Attractiveness

As figure 3–3 indicates, endgame attractiveness is determined by a combination of traits: demand outlooks must be favorable, industry structures must be conducive to high profit margins, and competitors must not engage in bloodletting warfare. Managers' assessments of how mature industries will evolve determine where in the endgame matrix their businesses will be placed. Chapter 3 provides a step-by-step checklist to help managers position their businesses in the matrix. It explains which traits are danger signals and which ones can be converted into advantages. The first step is forecasting how demand will grow.

Environmental Traits

● Demand-price insensitive	Demand-price sensitive ●
● Replacement units likely to be needed by some customers for a long time	Demand could deteriorate abruptly ●
● Loyal customer demand likely to endure	Low customer switching costs ●
● Revitalization likely, albeit remote	Competition usually volatile ●
● Firm serves protected (high entry barriers) market niche alone	Competitors face high exit barriers ●
● Suppliers willing to help firm compete	Customers likely to exert bargaining power ●

Aggressive _____ The Strategic Continuum _____ Cut losses
(increased   (divest now
investment   strategy)
strategy)

Figure 3–3. Relating Strategy Alternatives to Environmental Conditions within a Mature Industry

Slowing sales have different causes for different types of products. If the products in question are durable goods, demand growth declines when primary demand is saturated and replacement sales account for most new purchases. If vendors can foresee industry saturation and adjust their productive capacities accordingly, many of the problems associated with endgame competition can be avoided until demand declines with little hope for revitalization.

Types of Declining-Demand Growth

Overall, there are three major reasons for demand to slow (or decline) so harshly: (1) technological obsolescence, (2) sociological or demographic changes, and (3) changing fashion. If products are consumed on purchase, managers must forecast demand for end products sold further downstream in the value chain and adjust their operations accordingly. When capacity adjustments do not occur because managers believe that demand will revive (or because no firms are willing to retire their plants), endgame competition will be volatile and head-to-head competitors will suffer badly.

Expectations. Forecasting skills are critical if firms wish to avoid losses. Although competitors act on their expectations concerning (1) where demand will decline, (2) how quickly demand will deteriorate, and (3) whether demand is likely to revive, they are less likely to take any capacity-adjusting actions if they are highly uncertain about how demand will grow. Demand may deteriorate quickly, as was the case with rubber baby panties when disposable diapers were commercialized; or it may diminish slowly, as with cigar consumption, which has been declining intermittently for half a century. Demand may plummet and then reach a plateau; this has occurred with baby food consumption, which has fallen with the declining U.S. birth rate, and with various other products that are sustained by cores of replacement demand. Or demand may decline to zero without pausing. There may be substantial uncertainty regarding products' revitalizations, as in the case of millinery equipment for ladies' hats; or there may be relative certainty that products are indeed obsolete, as in the case of electronic receiving tubes. In general, sales declines induced by fashion or demographic changes produce greater uncertainty about future industry prospects because they are harder to predict. Sales declines created by technological change are easier to anticipate, especially when firms' scientists, engineers, and sales forces are involved in developing products that use substitute technologies.

If there were relative certainty regarding (1) which pockets of demand would decline first, (2) how rapidly demand would decline for different market niches, and (3) whether demand would be likely to revitalize, then competition within mature industries would be less volatile and the timing of exits would be more orderly. Where managers could easily forecast how demand would fall, their firms suffered fewer large write-off losses on asset disposal and firms that exited did so in nondisruptive fashions. When forecasting skills were well developed, managers improved their firms' timing in exit. However, when there was substantial uncertainty concerning where, when, and how fast demand would fall, chaos ensued. Errors in forecasting discontinuities in the rate and pattern of decline were especially disastrous because changes in these demand conditions trapped firms that were unable to sell their underutilized assets quickly. Trapped assets increased the likelihood that destructive price wars would erupt.

Automobiles. By 1988, many non-U.S. automotive firms had announced plans to build plants in or export cars to the United States. For example, Honda, Nissan, and Toyota were operating U.S. plants. Yugoslavia was exporting its Yugos to the United States. Toyota announced plans to expand its Georgetown plant's capacity to 200,000 cars by 1989. Mazda Motor (in a joint venture with Ford Motor) announced that in 1988 it planned to build a plant in Flat Rock, Michigan, with a manufacturing capacity of 135,000 cars. Mazda also announced plans to expand the Flat Rock plant's capacity to 240,000 cars by 1989. Malaysia planned to export its Proton Sagas to the United States by 1988. Diamond Star Motors (a joint venture between Mitsubishi and Chrysler) announced that in 1989 it planned to build a plant in Bloomington-Normal, Illinois, with a manufacturing capacity of 182,400 cars. Daihatsu Motor (in a joint venture with Bombardier) announced that in 1989 it planned to build a plant in Valcourt, Quebec, with a manufacturing capacity of 37,200 cars. Isuzu-Subaru announced that in 1990 it planned to build a plant in Lafayette, Indiana, with a manufacturing capacity of 240,000 cars. Suzuki/General Motors announced that in 1990 it planned to build a plant in Ingersoll, Ontario, with a manufacturing capacity of 200,000 cars. Kia Motors of Korea planned to export cars and vans worldwide by 1990. Thailand and Taiwan were also trying to export automobiles to the United States. If all of these announced plants were built, most U.S. automotive plants existing in 1988 would be rendered *obsolete* and forced to close because they would not be cost-competitive with global competitors' new, world-scale plants.

Electronic components. The successful introduction of the personal computer in the late 1970s created a one-time surge in demand for semiconductors. As global chip consumption jumped from $15 billion in 1982 to $29 billion in 1984, semiconductor firms raced to add productive capacity to meet what appeared to be insatiable demand. Worldwide semiconductor production increased by 33 percent in 1984 alone. But when global chip demand fell by 14 percent in 1985 due to falling personal computer sales, the worldwide semiconductor industry lost billions of dollars. In the United States and Japan (which together accounted for 87 percent of global chip-making capacity at that time), the rate of semiconductor-equipment use fell from nearly 100 percent in 1984 to about 60 percent in 1985. Price pressures created by the huge unused capacity of 1985 eased as orders picked up somewhat in 1986, but most semiconductor firms remained deeply troubled in 1987 because aggressive firms were ignoring market conditions while they pursued market share. In particular, Japanese producers continued to add productive capacity and slash prices on semiconductor products below marginal costs. By taking advantage of their access to lower-cost capital provided by patient investors and government research assistance, Japanese firms captured worldwide control of major commodity chip markets by 1988.

Enduring niches of demand. The presence of pockets of demand where customers' switching costs are financially high (or are perceived as being high as a result of fears about degradation of quality) make endgame environments more attractive than if there are no lucrative customers to serve. Some mature businesses look unattractive when, in fact, particular firms are merely not cost-competitive, as in the steel, semiconductor, and lift truck industries. Demand for troubled products continues, but a different group of vendors may serve ongoing customers as the endgame progresses. Other mature businesses truly are unattractive because no attractive customers continue to use products facing stagnant demand.

The most desirable customers to serve in mature industries are those who are least likely to convert soon to substitute products. They are laggards, customers who are least likely to adopt a new technology because they are too small or cannot afford it. For example, use of the electronic photocopier is not as widespread as one would think. A. B. Dick makes money selling mimeograph machines to small offices that do not want to switch to something newer. Gillette's Liquid Paper division is selling correction fluid to firms that do not use word processors for every typewritten document.

Favorable endgame environments must contain at least one pocket of enduring product demand of viable size. Examples of such pockets of demand include electronic receiving tubes for high-fidelity amplification uses or as replacement components in color television; leather goods and apparel designed and merchandised for the haute couture market; premium-branded cigars (retailing for $2 per cigar); belted, nonradial tires merchandised through discount outlets; hypoallergenic infant formula; sterling silver electric percolator coffee makers and plastic percolators; shiny acetate fabrics for evening wear and rayon filament fibers for high-quality menswear lining fabrics; and leather military boots. Among the post–World War II babies, the current "me-generation" of adults who have recently become parents is especially price insensitive; because these consumers have little free time, they try to compensate for their absence from home by denying their children nothing.

Steel. Excess steel-making capacity was created by poor investment decisions during the 1970s, when European and Japanese steel makers built new facilities in anticipation of capacity shortages while United States steel makers began to modernize their plants by incorporating technologies with improved cost structures. Not only did the anticipated scarcity of steel-making capacity never come, but steel consumption also fell sharply in industrialized nations because their economic infrastructures were already in place; their railroads, highways, and other steel-consuming infrastructures had already been built. Use by key customer industries—such as automobiles and containers—was expected to dwindle as these industries switched to the use of alternative materials.

Steel-making capacity in industrialized nations increased by 14 percent to 485 million metric tons from 1970 to 1980, while consumption dropped 8 percent to 334 million metric tons. By 1987 global excess capacity was between 75 million and 200 million metric tons—comprised of 570 million metric tons of total steel-making capacity in non-Communist countries and 455 million metric tons in industrialized nations. The only way that supply would shrink to meet 1988 demand in the non-Communist countries was if the entire United States steel industry shut down its operations, or if steel producers in Europe and Japan jointly reduced their respective capacities.

Predicting the effect of declining sales growth. If there is great uncertainty concerning whether demand will grow (or decline), endgame competition will be chaotic. If managers can recognize how demand for their firms' products will deteriorate, their reduced uncertainty will make capacity adjustments easier and reduce the likelihood that price cutting will erupt.[1]

Rayon fiber and filament. Demand for rayon declined due to substitutions by other natural and synthetic fibers and competition from imported fibers. Demand in the fashion market was highly unpredictable from year to year; demand in the industrial market fell suddenly when tire manufacturers switched to steel belting for their tire carcasses. Most U.S. firms were unable to foresee these changes in demand and they suffered losses. By 1968, environmental pollution standards had tightened so dramatically that the cost of bringing some rayon plants into compliance was prohibitive and most firms were forced to exit.

Baby foods. The number of births per thousand fertile U.S. women reached its peak in 1957, and baby-food manufacturers were estimating a 16 percent increase in births beyond that level for the next decades. Food-processing plants were built in anticipation of this forecast. Instead, births declined 12 percent by the mid-1960s and the presence of significant excess capacity propelled competitors into a vicious price war in which profits were eliminated and prices fell by more than 30 percent.

Synthetic soda ash. The discovery of natural soda-ash deposits in Wyoming made demand for synthetic soda ash easier to predict. When price levels rose to cover the higher transportation costs incurred by shipping inexpensive, natural soda ash to eastern customers, well-prepared producers of synthetic soda ash closed their plants. Inattentive firms faced large write-off losses and great disruption to ongoing activities because they did not act on readily available information about how quickly substitution would occur.

Electronic receiving tubes. Although the invention of the transistor made electronic receiving tubes technologically obsolete in 1947, the last television receiver containing receiving tubes was not manufactured until 1974. Substitutions from the older technology to the new one were easily predicted in each market where active electronic components were used. Producers of electronic receiving tubes kept prices high in the original equipment market (OEM) and replacement markets by keeping supply in line with demand. Managers phased out productive capacity so smoothly that import competition was unable to ruin the profitability of the electronic receiving-tube industry as it had destroyed so many others.

Speed of decline. If there is great uncertainty concerning the speed with which demand will deteriorate, chaos increases. When demand declines rapidly, firms are more likely to be stuck with assets that are no longer needed. If demand deteriorates slowly, managers have the necessary lead time to reallocate resources, change their firms' operating systems, and downsize their organizations.

Percolator coffee makers. The first automatic drip coffee maker was introduced in the United States in 1972. Sales of percolator coffee makers fell drastically; two years later, prices had decreased by 45 percent as surprised producers of percolator coffee makers undercut manufacturing costs to bolster declining demand.

Acetylene. One year after the largest volume of acetylene was produced as a chemical feedstock, acetylene was made obsolete by the discovery that the ethylene route to making plastics was cheaper. Although astute firms were able to plan orderly exits, many firms had recently built new acetylene plants, which they could not abandon easily. Those firms incurred losses when they exited.

Cigars. Cigar manufacturers had ample time to reposition themselves to cope with declining demand. Cigar consumption had been declining since the introduction of cigarettes in the 1920s, revitalized to a near-historic peak in 1964 when cigarette smoking was declared carcinogenic, and declined again in the face of bans on smoking in public areas. Complacent managers continued to chase market-share increases as industrywide demand fell; they suffered losses and threats of takeovers. Savvy managers divested as many assets as they could sell and retired other cigar-making assets. They prospered.

Whiskey. Whiskey consumption had been slowly declining since 1961, but many whiskey distillers had been building up their inventories instead of cutting back on production. Because U.S. consumers seemed to be more health conscious in the 1980s, complacent managers suffered losses when they awoke to find that whisky consumption fell by one million gallons from 1980 to 1981.

Revitalizing demand. If managers believe that there are chances that demand for their firms' products will revitalize, their hope leads them to take actions that make endgame competition more bitter. If managers see little chance that demand for their products will revive, they are more likely to bite the bullet in reaching difficult conclusions regarding the need for repositioning investments. Managers are more likely to overcome the exit barriers that prevented them from thinning out product lines, abandoning costly customers, closing redundant plants, and making other hard decisions if they believe that the end is near.

Bulk chemicals. In 1987, roughly half of all commodity chemical sales were made by European and U.S. firms to Latin American and Pacific Basin customers. In 1988, plastics and petrochemical plants worth $8 billion were announced by several South American nations. The capacity announcements threatened to ruin the attractiveness of the recently restructured chemicals industry for European and U.S. chemical firms because resulting bulk chemical capacity in Latin America would double to a total of 4 million tons; Latin America would then account for almost 10 percent of the world's chemical production. Morover, the new Latin American plants would eat into the European and U.S. chemical firms' small market shares in Latin America and threaten their big export markets in the Pacific Basin because Latin American producers planned to export bulk chemicals to Southeast Asia and the United States.

In 1988, Brazil planned to spend $4.2 billion on new bulk chemical plants. Venezuela allocated $2 billion to plastics and MTBE (an additive for lead-free gasoline). Argentina planned to spend $1 billion to build bulk chemical plants (and an ethylene cracker). Chile and Colombia were planning to build bulk chemical plants, as well. Before the mid-1990s, another 3 million tons of bulk chemical capacity was scheduled to be added in Korea, Taiwan, and Thailand. Finally, Japanese firms planned to reopen mothballed plants after the Japanese government removed the chemical production limits it set as part of a rationalization program during the worldwide chemical recession of the early 1980s.

Forecasting demand growth. Demographic and lifestyle changes will force growing industries into the endgame while new opportunities develop elsewhere. For example, the graying of populations in industrialized nations will increase interest there in products for physical fitness and the delay of aging. These patterns will exacerbate the differences in demand between industrialized and newly industrializing nations. The rapid influx of immigrants will account for one-third of U.S. population replacement by 2010. Their migrations will make demand in different geographic regions grow rapidly while other U.S. regions wither. These changes will result in different spending patterns as demand rises for products that reflect different tastes. Technological progress will replace vinyl phonograph records with compact audio disks, ironing boards with permanent-press fabrics, airplane propellers with jet engines, and metal gears with plastic gears. Greater productivity in farming will reduce demand for farming equipment. When managers recognize these trends soon enough, their firms can take measures to reduce their dependence on declining products.

Managers facing stagnant demand may revitalize demand by rethinking their products' uses. Just as demand for parachute nylon was revitalized by demand for nylon stockings, and demand for baking soda was revitalized by using it to deodorize refrigerators, managers must devise new ways to define their products when growth slows. For example, demand for baby foods can be replaced by a concern for infant nutrition. Demand for annual physical checkups can be replaced by an ongoing campaign for wellness. Demand for corsets, girdles, and brassieres can be sustained if they are specially designed for the lifestyle of the "fitness generation." In the textile industry, demand for polyolefin fibers in automobile upholstery fabrics was supplanted through a concerted effort by producers of cotton velour. Because 99 percent of all U.S. households have refrigerators, appliance manufacturers maintained their sales volumes by expanding their product lines to include small refrigerators for home bars, offices, and master bedrooms.

Summary. When positioning firms' mature businesses along the industry attractiveness axis in figures 3–1 and 3–2, great demand uncertainty indicates competitive volatility in the endgame. Sudden drops in demand will exacerbate the likely bitterness of competition, as will hopes that demand will revive later. As figure 3–1 implies, the most aggressive endgame strategy that is appropriate for such environments is "shrink selectively." This conclusion suggests that managers should evaluate the attractiveness of market segments that their firms serve to determine (1) which customers are most profitable to serve, (2) which new market segments should be developed, and (3) how to turn the most attractive market segments into defensible "niches" that their firms can serve better than all others.

Such analyses should be undertaken regularly while demand is still growing. Too often, this analysis is not done even when demand growth is stagnant. One of the biggest problems in mature industries is that managers refuse to acknowledge that the endgame has begun. Instead of making an educated guess about which market segments will deteriorate most rapidly (and taking precautions not to lock up their firms' wealth in investments for serving such customers), complacent managers hide the reality of industrywide maturity in clever recastings of data that disguise trends and aggregate information about important differences among market segments when they should be breaking down data more finely.

Industry Structure and Profitability Potential

The first step in formulating an endgame strategy is to assess the mature industry's attractiveness. Forecasting how different patterns of demand growth (or decline) will affect competitive behavior is one part of that assessment. After evaluating how demand is likely to grow (or decline), managers must also appraise the profitability potential of troubled industries, *without regard for how well suited their particular firm is to satisfy demand.* It is important to distinguish between sick industries that need restructuring and sick businesses that need to improve productivity, fine-tune product offerings, and increase cost effectiveness. Some mature industries offer attractive long-term sales potential and profitability. If restructured, they would offer environments of price stability and ease in recovering sunk-asset values. If analysis suggests that endgame industries are attractive (but a particular firm is weak), early divestiture may be the most attractive option to embrace. Industry attractiveness increases where firms are protected from incursions by displaced competitors whose primary markets have dwindled. It is easier to serve attractive customers successfully when there are no maverick competitors who instigate price wars. Finally, endgame industries are most attractive when firms can readily form coalitions with helpful suppliers and distributors.

Less favorable industries, by contrast, have no niches of enduring and lucrative demand, little product differentiation, and no mobility barriers to prevent competitors from copying firms' strategic approaches. Sick industries cannot be restructured effectively. Firms with large market shares in sick industries must prepare for very unpleasant endgame experiences. Other traits that decrease the attractiveness of mature industries include high reinvestment requirements, substantial diseconomies of scale, at least one maverick competitor who would cut prices below costs, opportunistic customers who possess and exert strong bargaining power,[a] and high exit barriers.

Product traits. Endgame industries are more attractive when patents are strong or firms' investments are effectively fortified from easy imitation. In such environments, would-be entrants are unable to hurdle entry barriers by using price cutting alone. Firms hold control over attractive customers best when their products can be effectively differentiated over those of competitors. If firms can

---

[a]"Opportunistic" customers are powerful retailers who appropriate their suppliers' fair share of value-adding profits by squeezing vendors' profit margins down but fail to pass on the benefits of their cost savings through lower prices for consumers.

differentiate their products, they can convert attractive market segments into protected niches.

Market "niches" are a unique way of serving customers that command price premiums. In order for endgame industries to be attractive, there must be traits in firms' product offerings that customers will pay premium prices for (otherwise products are "commoditylike"). Those traits—physical configuration, reliability, delivery, after-sale servicing, or other attributes—provide the basis for creating market niches. If product differentiability is impossible (or does not command price premiums), mature industries are less attractive for investments in aggressive endgame strategies.

Automobiles. As quality differences became more important to automobile buyers, car lines with fewer problems were more highly valued. Because reports of owners' problems were compiled and reported by consumer reporting agencies, customers could easily distinguish among different automobile brands. The most desirable product lines—Mercedes-Benz, Honda, and Lincoln-Mercury (among others)—sold higher volumes while commanding premium prices. The fact that car lines could be strongly differentiated from each other made the automobile industry a more attractive one for some firms to invest in aggressively.

Customer traits. Industries are most attractive if customers can afford to bear the increased costs that manufacturers will sustain by producing mature products even while their assets are underutilized. If these higher costs or others associated with maturity *cannot* be passed on to customers, there are fewer advantages to remaining for long in mature industries. For example, when hospital purchasing agents replaced x-ray technicians in making decisions regarding which vendors' x-ray films to buy, lower prices became more important than the ability to produce higher-resolution pictures. Because the U.S. system of third-party reimbursements to health-care providers paid a finite fee per x-ray film exposure, technicians were told to take more pictures with less costly x-ray films to provide equivalent diagnostic information.

The balance of power favors vendors in attractive endgame environments. In the continual tug-of-war for profits that exists between all vendors and buyers, the bargaining power of customers may be so strong that vendors are no longer compensated for providing endgame products. The balance of power favors *customers* when inexpensive and perfect substitutes are available. For example, the availability of inexpensive automobiles and television receivers makes customers more sensitive to the prices of costly automobile replacement-parts and electronic receiving tubes, respectively. When "Farina" hot breakfast cereal was discontinued, customers readily switched to "Cream of Wheat" hot breakfast cereal instead. The balance of power favors *vendors* when expensive and imperfect substitutes are customers' only available choices. For example, the only alternatives to costly ulcer and transplant nonrejection drugs is ulcer surgery and dialysis treatments, respectively.

Infant formula. As purchasing agents grew more sophisticated in 1988, manufacturers of infant formula were forced into using competitive bids to win federally funded contracts to supply infant formula. Leading firms, Abbott Laboratories' Ross Laboratories and Mead Johnson, controlled 90 percent of the U.S. infant formula market at that time, but Wyeth Laboratories, with a U.S. market share of 9 percent, underbid the two larger firms and started a nationwide battle using price warfare to win federally funded supply contracts. In many cases, Ross Laboratories and Mead Johnson gave Wyeth Laboratories these customers when they refused to bid on such contracts (rather than compete on price).

Steel. The global steel-making capacity glut in 1988 reflected burgeoning production in rapidly industrializing nations. When European and Japanese steel makers turned to export markets to consume their products, they discovered limits to growth because the U.S. markets were closed due to import curbs. Although newly industrializing nations were consuming more steel, they were also producing more of it themselves. Moreover, some customers in rapidly industrializing nations were becoming major exporters and had penetrated export markets that were traditionally served by European and Japanese steel exporters. Fewer customers wanted their steel products in 1988.

Supplier behavior. The same tug-of-war for profits that firms face with regard to their customers also exists with respect to their vendors. If sales to firms in mature industries are important to suppliers, they will extend help to them. Mature industries are most attractive where suppliers help customers weather the competitive turbulence of endgame by financing their sales, advertising on their behalf, or extending discounts and other forms of assistance.

As I explain in chapter 5, vendors can improve their quality controls, delivery systems, and value-adding tasks—frequently by undertaking activities that customers once did. Boundaries between supplier and buyer blur when both firms are working cooperatively to serve ultimate customers more effectively. Vendors invest in R&D activities to develop better inputs for customers; buyers invest in R&D to incorporate suppliers' superior components. Both parties enjoy the vertical synergies of a cooperative relationship as they strive for continual improvements in operations.

Computers. Because technological capabilities changed so rapidly in the computer industry, manufactuers of electronic components tried to keep abreast of changing customer needs by working closely with computer manufacturers and assemblers. Their willingness to help computer firms improve processing speeds and other performance attributes increased the attractiveness of the computer industry for pursuing aggressive endgame strategies.

Competitor behaviors. Strategy cannot be formulated in a vacuum; endgame strategies must be made with full consideration of the probable responses of competitors. Shrinking sales growth often means the end of nonprice competition. Stagnant growth forces firms from other strategic groups[2] to seek new customers. Penetration into new market segments brings firms with different approaches to and perceptions concerning the mature industry into head-to-head competition. Analysis of other firms' commitments to continued competition in the mature industry will suggest what other firms will do to gain customers when less committed rivals quit. Analysis will also suggest whether price levels can be maintained.

It is particularly difficult for publicly traded U.S. firms to compete in mature industries against competitors that possess differing time horizons or performance goals than theirs. Such competitors can be far more flexible in their approach to the vendor-supplier relationship because the resulting short-term "cross-subsidization" of other parties is a critical underpinning of their approach to doing business. Competitors with long-term horizons have deep pockets or "sugar daddies,"[3] they enjoy greater strategic flexibility in how they serve lucrative market segments, and they are often more willing to be extremely accommodating to win such customers away from their traditional vendors.

Oil refining. Endgame industries are more promising if competitors can signal their commitments to various actions well enough that other firms avoid incurring their wrath. For example, when oil prices rose during the 1970s and early 1980s, oil consumption fell due to higher prices and successful conservation efforts. Although the addition of excess refining capacity threatened to destroy price levels, Dow Chemical continued to build a new refinery. Its signaling procedure warned other firms not to follow its example. Briefly, Dow prolonged the construction process but launched major publicity campaigns that stressed how much capacity would be added by the completed oil refinery as each construction milestone was reached. In this manner, Dow ensured that all potential entrants to the refining industry (as well as all current competitors) would be deterred from adding redundant refineries.

Fiber-optic cable. In 1985, AT&T sent an unambiguous signal to would-be creators of high-volume, short-haul, long-lines competitors when it announced its intention to add 96,000 miles of fiber-optic cable to its long-distance network. At that time, specialized firms that were hoping to emulate the strategy of MCI Communications were forming telecommunications ventures with railroads by laying fiber-optic communications cable on lands occupied by railroad tracks. Because AT&T had little fiber-optic cable in its long-distance network at that time, the would-be specialized communications firms expected that their networks could be sold to AT&T in the event that their ventures failed. AT&T's much-publicized announcement of capacity expansion was intended to discourage the formation of such opportunistic ventures.

Farm machinery. By 1986, the world was teeming with food because many food-importing nations had made investments in new agricultural technology in previous years when they feared shortages, embargoes, and price-gouging by food-exporting nations. The resulting global surplus of food and feed grains harmed farmers, causing demand for tractors and larger farm equipment to fall markedly. Worldwide tractor output fell to 120,000 units in 1986, down from 230,000 units in 1979. Tractor makers produced only 20,000 over-100-horsepower tractors in 1986, down from 80,000 units in 1979.

Plunging demand blighted the farm equipment industry with substantial worldwide overcapacity, which persisted despite sharp cutbacks in the number of factories producing tractors, combines, and other agricultural equipment. Tractor makers were playing an industrywide game of "chicken." Although makers of farm and construction equipment were buried in overcapacity in 1988, firms in some countries—especially South Korea—were planning to add more plants. No firm wanted to get out of the business so that competitors could make money again.

Summary. If analysis concludes that mature industries have unfavorable structures and poor demand outlooks, endgame businesses belong in the lowest row of the strategy matrix of figures 3–1 and 3–2. Assessments that industries are not hospitable for further investments limit the range of strategy options to asset repositionings and disinvestments because businesses placed in the lowest row of the endgame strategy matrix are facing such inexorable decline or such a hostile competitive setting that *no* further investments can be justified.

Unfavorable industries have no niches of enduring, price-insensitive demand, low customer switching-cost barriers, opportunistic customers who exert their bargaining power, commodity-like products, substitutes that are perfect and cheaper, rapid or highly uncertain rates of declining demand, indifferent suppliers, highly specific and undepreciated assets, poor competitive signaling, and maverick competitors who insist on remaining in the troubled industry, among other inhospitable traits. Within unfavorable mature industries, demand was highly price sensitive and often plummeted abruptly—creating sizable write-off losses for firms that were forced to exit. Price cutting was severe, substantial reinvestment requirements often forced competitors to exit prematurely, and such great uncertainty prevailed regarding the duration of demand that firms were induced to invest in what was later revealed to be an unpromising industry. There was also substantial disorder in the patterns of firms' exits; the need for major asset write-offs deterred some marginal competitors from making timely exits. Indeed, the impact of competitors' actions on firms' endgame experiences was so important in the industries I studied that when managers believe competitors are especially committed to remaining in endgame industries, they should move their own firms' positioning to the right (a horizontal adjustment) on the strategy matrix shown in figures 3–1 and 3–2.

If analysis of mature environments indicates more undesirable traits than desirable ones, managers should *not* consider the aggressive strategy options shown in the top rows of figures 3–1 and 3–2. Instead they should investigate ways to divest their firms' assets immediately or milk them efficiently if outright sale of them is impossible. Fade-out joint ventures or other unorthodox arrangements may be needed to help firms to exit.[4] Sometimes government coordination through cartel schemes is needed to coax inefficient productive capacity out of troubled industries like fibers, bulk steel, steel castings, and petrochemicals (among others).

If analysis concludes that mature industries have favorable structures and good demand outlooks, the endgame businesses belong in the top row of the strategy matrix of figures 3–1 and 3–2. Businesses placed in the top row of the endgame matrix face the most promising industry environments. Such businesses often have products that require new infusions of cash in order to turn them around, and managers must also assess whether their firms are the ones to make those investments (using the tests of competitive strength developed in the next section). But first, managers must determine whether any promise of profitability remains in mature industries.

Large and enduring pockets of demand where customers will pay premium prices for differentiated products are most important to successful endgames. Without loyalty from such customers, firms cannot pursue the "last iceman" strategy successfully. In addition to sizable niches of enduring demand, favorable industries have differentiated product attributes (services) that customers value, high customer switching-cost barriers for sizable niches of demand, weak customers who do not exert buying power, slow and predictable rates of declining demand or hope for some revitalized demand (on a lesser scale), imperfect substitute products for some uses, helpful suppliers, flexible or depreciated assets (or ready markets for retired assets), few reinvestment requirements, low penalties for excess capacity, effective competitive signaling, and gentlemanly and statesmanlike competitors, among other hospitable traits.

Assessments that industries will remain attractive for continued investments opens up a wider range of strategy options, depending on firms' abilities to implement them. In favorable endgames, firms that possessed commitments to doing so increased the level of their investments in endgame by purchasing other firms' assets or improving their own operations. Guided by their analysis of the expected evolution of demand for mature products, other firms repositioned their investments to eliminate unpromising portions of mature businesses while fortifying more promising products or campaigns used in serving their best customers.

Assessing Competitor Strengths

After evaluating industrywide potential and determining whether mature industries are promising (or not), the next step in formulating endgame strategy is to assess which firms are best suited to serve any enduring pockets of demand that might exist. To perform this step of the analysis well, managers must have collected information about their competitors' strategic objectives, priorities, recent actions in mature businesses, and decision-making processes. Early in an industry's development—when demand is growing rapidly—knowledge about competitors and potential entrants is less critical. But when growth slows and firms must take actions with each other's reactions in mind—to set technological standards and avoid overbuilding—it is very important for managers to monitor their firms' competitors.[5]

Anticipating competitive behaviors. There is less room for competitive errors in the second half of industries' evolutions. Every decision that other firms make when competing in mature industries affects everyone's future prospects for profitability in that industry. When primary demand growth slows, most industrywide sales are to satisfy replacement demand and the emphasis in competition is on stealing other firms' customers. Managers must assess (1) which firms are most likely to remain to fight in endgame, (2) how quickly the less committed firms can be persuaded to exit, and (3) whether any new firms are likely to enter endgame industries (bringing with them new technologies for better operating economics or serving customers better).

Many corporate managers are uneasy about funding major rounds of factory modernization and automation in mature businesses because their firms' performance has not improved in spite of plant closings, layoffs, wage reductions, working practice concessions, and other cost-cutting measures. Their reticence in commiting to endgame competition could provide aggressive firms with opportunities to make preemptive investments in penetraing new market segments, modernizing plants, introducing new product features, and making other restructuring investments (including divestiture). Endgame competition is not for weak-kneed managers.

Textiles. Although the plants of many U.S. metals, textile, and paper firms were running near 95 percent of capacity utilization in 1987, their managers were unwilling to commit several hundred million dollars for new plants that would come onstream three years later—especially when they were uncertain of future demand growth and their firms' own relative competitive strengths. In many mature U.S. industries, such doubts resulted in an eroding capital base.

Aluminum and paper. By contrast, ALCOA pursued its customary strategy of building capacity in anticipation of demand growth by spending $800 million to build an aluminum sheet plant for making cans, largely for export sales. Great Northern Nekoosa spent $500 million on a new paper mill. Its competitor, Georgia-Pacific, appeared to be milking its paper-making investment as it raised prices to earn more money on smaller sales volumes.

Recognizing sources of strength. The strengths that help firms most to thrive in endgame include established relationships with customers who make up enduring (and lucrative) pockets of demand; highly valued brand names; plants that can operate efficiently when underutilized; strong and substantial distribution networks; favorable locations for operations; advantageous raw material contracts; good sourcing alternatives; international market links (and low shipping costs); able technicians who can jimmy-rig productive assets; low manufacturing costs (best economics and technology); good competitive-scanning systems and data collection of liquidation options; and advantageous postures of diversification, among others. Many strengths that become important for successful endgame competition can be cultivated while demand is still growing. For example, most managers desire logistical systems that allow them to recognize ethnic differences in consumer tastes due to changing population demographics. Because demand traits in most industries are becoming increasingly similar in many worldwide markets,[6] most managers want links to international markets and the wherewithal to coordinate global operations effectively. Because reputation is important to endgame competition, the "tall tales" that circulate among customers about how well particular vendors treat them are desired by managers also. All of these sources of strength have their basis in actions taken long before industries matured. To enjoy these strengths, managers should invest in ways of delivering high value to customers that are difficult for competitors to emulate long before they must also start thinking about how to keep up historical momentun in sales and profits.

Strengths become liabilities. As chapter 4 explains, some of the attributes that give competitors positions of relative strength to serve mature or declining demand are also sources of exit barriers that will make competitors difficult to dislodge. Weaker competitors may not realize that they are ill suited to remain and do battle in the endgame. Managers may have to take actions or adjust their firms' tactics to help weaker competitors to exit. Too much excess capacity makes weak firms especially nervous. Weak firms are too eager to use unwarranted price cutting—the easiest short-term competitive response and the most difficult to reverse.

The key to effective use of the endgame strategies lies in recognizing the depth of competitors' commitments to various products (and markets) and moving their attentions to arenas where managers would prefer that their firms compete against them. It is also a strength to understand why traditional sources of competitive advantage—such as closely coordinated vertical integration, shared facilities, and high scale economies in production—may be *disadvantageous* in endgame. Firms are most successful in endgames where firms' products can be differentiated effectively or where diverse market segments can be served by different firms without skirmishes due to attempted crossovers. If mature product offerings have been effectively differentiated in some way, managers can justify making new investments in them. If firms' products do not service customers that respond well to differentiation efforts—for example, if mature products are developing commoditylike traits that make customers increasingly price sensitive—reinvestments for aggressive endgame strategies may *not* be justified because no bases for enduring relationships between vendor and customer are likely to exist. Without the protection of high mobility barriers that effective investments in product differentiation usually provide, high-cost firms are vulnerable to market invasions by lower-cost competitors. If firms have allowed their products to become commoditylike such that no firm can distinguish its products from those of other vendors, strength in endgame may come from having flexible assets (or highly depreciated ones that can be quickly removed without substantial costs or disruptions to ongoing operations).

Market share and mature businesses. Although high market share is beneficial while industrywide sales volumes are stable, many of the advantages associated with high market are eroded when industrywide sales volumes decline. Scale economies become *diseconomies* if large-scale plants are not fully utilized. The impact of drops in sales growth is most exaggerated for firms that formerly dominated 60 percent (or more) of industrywide sales. If industries' structures are also sick, dominant firms' problems are exacerbated.

If firms are not lowest-cost competitors in industries where products' configurations are becoming commoditylike, they must often surrender market share during endgame competition until excess capacity is removed. If firms possess large market shares but do not possess lowest operating costs, strong distribution systems, or loyal niches of customers, they may wish to overcome their own exit barriers early by selling out to competitors (or even to suppliers). This is particularly true if high-cost but dominant firms possess large proportions of undepreciated assets.

As chapter 5 argues, managers should not necessarily be rewarded for increasing their firms' market share as endgames evolve to environments of stagnant industrywide sales growth. Profitability and cash flow become more important to endgame success than market share increases then because even committed firms may have to divest their endgame product lines if industry conditions turn sour. When managers pursue market share too aggressively by trying to maintain historic sales volumes in settings where sales are flat (or declining), they create environments of extreme price volatility and no profit margins. Their short-sightedness results in uneven financial results and wastes precious employee time and talent. If managers become too obsessed with maintaining their firms' leadership positions in endgame industries, their firms could suffer technological lags from which they may never recover.

If analysis concludes that particular firms have relevant strengths for remaining in endgame industries, they belong in the left column of the strategy matrix in figures 3–1 and 3–2. The benefits of being strong endgame competitors can be realized only by clearing mature industries of weaker firms. Recalling that the continued presence of highly determined (but potentially weaker) firms can have adverse effects on the endgame experiences of healthier firms, it is important for managers to make necessary capacity adjustments (in their firms' or other firms' plants) early enough for them to be helpful.

The strongest firms in endgame can pursue survival strategies—the increased investment, holding pattern, and selective shrinking strategies. Weaker firms should begin to implement exit strategies—by selling out to stronger firms if possible or by milking their investments if outright sale is not possible. Business units above the southwest-to-northeast diagonal in figures 3–1 and 3–2 are the only candidates that should receive funding as endgame competition progresses.

Staying flexible. In competitor analysis sessions, managers can position other firms on the endgame strategy matrix to determine which competitors are not yet pursuing appropriate strategies. Because all of the endgame competitors should be arrayed in the same row of the matrix, discrepancies between predicted and actual positionings may suggest that other firms see promise in industries that managers have missed. Alternatively, discrepancies may predict that overzealous firms will become sources of volatile price cutting later when they realize that their investments are trapped.

I have found high correlations between the strategies recommended in figures 3–1 and 3–2 and success in endgame. Figure 3–4 depicts this correlation. Briefly, 92 percent of the firms that followed these recommendations were successful, and 7 percent of the firms that followed the recommendations were

	Number of relatively successful outcomes	Number of relatively unsuccessful outcomes	
Number of firms that followed recommendations	39	3	(42)
Number of firms that did not follow recommendations	3	16	(19)
	42	19	

Figure 3–4. Correlation between Model and Success

unsuccessful; 16 percent of the firms that did not follow recommendations were successful, while 84 percent of the firms that did not follow recommendations were unsuccessful. Firms' endgame successes were determined by (1) accurately forecasting how demand will decline, (2) having favorable industry structures, (3) building positions of relative competitive strength, (4) adapting the tactics of chosen strategies to differing competitor activities, (5) maintaining good coordination between intelligence gained from scanning activities and actions taken, and (6) preempting competitors when executing chosen strategies. Successful firms maintain their strategic flexibility by developing sophisticated scanning systems that help them to implement tactics with greater precision.

Receiving tubes and rayon. As they implement their chosen endgame strategies, managers must watch competitors' actions closely. Their firms must be able to turn on a dime, as General Electric (GE) did in the electronic receiving-tube endgame where its analysis suggested that GE was the number-three competitor in what would be a comfortable two-firm endgame. When an organizational restructuring within the leading electronic receiving-tube producer (RCA Corporation) led it to shut down its plants and exit abruptly, General Electric shifted gears almost overnight and changed its endgame strategy from milking to a holding pattern. (Failure to change strategies in time to serve the customers that RCA was abandoning would have opened the U.S. replacement market for electronic receiving tubes to offshore competitors that had histories of using below-cost price cutting rather than more subtle ways of competing.) Similarly, when FMC Corporation threatened to shut down its Avtex Fiber rayon unit, competitors hurriedly announced capacity expansions and took other preventative measures to deter offshore competitors with histories of dumping from entering the U.S. fibers market. (At the last minute, the Avtex management team found funding for a leveraged buyout. Customers enjoyed uninterrupted supplies of rayon fibers, and new capacity did not enter the U.S. market.)

Summary. Survival and prosperity are possible even when mature industry environments become structurally unfavorable if managers make necessary investments soon enough. Other firms' actions can shift the competitive balance in mature industries, however, and inhibit firms from undertaking the most appropriate strategies. Weaker firms were able to preempt larger, complacent firms in many of the industries I studied.

Notes

1. The examples of differences in industry demand traits are taken from the industry studies comprising chapters 4 to 10 of K.R. Harrigan, *Strategies for Declining Businesses,* Lexington, Mass.: Lexington Books.

2. See Y. Ijiri and H.A. Simon, 1964, "Business Growth and Firm Size," *American Economic Review,* vol. 54, March:77–89; M. Hunt, 1972, "Competition in the Major Home Appliance Industry, 1960–1970, "Unpublished doctoral dissertation, Boston: Harvard Business School; K.J. Hatten, 1974, "Strategic Models in the Brewing Industry," Unpublished doctoral dissertation, West Lafayette: Purdue University; R.B. Manke, 1974, "Causes of Interfirm Profitability Differences: New Interpretations of the Findings," *Quarterly Journal of Economics,* vol. 88, no. 2, May:181–193; K.J. Hatten, 1975, "Strategy, Profits and Beer," *Proceedings, National Academy of Management;* R.E. Caves, B.T. Gale, and M.E. Porter, 1977, "Interfirm Profitability Differences: Comment," *Quarterly Journal of Economics,* vol. 91, November:667–675; K.J. Hatten and D. E. Schendel, 1977, "Heterogeneity within an Industry: Firm Conduct in the U.S. Brewing Industry, 1952–1971," *Journal of Industrial Economics,* vol. 26, no. 2, December:97–113; K.J. Hatten, D.E. Schendel, and A.C. Cooper, 1978, "A Strategic Model of the U.S. Brewing Industry, 1952–1971," *Academy of Management Journal,* vol. 21, no. 4, December:592–610; M.E. Porter, 1979, "The Structure within Industries and Companies' Performance," *Review of Economics and Statistics,* vol. 61, May:214–227; K. Vesper, 1979, "Strategic Mapping—A Tool for Corporate Planners," *Long Range Planning,* December:75–92; K.R. Harrigan, 1980, "Clustering Competitors by Strategic Groups," *Proceedings, Southwest Academy of Management Conference,* San Antonio; D. Miller and P.H. Friesen, 1980, "Archetypes of Organizational Transition," *Administrative Science Quarterly,* vol. 25, June:268–299; J.G. Wissema, H.W. Van Der Pol, and H.M. Messer, 1980, "Strategic Management Archetypes," *Strategic Management Journal,* vol. 1:37–47; S. Oster, 1982, "Intra-industry Structure and the Ease of Strategic Change," *Review of Economics and Statistics,* vol. 64:376–383; D.C. Hambrick, 1983, "High Profit Strategies in Mature Capital Goods Industries: A Contingency Approach," *Academy of Management Journal,* vol. 26:687–707; D.C. Hambrick, 1983, "An Empirical Typology of Mature Industrial-Product Environments," *Academy of Management Journal,* vol. 26, no. 2, June:213–230; D.C. Hambrick, 1983, "Some Tests of the Effectiveness and Functional Attributes of Miles and Snow's Strategic Types," *Academy of Management Journal,* vol. 26:5–26; M.L. Hergert, 1983, "The Incidence and Implications of Strategic Grouping in U.S. Manufacturing Industries," Unpublished doctoral dissertation, Boston: Harvard Business School; B. Kogut, 1984, "Normative Observations on the International Value-Added Chain and Strategic Groups," *Journal of International Business Studies,* vol. 15, no. 2, Fall: 151–167; K.R. Harrigan, 1985, "An Application of Clustering for Strategic Group Analysis," *Strategic Management Journal,* vol. 6, no. 1:55–74; K.J. Hatten and M.L. Hatten, 1985, "Some Empirical Insights for Strategic Marketers: The Case of Beer," in H. Thomas and D. Gardner (eds.), *Strategic Marketing and Management,* London: John Wiley; and K.J. Hatten and M.L. Hatten, 1987, "Strategic Groups, Asymmetrical Mobility Barriers and Contestability," *Strategic Management Journal,* vol. 8, no. 4, July–August: 329–342.

3. The "sugar daddy" that finances competitive efforts for firms with long-term horizons could be family members, a religious order, a bank (or other institutional provider of capital), a government agency, or firms' shareholders—especially where firms' employees are also their owners. If the subsidized business were in a growing industry, such behavior would be called "venture capital" and would be accepted as reflecting typical "Payback Analysis" cash-flow patterns. When the subsidized business is in a mature (or declining) demand industry, however, the economic theory guiding U.S. antitrust policy considers such behavior to be that of a monopolist.

4. See chapter 11 of K.R. Harrigan, 1985, *Strategies for Joint Ventures,* Lexington, Mass.: Lexington Books.

5. See W.R. King and D.I. Cleland, 1977, "Information for More Effective Strategic Planning," *Long Range Planning,* February:59–64; W.R. King and D.I. Cleland, 1977, "Decision and Information Systems for Strategic Planning," *Business Horizons,* April:29–36; W.R. King, B.K. Dutta, and J.T. Rodriguez, 1978, "Strategic Competitive Information Systems," *OMEGA: The International Journal of Management Science,* vol. 6, no. 2:123–132; P. Wack, 1986, "Scenarios: Shooting the Rapids," in Harvard Business Review (ed.), *Strategic Planning Comes of Age,* no. 11014:135–146.

6. R.B. Stobaugh, Jr., 1969, "Where in the World Should We Put That Plant?," *Harvard Business Review,* vol. 47 no. 1:132–134; W.J. Keegan, 1969, "Multinational Product Planning: Strategic Alternatives," *Journal of Marketing,* January:58–62; J.M. Stopford and L.T. Wells, Jr., 1972, *Managing the Multinational Enterprise,* New York: Basic Books; F. Knickerbocker, 1973, *Oligopolistic Reaction and Multinational Enterprise,* Cambridge, Mass.: Harvard University Press; W.V. Rapp, 1973, "Strategy Formulation and International Competition," *Columbia Journal of World Business,* Summer:98–112; P. Nueno, 1974, "A Comparative Study of the Capacity Expansion Decision Process in Steel Industry: U.S. and European Economic Community," Unpublished doctoral dissertation, Boston: Harvard Business School; C.L. Pomper, 1974, "International Facilities Planning: An Integrated Approach," Unpublished doctoral dissertation, Boston: Harvard Business School; U. Wiechmann, 1974, "Marketing Management in Marketing-Intensive Multinational Firms," Unpublished doctoral dissertation, Boston: Harvard Business School; R.Z. Sorenson and U. Wiechmann, 1975, "How Multinationals View Marketing Standardization," *Harvard Business Review,* vol. 53, no. 3, May–June:38–56; R.B. Stobaugh, Jr., 1977, "Multinational Competition Encountered by U.S. Companies That Manufacture Abroad," *Journal of International Business Studies,* vol. 8, no. 1, Spring:33–43; D. Channon and R.M. Jalland, 1978, *Multinational Strategic Planning,* New York: Macmillan; T.A. Pugel, 1978, *International Market Linkages and U.S. Manufacturing: Prices, Profits and Patterns,* Cambridge, Mass.: Ballinger; R.D. Ronstadt, 1978, "International R&D: The Establishment and Evolution of Research and Development Abroad by Seven U.S. Multinationals," *Journal of International Business Studies,* vol. 9, no. 1, Spring:7–24; J.W.A. Fischer and J.N. Behrman, 1979, "Coordination of Foreign R&D Activities by Transnational Corporations," *Journal of International Business Studies,* vol. 10, no. 3, Autumn:28–35; W.J. Keegan, 1979, "Future of the Multinational Manufacturing Corporation: Five Scenarios," Journal of International Business Studies, vol. 10, no. 1, Spring:98–104; A.M. Rugman, 1979, *International Diversification and the Multinational Enterprise,* Lexington, Mass.: Lexington Books; J.N. Behrman, 1981, "Transnational Corporations in the New International Economic Order," *Journal of International Business Studies,* vol. 12, no. 1, Spring:29–42; Y.L. Doz, C.A. Bartlett, and C.K. Prahalad, 1981, "Global Competitive Pressures and Host Country Demands: Managing Tensions in MNCs," *Sloan Management Review,* Spring:63–74; R.E. Caves, 1982, *Multinational Enterprise and Economic Analysis,* Cambridge, Mass.: Cambridge University Press; T. Hout, M.E. Porter, and E. Rudden, 1982, "How Global Companies Win Out," *Harvard Business Review,* vol. 60, no. 5, September–October: 98–108; J.K. Johansson, 1982, "The Managerial Relevance of Interdependence," *Journal of International Business Studies,* vol. 13, no. 3, Autumn:143–145; V. Terpstra, 1982, *International Dimensions of Marketing,* Boston: Kent; M.R. Cvar, 1984, "Competitive Strategies in Global Industries," Unpublished doctoral dissertation, Boston:

Harvard Business School; W.H. Davidson, 1984, "Administrative Orientation and International Performance," *Journal of International Business Studies,* vol. 15, no. 2, Summer:11–23; W.A. Dymsza, 1984, "Global Strategic Planning: A Model and Recent Developments," *Journal of International Business Studies,* vol. 15, no. 2, Summer:169–183; W.A. Dymsza, 1984, "Trends in Multinational Business and Global Environments: A Perspective," *Journal of International Business Studies,* vol. 15, no. 3, Autumn:25–46; A. Edstrom and P. Lorange, 1984, "Matching Strategy and Human Resources in Multinational Corporations," *Journal of International Business Studies,* vol. 15, no. 2, Summer:125–137; B. Kogut, 1984, "Normative Observations in the International Value-Added Chain and Strategic Groups," *Journal of International Business Studies,* vol. 15, no. 2, Fall:151–167; B. Mascarenhas, 1984, "Coordination of Manufacturing Interdependence in Multinational Companies," *Journal of International Business Studies,* vol. 15, no. 3, Autumn:91–106; B.S. Chakravarthy and H.V. Perlmutter, 1985, "Strategic Planning for a Global Business," *Columbia Journal of World Business,* vol. 20, no. 2, Summer:3–10; G.A. Daneke, 1985, "The Global Contest over the Control of the Innovation Process," Paper presented at the Academy of Management Meetings, San Diego; W.H. Davidson and D.G. McFetridge, 1985, "Key Characteristics in the Choice of International Technology Transfer Mode," *Journal of International Business Studies,* vol. 16, no. 2, Summer:5–21; W.R. King, 1985, "Information, Technology, and Corporate Growth," *Columbia Journal of World Business,* vol. 20, no. 2, Summer:29–34; T.H. Naylor, 1985, "International Strategy Matrix," *Columbia Journal of World Business,* vol. 20, no. 2, Summer:11–20; K. Ohmae, 1985, *Triad Power: The Coming Shape of Global Competition,* New York: Free Press; D.J. Teece, 1985, "Multinational Enterprise, Internal Governance, and Industrial Organization," *American Economic Review,* May:223–238; J. Thackray, 1985, "Much Ado about Global Marketing," *Across the Board,* vol. 22, no. 4:38–46; C.A. Bartlett, 1986, "Building and Managing the Transnational: The New Organizational Challenge," in M.E. Porter (ed.), 1986, *Competition in Global Industries,* Boston: Harvard Business School Press; A.D. Chandler, Jr., 1986, "The Evolution of Modern Global Competition," in M.E. Porter (ed.), *op. cit.*; D.S. Cho and M.E. Porter, 1986, "Changing Global Leadership: The Case of Shipbuilding," in M.E. Porter (ed.), *op. cit.*; M.R. Cvar, 1986, "Case Studies in Global Competition: Patterns of Success and Failure," in M.E. Porter (ed.), *op. cit.*; D.J. Encarnation and L.T. Wells, Jr., 1986, "Competitive Strategies in Global Industries: A View from Host Governments," in M.E. Porter (ed.), *op. cit.*; M.T. Flaherty, 1986, "Coordinating International Manufacturing and Technology," in M.E. Porter (ed.), *op. cit.*; P. Ghemawat and A.M. Spence, 1986, "Modeling Global Competition," in M.E. Porter (ed.), *op. cit.*; P. Ghemawat, M.E. Porter, and R.A. Rawlinson, 1986, "Patterns of International Coalition Activity," in M.E. Porter (ed.), *op. cit.*; M.E. Porter, 1986, "Competition in Global Industries: A Conceptual Framework," in M.E. Porter (ed.), *op. cit.*; H. Takeuchi and M.E. Porter, 1986, "Three Roles of International Marketing in Global Strategy," in M.E. Porter (ed.), *op. cit.*; J.K. Johansson and H.B. Thorelli, 1987, "International Marketing Policy: A Discussion of the Standardization Construct and Its Relevance for Corporate Policy," *Journal of International Business Studies,* vol. 17, no. 2, Summer:55–69; S. Ghoshal, 1987, "Global Strategy: An Organizing Framework," *Strategic Management Journal,* vol. 8, no. 5, September–October:425–440.

4
Restructuring Industries

As chapter 3 has explained, when managers prepare to maneuver through the endgame, they analyze the causes of depressed demand in order to identify *whether* enduring niches of lucrative customers exist. Next, they evaluate *which firms* are best suited to serve the most attractive customers and estimate whether their own firms can justify the repositioning investments needed to serve attractive market niches. If analysis suggests that their firm is not the strongest or that no attractive market niches exist, managers should divest troubled business units immediately (assuming that ready markets exist for their firms' assets). If outright sale is impossible, managers should begin milking their firms' asset bases quickly.

If their analyses suggest instead that their firms are among the stronger competitors and that demand within attractive customer niches will endure, managers progress to the next step. They assess the heights of their firms' and competitors' exit barriers to assess *whose* barriers would be easier to overcome, and how to help those firms to exit. That is the subject of this chapter.

It is necessary to overcome firms' exit barriers to restructure mature industries advantageously. If excess capacity is not removed (and destroyed), the threat of price warfare will undermine firms' willingness to replenish their assets during endgame competition. If firms do not reinvest in mature businesses, they risk losing advantages based on their problem-solving skills and manufacturing base to competitors.

Exit Barriers

Exit barriers are factors that dissuade firms from making smooth and timely exits from their various lines of business.[1] They may assume a variety of forms, as table 4–1 indicates. Exit barriers harm firms' strategic flexibility because opportunity costs are incurred from the blocked assets and diverted resources arising from them.

Table 4–1
Forms of Exit Barriers

Strategic exit barriers:
   Customers that are cut off may harm other businesses;
   Quality image;
   Shared customers, shared physical facilities, or other shared facilities;
   Centerpiece of corporate strategy (mother business).

Accounting-loss treatments:
   Poor performance undermines confidence in management's capabilities;
   Optimistic valuation induces firms to prolong their presence in industry.

$$\frac{\text{Barrier}}{\text{height}} = \frac{\text{Expected value of cash flows earned through future operations}}{\text{Immediate salvage value realizable}}$$

Managerial exit barriers:
   Emotional (prestige) investments;
   Turf battles (interdepartmental transfers or other lack of cooperation).

Source: Adapted from M.E. Porter, 1976, "Please Note Location of Nearest Exit: Exit Barriers, Strategy and Organizational Planning," *California Management Review,* vol. 19, no. 2, Winter: 21–33.

Strategic flexibility. Firms' abilities to reposition themselves in markets, change their game plans, or dismantle their current strategies when the customers they serve are no longer as attractive as they once were are tests of firms' *strategic flexibility.* When managers ignore questions of strategic flexibility, their firms often get stuck in obsolete strategic postures while competitors move on. (Exit barriers are called "mobility barriers" when they prevent firms from repositioning themselves easily, or decrease firms' strategic flexibility in other ways.[2])

Harm Caused by Exit Barriers

The barriers to flexibility can be asset-specific, but they are more likely to be mental. Too many managers refuse to face the ugly reality that they are in sick businesses or that their firms' strategic postures are simply wrong for serving remaining market segments. Even when it comes to phasing out their no-longer-profitable products or product lines, many otherwise well-managed companies hang on for too long. The worst offenders are plant or brand managers who recognize the trouble but cannot face giving up their own positions or laying off loyal workers. Thus bad news is kept from top management for as long as possible.

Firms face strategic inflexibility when they cannot redeploy their assets without friction. When exit (or mobility) barriers are high, firms cannot respond effectively to the innovations of new entrants (or ongoing competitors). They fall behind technologically and cannot respond adequately to changes in demand. Exit barriers prevent firms from repositioning themselves to serve more attractive customers, and they induce technological lags by misdirecting managers' attentions from other, more critically troubled businesses. High exit barriers keep firms operating in a status quo fashion even when they earn subnormal returns on their investments. Because they convince managers that their firms cannot afford to divest (or milk) businesses, exit barriers divert excessive managerial resources to endgames that cannot be won. Exit barriers are the major reason for bloodletting competitive behavior in endgames. Because high exit barriers can trap competitors within mature industries, they incite the kind of price-cutting behavior that ruins industry profits for all. Because high exit barriers ruin mature industries' attractiveness, few firms reinvest in such environments.

Managers that understand the pressures that exit barriers can exert on competitive behaviors could use this knowledge to their firms' advantage in shaping mature industries' contours. If managers believe adequate reasons to remain in troubled businesses exist, early analysis of competitors' barriers could suggest which other firms might be most responsive to their attempts to alleviate high exit barriers. Skillful manipulation of industry exit barriers can be used to influence an endgame's evoluation. The objective is to fashion favorable environments by rationalizing excess capacity, instead of allowing unfavorable environments plagued by destructive price cutting and no improvements in operating skills to evolve by doing nothing.

Strategic Exit Barriers

Exit barriers emanate from managers' reluctance to sacrifice the benefits of cumulative, intangible assets that their firms created through previous investments. Strategic exit barriers are created by customer-service obligations, potential harm created to ongoing businesses through the loss of shared customers or distribution channels, internal synergies between related businesses, shared facilities, image-maintenance goals, or highly successful market positions.

Customer-oriented exit barriers. In most mature industries, strong relationships with customers are the most valuable asset that any firm can possess and the most difficult to create. Many smaller firms grow, diversify, and thrive by finding new products to offer to their original customers. All fears created by strategic exit barriers concern potential harm that may be done to lines of business that will go on after the contemplated rationalization occurs. Managers fear that discontinuing products will erode their firms' overall images as reliable suppliers.

Managers must be aware of the strength of customer-oriented exit barriers. Table 4–2 indicates that in my tests of exit barrier heights, concerns arising

Table 4–2
Exit Barrier Heights

Probability of exit given the presence of:	
Customers with strong bargaining power	− .53
Substantial promotional and advertising investments	− .45
Physical facilities shared with ongoing businesses	− .42
Expectations that demand will revive	+ .41
Reputation for high-quality products	− .35
Undepreciated capital assets	− .26
Strategic importance to future activities	− .11

from customers created the highest probability that exit would *not* occur (53 percent likelihood).[3] Customers that are sick can contaminate their suppliers, as in the leather-tanning and man-made fibers indutries where weak companies carried their customers—by financing their inventories, advertising on their behalf, and granting lenient return and credit terms—largely because they feared losing *any* customers, regardless of the cost to the firm. As long as their sales volume was high, managers excused these losses as being temporary industry aberrations rather than fundamental, industrywide decreases in demand for their products.

Vertical integration as an exit barrier. Relationships among firms' business units—vertical-integration arrangements—can become sources of strategic exit barriers in mature industries.[4] The many benefits that can be enjoyed through vertical integration may result in frozen assets and illiquidity if managers are not flexible about adjusting the degree, breadth, stages, and form of their firms' buyer-supplier relationships—with outsiders as well as with sister business units.[5] Fears regarding losses of synergies that originate from sharing resources also discourage timely exits.

Firms engaged in several stages of processing will face high exit barriers because several vertical links represent larger investments to dispose of than few links. High degrees of backward integration with sister strategic business units (SBUs) will be more difficult to disrupt than high degrees of forward integration because the higher minimum-efficient-scale (MES) plant sizes of upstream units usually make them more dependent on downstream SBU purchases than downstream stages are on upstream sales. Also, the throughput volumes involved in the deintegration decision will seem more substantial when vendors are divested than when downstream linkages must be severed, especially when upstream SBUs sell to outsiders.

The power of vertical-integration exit barriers means that panicking firms might integrate backward to ensure supplies of necessary inputs at the very time when divestiture or abandonment would cost less than acquiring supplying business affiliates. Because new investment redoubles firms' commitments to mature industries at the very time when they should be investigating ways of easing down exit barriers, firms that would be their industries' last icemen must provide for ways of overcoming other firms' impulses to integrate vertically in endgame.

Economic Exit Barriers

Economic exit barriers arise from financial concerns. These barriers can be the costs associated with eliminating plants (such as the cost of dismantling chemical plants and treating the land beneath them) or the lack of resale markets for plant and assets that are not fully depreciated. If the expenditures for other types of investments—advertising, R&D, or plant improvements—are not expensed, they too could constitute economic exit barriers in the sense that they might appear as undesirable reported losses on disposal when firms exit. (All assets that have been capitalized could act as exit barriers by virtue of the reporting losses they could create if firms exited before depreciating them, but physical assets—such as plant, machinery, and inventory—are major sources of economic exit barriers.)

Managers within publicly traded firms are especially susceptible to economic exit barriers because they let their firms' accounting policies entrap them in unattractive industries. For example, when firms are required to eliminate the reserves that offset losses on asset disposals, the resulting poor reported performance undermines the capital market's confidence in management's abilities. Because their firms need ready access to outside sources of capital to finance growth strategies, managers that are entrapped by exit barriers prolong their firms' presence in industries where they are ill equipped to compete (rather than realize write-offs on asset disposals). In their desire to show pretty financial results to short-term investors, managers may divest promising businesses for quick profits to offset the effect of losses incurred in writing off mature businesses' assets.

The extent to which past asset investments become millstones when firms try to reposition themselves depends on the types of assets they have created. New physical assets—for example, recent investments in factory automation— are not barriers until they cannot be used readily elsewhere. Investments in machinery capable of doing one specific task are more inflexible than investments in general-purpose, flexible-manufacturing machinery, and U.S. firms are especially likely to become hamstrung by investments in inflexible assets because their managers act as though they believe that each "technological fix" of new physical assets will solve their fundamental operating problems. Where managers can devise ways to improve operating systems continually, old plants and equipment can be nurtured, preserved, and run efficiently while economic exit barriers are lowered.

Steel. Despite considerable evidence that expected rises in demand would not materialize, managers of steel firms refused to abandon their illusions that steel consumption would increase and refused to face the high financial (and political) barriers to closing their steel mills.[a] In Europe, procrastination resulted in the most efficient firms being forced to exit first.

West German steelmakers—which specialize in making high-quality, specialty steel products that bring higher profit margins and boast some of the most modern and efficient plants in the world—must close their plants under rationalization schemes of the EEC's "crisis cartel," which has existed since 1980. The West German steel industry has remained in private hands while those in many other European nations have been nationalized and subsequently subsidized (despite a formal 1985 agreement to stop subsidies).

There was much unused capacity in the European steel industry, yet prices were rising. Spanish buyers of stainless steel complained that imports were so restricted that they could buy only from Acerinox (a big Spanish firm). British customers were angry about 7.5 percent price increases because they could not obtain cheaper quotes from any suppliers. The West German steelmakers opposed the commissions' plan for members to share the need to retire unused capacity by 20 million tons or more because they were reluctant to sacrifice their "efficient" steelworks to save other nations' "inefficient" plants.

Falling Demand

Expectations concerning demand growth are important because they affect firms' abilities to change strategic postures. In embryonic and emerging industries, expectations affect firms' abilities to raise capital or dispose of obsolete assets. Expectations also affect firms' strategic flexibility in endgame because their exit barriers increase substantially when it becomes clear that demand is no longer growing. It is inevitable that the liquidation value firms can realize on assets committed to endgames will shrink as competition within mature industries progresses, especially if these assets cannot be easily converted to other productive uses. When it becomes widely recognized that demand will not recover within mature industries, excess capacity will become endemic. Competitors that are locked into troubled industries by high exit barriers will engage in contorted maneuvers to exit later when it becomes imperative to do so. To avoid such disruptions, surviving firms may find ways to ease erratic competitors out of mature industries.

---

[a]Chase Econometrics estimated that the cost of closing a typical integrated steel mill would exceed $300 million ($75,000 per employee) in 1987. Some steel makers were unable to retire even their unprofitable unused capacity because their pension fund obligations were unfunded. Other steel firms could not absorb the cost of paying off workers and other closing expenses.

Managerial Exit Barriers

Even when managers know that business units are in trouble, they may continue bleeding operations until the hemorrhage weakens their entire firm if they feel responsibilities to go on for employees, customers, or vendors. Managers may have emotional attachments to mature businesses or fear loss of prestige in their business communities. More frequently, their inaction arises from long-standing and deeply rooted beliefs that their corporate cultures reinforce. Exit barriers are mental baggage that managers carry with them into problem solving. These barriers are their firms' established ways of looking for solutions to problems, and the traditional excuses for why actions are not undertaken. Exit barriers are mind-sets that inhibit firms' strategic flexibility in the midst of competitive turmoil.

The barriers that permeate firms' cultures—creating a "no-can-do" atmosphere—prevent people from taking risks and abandoning mediocre behaviors. These barriers are reflected in managers' outlooks as well as in their ways of conceptualizing what customers want and how to serve them. These barriers also reflected in firms' faulty management systems—in the wrong types of performance measures and the wrong competitive behaviors they reward. Flexible firms must be willing to create flexible systems wherein people (the critical differentiating factor in competition) are given autonomy to change their organizations and their focus.

It is difficult to overcome inertia barriers by fostering new ways of thinking when managers are scrambling to revitalize demand, contain costs, and remain innovative. The do-nothing solution that seemed so right in the past is a difficult life preserver to sacrifice when one is afloat in the vast, cold ocean of competition. But it is necessary to overcome these mental barriers in order to reposition firms with ease in endgame industries.

Reducing Exit Barriers

If analysis suggests that their firms are one of the stronger competitors and that attractive customer niches will endure, managers must assess the heights of their firms' and competitors' exit barriers to assess *whose* barriers would be easier to overcome and to decide how they might influence endgames' evolutions. Because the strongest barriers to strategic flexibility tend to be shared customers that can harm firms' other business units when they are cut off, managers begin shaping their endgame environments by assessing how they might change customers' exit barriers. If managers do not take actions to lower exit barriers that threaten to turn their industries into cash traps, their mature businesses may turn abruptly from healthy cash cows to those with tapeworms that consume more resources than they generate. When managers reduce exit barriers, they take actions to (1) move customers to products that their firms prefer to offer, (2) help weaker competitors to exit, and (3) lower their own barriers. In concert with competitors, managers keep industrywide capacity in line with stagnant (or declining) demand while using unorthodox sourcing and selling arrangements to utilize existing capacity better. Whether particular firms invest in restructuring mature industries (or not) depends on which endgame strategy alternatives they pursue and their sensitivity to outsider criticisms. The U.S. capital markets overvalue firms that "bite the bullet" by *divesting* sick businesses when they first begin to sour. Other cultures reward the heroism of managers who retrieve the value embedded in sick businesses that other firms have sold by *turning them around* (see chapter 5).

Managing Relationships with Customers

Managers begin shaping their endgame environments by assessing how they might change customers' exit barriers. Effective management of highly valued customers' switching-cost barriers is especially important if firms intend to continue serving those customers with products that are *not* being deleted. To avoid harming ongoing products, firms sometimes resell products that they have purchased from surviving manufacturers long after their own plants have been closed. They do this as a service to highly valued customers while they try to ease customers into using new products. Firms take fewer pains to inconvenience less valued customers because they realize that these customers are so price sensitive, fickle, and opportunistic in their use of bargaining power over vendors that they will readily abandon reliable vendors. Sales representatives that are compensated for bulk sales (instead of *mix* of sales) are often unwilling to admit that customers are not equally attractive to serve. Distinguishing among different types of customers is an important part of managing the endgame effectively.

Many managers believe that policies to lock in customers—such as take-or-pay contracts[6]—are advantageous to their firms. In fact, having customers that face high switching-cost barriers can be a two-edged sword. Although contractually bound customers guarantee some cash flow, firms often need several customers whose purchases each represent substantial portions of their plants' productive capacities to justify remaining in endgame businesses. If one of those customers fails and the others will not renegotiate their contracts to absorb its slack, dependence on a few customers who are bound by take-or-pay contracts can stymie firms' strategic flexibility. Enterprising managers should recognize that when the dangers of locking customers into purchasing contracts outweigh the possible benefits of continuing such relationships, they must find ways to ease contractually committed customers to other products. Perhaps their firms can create new business opportunities by helping key customers to develop new technologies or services that depend on their substitute products instead of endgame products.

Lowering Competitors' Exit Barriers

Enterprising managers can help marginal firms to exit by (1) offering to honor competitors' obligations to service installed bases of products or supply replacement parts (thus lowering rivals' customer-related exit barriers), (2) acquiring their plants or other productive assets, and (3) intercepting suppliers who appear eager to assist marginal competitors. Desperate firms have gone public in a plea to persuade competitors to exit, as Gerber Products did. Managers may even start price wars (but only if their firms can win) or alert regulatory agencies of competitors' transgressions in pollution control or infringements of other regulations, if their firms are blameless.

Buying competitors' assets. Competitors' staying power—that is, their abilities and willingness to stay in industries and fight for shrinking numbers of customers—is determined by the exit barriers they face or inflict on themselves. An understanding of competitors' exit barriers is essential in order to determine whether aggressive restructuring investments should be undertaken. If analysis suggests that, despite its efforts to avoid a price war, firms will be drawn into bloodbaths by competitors that will not yield market share despite their competitive disadvantages, managers might consider purchasing the assets of those disruptive competitors.

Managers should realize that announcing firms' intended departures precipitates shifts by former customers to alternative sources of supply and price rises for endgame products. For example, Olin Corporation was left with warehouses full of soda ash when customers abruptly switched suppliers following a rumor that Olin planned to shut down its synthetic soda-ash plants. Cigar makers raised their prices as smaller firms left the industry. Even if the capacity of exiting firms is operated by competitors, exit provides an opportunity for surviving firms to establish wider profit margins for their endgame products. The confusion created by competitors' exits may also provide the lag time needed by survivors to improve operations and regain customers that were temporarily lost. In this manner, remaining firms can prosper in subsequent years of endgame competition if they are poised to exploit this period of temporary confusion. To do so, managers must assess whether expenditures made to lower competitors' exit barriers are cost justified. Decisions to purchase marginal competitors' assets must be guided by the conclusion that acquiring firms should increase their commitments to the mature industry. (The proper calculation is a comparison of (1) the discounted cash flows expected from continued operations in the rationalized industry to (2) the cost of lowering other firms' exit barriers.) When Sylvania drowned the electronic receiving-tube assets of Union Electric in the Bashi Channel, it improved industry profitability for surviving firms, as did Broken Hill Proprietary Ltd. when it bought the assets of several barbed-wire firms and destroyed them. When Norsk Hydro rationalized its fertilizer-producing assets, it signaled its continued commitment to enhance industry profitability.

Cross-production agreements and asset swaps. If stronger firms are to retire weaker firms' assets, arrangements must be made to ease them smoothly out of mature industries. As a first step, stronger firms might manufacture products for weaker firms under private-branding arrangements. Later, acquiring firms can take over responsibility for serving departing firms' customers. As endgame competition progresses, surviving firms must ensure that new firms do not acquire the assets of departing firms or invest in new productive capacity. Otherwise their restructuring efforts are wasted.

Bulk chemicals. Dow Chemical was not the only firm to take write-downs in achieving the shift in emphasis from bulk chemicals to specialty products. An industrywide restructuring occurred. In 1982, Exxon shut in one-fourth of its ethylene capacity in Baton Rouge, Louisiana, and Occidental Petroleum mothballed 20 percent of its capacity for making polyvinyl chloride (PVC). In 1984, du Pont sold Conoco's chemicals business to Vista Chemical. Two years later, Monsanto sold Sterling Chemical, its Texas City Petrochemical complex to Vista Chemical.

Imperial Chemical Industries (ICI) swapped its polyethylene business for British Petroleum (BP)'s polyvinyl chloride (PVC) business and formed a joint venture with Enichem to sell PVC jointly in Europe in 1986. Firms in West Germany and Japan took similar actions to prune excess capacity, but Italian and French governments nationalized (or subsidized) chemical firms rather than close noncompetitive facilities. In 1983, the French government gathered several loss-making bulk-chemical businesses under the umbrella of Elf-Aquitaine (the state-owned energy group). Rhône-Poulenc was persuaded to acquire several other troubled chemical, drug, and fiber firms. Elf-Aquitaine and Rhône-Poulenc both received generous government grants for taking on the excess capacity, but they were not allowed to restructure these businesses quickly by closing plants. In 1983, the Italian government bailed out six troubled chemical firms. Enichem was persuaded to take on bulk chemicals. Montedison absorbed the more valuable specialty chemical firms. More than half of the bulk-chemical capacity had to close, and the process of capacity rationalization was painful because of the gradual pace at which surviving firms were allowed to cut capacity.

From 1982 to 1988, one-fourth of the developed world's bulk-chemical capacity was retired. The number of European ethylene producers dropped from thirty-one to twenty-eight, and the number of plants in operation fell from sixty-five to forty-four. As a result of this downsizing, chemical plants were using more than 80 percent of productive capacity in 1987, as compared with utilization rates of 66 percent in 1982. Most surviving chemical firms were profitable, but there were fewer manufacturers for any given specialty chemical after the restructuring occurred.

Lowering Firms' Own Exit Barriers

Only the strongest firms should work to improve working practices and operating systems in quests to become endgames' last icemen. Other firms should retrieve as much value as possible by reducing their own exit barriers early.

Financially oriented barriers. There are numerous accounting tricks that managers could use to lower their firms' own exit barriers, if financial concerns are their major sources of strategic inflexibility. Managers can help their firms to overcome exit barriers with greater ease by changing their firms' planning processes and accounting policies. For example, managers could institute "horizon budgets" whereby they routinely evaluate whether to exit from a line of business when demand growth falls below a prescribed performance level. Horizon budgets force managers to prepare contingency plans for workforce reductions, replacement parts for their installed products, and so on, in case top management decides to ease out of endgame businesses. Horizon budgets warn managers when purchasing policies should be changed so that contracts are timed to parallel plant depreciation schedules, and when accounting losses on disposal should be matched with gains by divesting winning product lines with losers (a practice that is especially commonplace if accounting exit barriers are high for firms). Money managers and other providers of financing often reward firms that make early divestitures with increased price-earnings ratios and higher bond ratings because they believe them to be well managed. Although early exits may actually shortchange firms of higher returns available after endgame industries have been restructured, capital markets are not as willing to reward managers for taking the higher risks of managing maturing businesses well.

Managers can lower their firms' own exit barriers by reducing their capital base, perhaps by leasing replacement assets instead of purchasing them. They could use technological tactics, such as trading off highly specialized plant and equipment for general-purpose, flexible assets as industrywide growth in unit shipments slows. Or they could find ways to run old plants more effectively. If firms operate in several international geographic markets, multinational tactics for lowering their exit barriers could include moving assets abroad on a scheduled basis, thereby forcing "jump-off" points of reevaluation each time firms are asked to fund new generations of assets for specific geographic sites.

Retrieving investments in intangibles. Firms that have the largest stakes invested in R&D and other intangible assets—those that differentiated their products effectively—face the greatest impediments in repositioning their competitive postures, closing plants, or exiting completely. Briefly, intangible sunk costs act as economic sunk costs because managers let them increase the heights of their exit barriers. If managers with differentiated products conclude that their firms possess no relative advantage as manufacturers, firms might lower their own exit barriers by appealing to staunchly committed competitors to purchase their productive assets and act as suppliers thereafter. Firms may cooperate by sharing production outputs, as well as information, marketing efforts, or other activities and resources to utilize resources that are trapped in mature businesses. Effective use of strategic alliances in mature businesses is similar to that of effective cartel arrangements; it reduces excess capacity while allowing members to recover their investments in intangible assets through continued marketing activities. Joint ventures provide firms that want to divest troubled businesses with an incremental means of doing so.

Selling assets. If exit appears imminent, overseas investors should not be overlooked as conduits for disposing of assets that cannot be used elsewhere. Suppliers sometimes purchase their customers (but customers often prefer lifetime-buyout sales instead of backward integration). Where divestiture is management's strategy choice, the most logical and appropriate candidates for buyouts are frequently right under their noses. Employees are often fruitful avenues for the disposal of business units that large firms cannot manage profitably. In cases where plant assets are old but serviceable, employee groups assisted by local banks have acquired spun-off business units to save their jobs. Without the burdens allocated by corporate overhead charges, spun-off companies have been able to survive and perform adequately for their new owners. Finally, managers could shut down obsolete facilities or convert them (and their work forces) to other uses by selling endgame businesses to employees (by using Employee Stock Option Plans (ESOPs), leveraged buyouts, or other plans whereby workers purchase assets). Redundant assets could be retired through "fade-out joint ventures," a form of incremental divestiture in which one partner fades out while the other joint-venture partner assumes majority ownership.[7]

In 1987, U.S. labor unions began to initiate buyouts and mergers to save jobs and control investment decisions. In 1985 and 1986, the United Steel Workers (USW) union set up ESOPs to purchase several facilities that steel companies such as LTV Corporation wanted to close or sell. Weirton Steel became wholly owned by employees in 1983. Employees purchased the Hyatt-Clark Industries roller-bearings plant from General Motors in 1981. In this last example, board members from the United Auto Workers (UAW) and management constantly argued over managerial appointments and salaries, as well as proportions of profits that should go to profit-sharing bonuses instead of reinvestment in new equipment. Demand for roller bearings declined in 1987, and Hyatt-Clark was pushed into chapter 11 bankruptcy proceedings.

Unions have won seats on the boards of Chrysler, Wheeling-Pittsburgh Steel, Pan Am, Kaiser Aluminum, Weirton Steel, CF&I Steel, PIE Nationwide, Transcom, and several smaller firms. When unions appoint board representatives, their interests are different than those of management appointees. Unlike owners that focus on short-term, financial performance criteria—most union board representatives tend to be interested in long-term issues—plant closings, layoffs, contracting out, and (most important) new investment.

Vertical-integration barriers. Vertical-integration arrangements need updating just as other dimensions of competitive strategy do. Because vertical-integration strategies coordinate activities in several divisions, changes in such strategies must lower exit barriers without destroying firms' vertical frameworks for realizing benefits at several stages of the value chain. If firms want their SBUs to supply (or buy from) each other, they should frequently reexamine their premises for encouraging such arrangements because the strategic window that may once have favored vertical integration can close. When demand growth slows, managers can avoid selling too much of the firm's products in-house and wide-ranging buyer-seller relationships between business units. To realize scale economies, only high-volume or high-margin products and activities should be produced in-house as endgames progress. (Outsiders can provide low-volume and low-margin products.) Because these changes should be made in stages and continuously—*not* by using radical surgery—managers may begin to create intracompany competition early by encouraging in-house customers to use the best local suppliers for some of their requirements and by helping in-house suppliers to create new products and services to fill the void created by de-integration. Ineffective firms tend to transfer more goods and services internally in adverse industries. They also perform more tasks in-house and engage in longer chains of processing, even when they possess the bargaining power needed to use outsiders advantageously.

To maintain strategic flexibility, it may be necessary to introduce duplicate assets (or service facilities) while managers separate units that were formerly linked. Downstream intrafirm linkages are easier to restructure than upstream intrafirm linkages are. Conceptually distinct accounting entities may be created by redefining business unit boundaries, but being engaged in several stages of processing creates inflexibilities that could best be avoided by using outsiders for some production steps. In doing so, firms remain more flexible to changes in technology and demand.

Soft drinks. In January 1988, the bottling operations of Coca-Cola USA were reorganized to reflect changes in how Coca-Cola's syrup and concentrate were sold to fountain and bottling customers. In the past, the bottling division had focused on providing services to, watching over, and smoothing relationships with Coca-Cola's independent and strong-minded bottlers. Since 1978, however, the number of independent bottlers had shrunk to 185 from 365.

As the consolidation of bottlers occurred, the larger resulting firms became increasingly more capable of providing their own services. (Coca-Cola's ten largest U.S. bottlers represented 75 percent of its U.S. sales in 1987, and has included firms such as Kirin Brewery, General Cinema, Beatrice Foods, IC Industries, and Procter & Gamble.) The number of bottling franchises granted by the five largest soft drink concentrate producers had fallen by approximately 15 percent between 1974 and 1984. Pepsico had repurchased several of its bottling franchises after World War II in order to strengthen their operations for the war Pepsico launched against Coca-Cola. As the "cola wars" intensified in the 1980s, Coca-Cola replaced bottlers in key markets where they were not deemed to be sufficiently aggressive, sometimes taking an equity position in the new ownership.

Major soft drink firms owned 15 to 20 percent of their own bottlers in 1985. Franchisees were allowed to bottle other firms' soft drinks, provided that the new beverage was not in the same product category, for example, a Coca-Cola bottler could not bottle another cola beverage. Despite their seemingly "independent" status, soft drink firms were known to exert duress over their bottlers, as in the case when Philip Morris introduced "Like" cola in 1982 and wanted its Seven-Up bottlers to drop their existing cola franchises to bottle its "Like" cola, instead of Coca-Cola, Pepsi-Cola, Royal Crown Cola, or another brand.

Overcoming Implementation Barriers

A frequent knee-jerk response to the news that businesses are entering endgame is to sell those businesses, but mature businesses are often worth more if they are retained and managed for continual improvement, than if they are sold. Careful study of mature industries may reveal that no firms could hope to operate there as well as present managers can and that even fewer knowledgeable buyers would pay the current value of mature businesses' assets on sale.

Mature businesses pose a vexing managerial puzzle. Endgame is an opportunity to introduce major changes in management policy companywide, but "sick pussycat" businesses can absorb valuable and unjustified managerial attentions. Top management must assess which sick industries can be cured and must guide the strategies of endgame businesses through their choices of leadership for mature business units, their overt attentions to the progress of turnarounds, and the management systems they create.

If top management cannot overcome its prejudices concerning the potential of mature businesses, they will bungle decisions concerning (1) who are the right managers to run mature businesses and (2) how to motivate them. The negative attitude top management holds regarding mature industries can quickly be sensed by plant managers and workers. If they mistrust top management, an unhealthy cynicism regarding support for operations can develop, which will lessen the value received from potential buyers later.

Make employees become allies. Implementation of endgame strategies hits snags when managers must deal with customers, activist community groups, militant unions, and other affected parties. Workers at heavily unionized plants may request access to corporate books (to evaluate proposed reductions in wages or in production volumes). Union representatives may hold their own press conferences regarding the future of the mature business. Unexpected workers' compensation suits may be filed following plant closings or organizational restructurings. To reduce these problems, top management must educate their firms' managers and employees about the implications of demand maturity. They should warn employees about the effects of losing competitive tranquility. It is wise to lower employee expectations in advance because it may later be necessary to reduce salary differentials and roll back wage increases. Employee motivation must be high to implement many of the endgame strategies of chapter 3, and top management support is needed if the highly motivated and charismatic endgame cadres in charge of mature businesses are expected to surmount the implementation barriers that plague troubled industries.

Do not prolong the agony. Line managers find it frustrating to keep obsolete factories operating, knowing that they may face an uncomfortably near-term termination date. Top management cannot afford to dally in deciding the future of mature business units. While top management deliberates mature businesses' fates, line management tries to avoid losing key workers and valued executives who might leave if they knew that exits or abandonments were being contemplated. If mature businesses must be sold, their value must be conserved until buyers have been found and sales have been consummated. If top management is not willing (or able) to support the efforts needed to run mature businesses skillfully, it may be better for all parties involved to locate buyers quickly and transfer ownership before significant damage has been incurred. Timely implementation is a critical aspect of this management problem.

If fade-out joint ventures (or other forms of strategic alliance) are planned, managers should identify and link up with the best partners for joint ventures, contract processing, or sourcing arrangements *early*—before their competitors reach the same conclusion and lock up the best outsiders. If managers wish to enhance *internal* joint ventures, they must also plan ahead.[8] Although managers may wish to use the leverage of their firm's bargaining power to shift inventory risks to suppliers or distributors (in a *kanban*-like arrangement), the benefits of internal resource sharing may be greater. Managers must anticipate the implementation problems most likely to arise in creating internal joint ventures and provide ways of overcoming animosities between sister business units that are not accustomed to cooperation. Many firms sacrifice synergistic (or scope) economies for lack of effective coordination systems. Most frequently, business intelligence is not communicated up and down vertical chains adequately because business units do not share top management's long-term vision of their roles in firms' global systems.

Keeping plants fully utilized and critically skilled laborers fully employed is important for firms if they desire the flexibility to reposition in endgame or sell out with ease. For example, in the oil-refining industry—where minimum-efficient-scale plants processed large volumes of throughput (175,000 barrels per day)—higher operating costs were incurred when refineries ran at lower levels of capacity utilization. Unfavorable economics exacerbated the difficulties that oil firms faced when they tried to rationalize their positions by disposing of excess facilities. If managers conclude that their best strategies are continued presences in the mature industries, it will be necessary for them to introduce changes in their operating systems that lead to quality, logistical, and servicing improvements. Chapter 5 addresses these programs for improvement.

Notes

1. G. Shillinglaw, 1959, "Profit Analysis for Abandonment Decision," in E. Solomon (ed.), 1959, *Management of Corporate Capital,* Glencoe, Ill.: Glencoe Press; L. Davis, 1965, "Corporate Separations," *Journal of Accountancy,* September:35–42; A. Robichek and J.C. Van Horne, 1967, "Abandonment Value and Capital Budgeting," *Journal of Finance,* December:577–589; R.H. Hayes, 1969, "Optimal Strategies for Divestiture," *Operations Research,* March–April:292–310; M.M. Speiser, 1969, "Corporate Divestitures: How to Sell Off a Subsidiary," *Management Review,* April:2–8; F. Lovejoy, 1971, *Divestment for Profit,* New York: Financial Executives Research Foundation; R.H. Hayes, 1972, "New Emphasis on Divestment Opportunities," *Harvard Business Review,* vol. 50, no. 4, July–August:55–64; P. Hilton, 1972, "Divestiture: The Strategic Move on the Corporate Chessboard," *Management Review,* March: 16–19; H. Wallender III, 1973, "A Planned Approach to Divestment," *Columbia Journal of World Business,* Spring:33–37; L. Vignola, 1974, *Strategic Divestment,* New York: AMACOM; K.J. Boudreaux, 1975, "Divestiture and Share Price," *Journal of Financial and Quantitative Analysis,* vol. 10:619–626; R.E. Caves and M.E. Porter, 1976, "Barriers to Exit," in R.T. Masson and P.D. Qualls (eds.), 1976, *Essays on Industrial Organization in Honor of Joe S. Bain,* Cambridge, Mass.: Ballinger, pp. 39–69; A. Easton, 1976, *Managing for Negative Growth: A Handbook for Practitioners,* Reston, Va.: Reston; M.E. Porter, 1976, "Please Note Location of Nearest Exit: Exit Barriers, Strategy and Organizational Planning," *California Management Review,* vol. 19, no. 2, Winter:21–33; D.J. Teece, 1976, *Vertical Integration and Vertical Divestiture*

in the U.S. Oil Industry, Stanford, Calif.: Stanford University, Institute for Energy Research; R.E. Caves and M.E. Porter, 1977, "From Entry Barriers to Mobility Barriers: Conjectural Decisions and Contrived Deterrents to New Competition," *Quarterly Journal of Economics,* May:241–261; W. Matthews and W.I. Boucher, 1977, "Planned Entry–Planned Exit: A Concept and an Approach," *California Management Review,* vol. 20, no. 2, Winter:36–44; G. Bing, 1978, *Corporate Divestment,* Houston: Gulf; K.R. Harrigan and M.E. Porter, August 1978, "A Framework for Looking at Endgame Strategies," Paper presented at the National Meetings of the Academy of Management, San Francisco; F.T. Magiera and A.E. Grunewald, 1978, "The Effect of Divestiture Motives on Shareholder Risk and Return," Paper presented at the Western Finance Association Meeting, Kona, Hawaii; G.R. Patton and I.M. Duhaime, 1978, "Divestment as a Strategic Option: An Empirical Study," Paper presented at the Academy of Management Meetings, San Francisco; K.R. Harrigan, 1979, "Strategies for Declining Businesses," Unpublished doctoral dissertation, Boston: Harvard Business School; B.D. Wilson, 1979, "The Disinvestment of Foreign Subsidiaries by U.S. Multinational Companies," Unpublished doctoral dissertation, Boston: Harvard Business School; B.C. Eaton and R.G. Lipsey, 1980, "Exit Barriers Are Entry Barriers: The Durability of Capital as a Barrier to Entry," *Bell Journal of Economics,* vol. 11, no. 2, Autumn:721–729; K.R. Harrigan, 1980, "The Effect of Exit Barriers upon Strategic Flexibility," *Strategic Management Journal,* vol. 1, no. 2, April–June:165–176; K.R. Harrigan, 1980, "Strategies for Declining Businesses," *Journal of Business Strategy,* vol. 1, no. 2, Fall:20–34; K.R. Harrigan, 1980, "Strategy Formulation in Declining Industries," *Academy of Management Review,* vol. 5, no. 4, October:599–604; I.M. Duhaime, 1981, "Influences on the Divestment Decisions of Large Diversified Firms," Unpublished doctoral dissertation, Pittsburgh: University of Pittsburgh; "American Divestment: Back to Basics," 1981, *The Economist,* May 2:74; K.R. Harrigan, 1981, "Deterrents to Divestiture," *Academy of Management Journal,* vol. 24, no. 2, June:306–323; K.R. Harrigan, 1982, "Exit Decisions in Mature Industries," *Academy of Management Journal,* vol. 25, no. 4, December:707–732; I.M. Duhaime and J.H. Grant, 1984, "Factors Influencing Divestment Decision-Making: Evidence from a Field Study," *Strategic Management Journal,* vol. 5, no. 4, October–December:301–318; K.R. Harrigan, 1984, "The Strategic Exit Decision: Additional Evidence," in R. Lamb (ed.), *Competitive Strategic Management,* Engelwood Cliffs, N.J.: Prentice-Hall, pp. 468–497; C.A. Montgomery, A.R. Thomas, and R. Kamath, 1984, "Divestiture, Market Valuation, and Strategy," *Academy of Management Journal,* vol. 27, no. 4, December:380–840; K. R. Harrigan, 1985, "Exit Barriers and Vertical Integration," *Academy of Management Journal,* vol. 28, no. 3:686–697; K.R. Harrigan, 1985, *Strategic Flexibility: A Management Guide for Changing Times,* Lexington, Mass.: Lexington Books; K.R. Harrigan, 1986, "The Cost of Bailing Out," *Strategic Direction,* May:5–7; C.A. Montgomery and A.R. Thomas, 1988, "Divestment: Motives and Gains," *Strategic Management Journal,* vol. 9, no. 1, January–February:93–97; C. Baden Fuller, 1988, "Cartels, Government Intervention and Firm Decision-Making in Declining European Industries," in C. Baden Fuller (ed.), 1988, *Management of Excess Capacity in the European Environment,* London: Basil Blackwell; P. Bianchi and G. Volpato, 1988, "Excess Capacity from Rigidity to Flexibility: The Case of the Automobile Industry," in C. Baden Fuller, *ibid.*; J.L. Bower, 1988, "The Management Challenge to Restructuring Industry," in C. Baden Fuller, *ibid.*; F. Fortan, 1988,

"Rationalization Schemes and the European Steel Industry," in C. Baden Fuller, *ibid.*; P. Ghemawat and B. Nalebuff, 1988, "Excess Capacity, Efficiency, and Industrial Policy," in C. Baden Fuller, *ibid.*; P. Lorange and R.T. Nelson, 1988, "Maintaining Organizational Momentum: Managing Denial and Complacency Factors," in C. Baden Fuller, *ibid.*; and R. Shaw and P. Simpson, 1988, "Rationalisation within an International Oligopoly: The Case of the West European Synthetic Fibres Industry," in C. Baden Fuller, *ibid.*

2. R.E. Caves and M.E. Porter, 1977, "From Entry Barriers to Mobility Barriers: Conjectural Decisions and Contrived Deterrents to New Competition," *Quarterly Journal of Economics,* May:241–261; M.E. Porter, 1980, *Competitive Strategy: Techniques for Analyzing Industries and Competitors,* New York: Free Press.

3. K.R. Harrigan, 1980, "The Effect of Exit Barriers upon Strategic Flexibility," *Strategic Management Journal,* vol. 1, no. 2, April–June:165–176; K.R. Harrigan, 1981, "Deterrents to Divestiture," *Academy of Management Journal,* vol. 24, no. 2, June:306–323; K.R. Harrigan, 1982, "Exit Decisions in Mature Industries," *Academy of Management Journal*, vol. 25, no. 4, December:707–732; K.R. Harrigan, 1984, "The Strategic Exit Decision: Additional Evidence," in R. Lamb (ed.), 1984, *Competitive Strategic Management,* Englewood Cliffs, N.J.: Prentice-Hall, pp. 468–497; and K.R. Harrigan, 1985, *Strategic Flexibility: A Management Guide for Changing Times,* Lexington, Mass.: Lexington Books.

4. K.R. Harrigan, 1983, *Strategies for Vertical Integration,* Lexington, Mass.: Lexington Books; K.R. Harrigan, 1985, "Exit Barriers and Vertical Integration," *Academy of Management Journal,* vol. 28, no. 3:686–697; and K.R. Harrigan, 1985, *Strategic Flexibility: A Management Guide for Changing Times,* Lexington, Mass.: Lexington Books.

5. "Stages" are the number of and total value-added by steps in firms' vertical chains of processing—from ultraraw materials to final consumers—in which their strategic business units (SBUs) are engaged. "Degree" of integration indicates the percentage of a particular upstream or downstream need that SBUs satisfy through product (or service) transfers from (or to) sister SBUs. The number of activities firms perform in-house at any particular level of their vertical chains of processing determines particular SBUs' "breadth" of integrated activity (and different firms define the boundaries of SBUs differently). "Form" refers to firms' proportions of equity ownership in particular vertically related SBUs (and powerful firms need not own vendors or distributors in order to control their respective activities). See K.R. Harrigan, 1983, *ibid.*

6. "Take-or-pay contracts" bind customers to purchase specified quantities of vendors' outputs or pay a penalty for not doing so. Such contracts are often used as collateral in financing capacity expansions when demand is growing because they guarantee revenues even when demand declines.

7. K.R. Harrigan, 1985, *Strategies for Joint Ventures,* Lexington, Mass.: Lexington Books; K.R. Harrigan, 1986, *Managing for Joint Venture Success,* Lexington, Mass.: Lexington Books.

8. K.R. Harrigan, *Strategies for Synergy* (forthcoming).

5
Matching Management Systems to Maturity

I n the last four chapters, I have suggested that survival and prosperity are possible even when mature industry environments become unfavorable if skillful managers can reposition their firms better to serve loyal customers. This chapter discusses how managers implement endgame strategies by making changes in their firms' operating systems and working practices.

It is not enough for managers to recognize that widespread industry maturity will create competitive problems and decree that their firms will rank among the survivors. If managers conclude that mature industries offer adequate profitability potential, or that the benefits expected from restructuring industries justify the costs, they must also change their firms' working practices to support the competitive requirements of maturity. The changes that are necessary affect how managers approach the task of *cash generation*. These changes determine how assets are used, which strengths are fortified, which behaviors are rewarded, and how quickly changes are made. Deeply held organizational beliefs and values may be undermined by these changes in working practices.

Cash Generator Businesses

The analytical frameworks of chapters 2, 3, and 4 are the justifications for making investments in troubled, mature industries to change them into cash generators. The nature of the changes that must be effected, this chapter's topic, is very important because without continual operating improvements in mature businesses, there will be no cash for firms' new projects. Firms remain competitive in mature industries only if they are not allowed to become complacent. Only skillful "endgame masters"—the managers who can enable their firms to realize the full potential of mature businesses—understand what types of R&D activities support improvements in working practices or what types of marketing efforts are needed to be of greater service to valued customers. Endgame masters have the thankless task of being endgame businesses' champions when defending funding requests to corporate managers (and providers of capital).

Risk versus Return Tradeoffs

Although cash-generating businesses often need new investments to execute specific endgame strategies, expenditures for steel and concrete that increase firms' asset bases should not be considered substitutes for human ingenuity. Endgame masters should not expect to rely on technological "quick fixes" to solve fundamental operating problems. Investments in new manufacturing assets—especially those in factory-automation systems that assume levels of intra-firm cooperation that have never existed previously—will require time to show improvements in productivity. Such investments carry risks that may be unacceptable because most U.S. owners expect a *quick* payback on any resources allocated to mature businesses; they are not expecting to bear the same deferred cash risks that projects in embryonic industries entail. Because investors expect managers in mature industries to recover risked capital earlier, they often have difficulty understanding why they should risk any more capital or defer cash flow any longer to implement endgame strategies. Endgame masters must disabuse investors of this prejudice; they must help investors to see that the short-term disinvestments necessary to provide the cash flows that investors prefer very likely *will* harm mature businesses' long-term abilities to generate cash.

Managers of mature businesses are usually expected to maximize cash returns on their investment bases. It has become traditional to assume that immediate gratification is more attractive than reinvestments for future competitive health (see chapter 7). Thus, few investments that do not offer short paybacks are readily undertaken in mature industries (unless required by law). Having impatient investors means that firms cannot stay in troubled industries too long without receiving just rewards for doing so. Endgame masters must educate investors about the need to be patient to realize the rewards of endgame competition (assuming that their analyses indicate that continued presences in mature industries are wise).

Patient capital. Some investors will resist the notion that patience is necessary to realize the benefits of well-placed investments in aggressive endgame strategies. Some providers of capital will face barriers to accepting new approaches to endgame competition, just as some managers of mature businesses do. Corporate managers that are unwilling to wait for the payoff on endgame (or are unwilling to believe there will be any payoff) also need to be educated. Otherwise the funding that endgame masters require will be withheld.

In an extreme example I studied, a diversified firm inherited several mature businesses as part of a package acquisition (by merging with another diversified firm). Because one acquired business was in an industry that faced declining demand, corporate managers assumed the business had no promise and were not very interested in its efforts to implement an aggressive endgame strategy. The managers of the mature business unit, by contrast, were very interested in performing well for their new parent and eager to play the endgame well. But after months of inattention from corporate managers with no responses to their action proposals and increasing corporate impatience for rapid cash generation, the eager cadre of endgame masters became frustrated. They stopped submitting proposals for revitalizing the endgame business. With no funding for repositioning activities, employees were forced to stop their kamikaze-like campaign to change how customers used the mature business's products. Despite divisional protests that the mature business could be a winner, corporate management was so convinced that the unit was a loser that they began milking resources from it. Eventually, they completely killed the business because no other firm would buy what remained of it. The second-strongest firm (the remaining competitor) stepped into the market niche that the first firm had been preparing and coined money on the first firm's mistake. The endgame masters had correctly identified the most profitable customer niche to serve (the one where high switching costs would have bound price-insensitive customers to their firm for several years) and their endgame strategy was apt. They were never given a chance to implement their strategic plans.

Clear trade-offs. If diversified firms are to survive when their industries become troubled, managers must create internal cultures that recognize the importance of products that generate cash and make personnel assignments to cash-generating businesses sought after. Doing so will require adjustments in mature businesses' performance measures and support from top management. It will also require discussion of the strategic objectives top management considers reasonable to pursue. Corporate management must clarify whether low-risk cash-flow maximization is more desirable than pursuing high-risk strategies such as maintaining leadership in technology, market share, or cost reductions. Top management must indicate their firms' risk preferences.

Assumptions Underlying Strategies

This section briefly reviews the assumptions underlying strategies that pursue technology, market share, and cost leadership in order to suggest where a particular strategic approach may be at odds with firms' endgame strategy objectives. Top management must determine whether resource allocations for mature businesses that pursue these objectives are warranted.

Technology leadership. Technology-leadership strategies are like being on a treadmill. Where technology changes rapidly, sophisticated customers become ever more demanding. Established firms must invest in ongoing applied engineering projects, as well as basic research that could lead to quantum technological leaps, just to keep abreast of technological changes. Firms that rely on their innovative skills to propel them up the next growth curve pursue the riskiest strategies because so many technological routes that firms invest in do not prove to be efficacious later. Smaller competitors—underdogs that challenge existing ways of satisfying customers—are more likely to rely heavily on the risky strategy of pioneering innovations than established firms because successful commercialization of a breakthrough is the *only* way underdogs can take on the products of current technology leaders.

Ethical pharmaceuticals. Strategies of continued technology leadership are very expensive. Patents must be strong and customers must be insensitive to high prices in order to reap the benefits of innovation. In ethical pharmaceuticals (one of the few industries where these conditions are present), technology leaders lose at least 40 percent of their market to price competition from generic drugs when patents on drugs expire. Laws encouraging the subsitution of generic drugs for prescribed, off-patent drugs drive down profit margins on technology leaders' remaining sales volumes. Lower prices for off-patent drugs mean funding for future research must be covered by the high prices firms charge for pharmaceuticals while they are still under patent protection, and the risk that patented drugs' competitive lives will be *shorter* than their legal lives has risen sharply since 1982. Each patented substance now faces increased competition from the greater number of new drugs in new therapeutic categories introduced by formerly undiversified, established drug firms and from new entrants. Each new drug introduction reduces the likelihood that legal monopolies on previously patented substances will be unchallenged before their respective patent protections end.

As more pharmaceutical products are exposed to the risk of shorter technological half-lives, drug firms are entering greater numbers of strategic alliances—most frequently cross-licensing and cross-marketing arrangements with overseas firms, but also research joint ventures and other cooperative ventures. Capacity-sharing arrangements for off-patent drugs have become commonplace, and sales-force sharing for patented substances (like Glaxo's Zantac anti-ulcer drug or Squibb's Capoten antihypertensive) have started. Revitalization efforts—campaigns to earn regulatory approval for use in a second therapeutic category—have given some drugs a second life. Finally, although new firms (like Procter & Gamble and du Pont) have entered the U.S. drug industry, mergers are consolidating the industry—as firms like A.H. Robins and Sterling Drug are acquired—and making financial success more difficult to achieve by undercapitalized firms.

Market-share leadership. Strategies to capture high market share are volume driven. Pursuit of market-share leadership assumes that the particular group of customers served is large enough to provide the necessary scale- and experience-curve-economies that justify lower profit margins. Firms forgo short-term profit maximization while they are capturing and maintaining high sales volumes by operating efficiently. When demand is deteriorating, firms recover postponed profits by surrendering market share.

Continued market-share leadership is very expensive. Firms must invest in the lower prices needed to steal market share away from other firms in order to push down the experience curve ahead of competitors. Volume objectives call for less profitable penetration-pricing policies rather than price-skimming policies. Firms must also support broad (perhaps slowly moving) product lines, stand their ground during price wars to give credibility to their entry-deterring threats, and move aggressively to preempt control of emerging pockets of demand. Finally, market-share leaders must devise ways to placate customers whose product requirements are deviating from the way in which demand was previously satisfied. (This last point is especially salient where firms pursue global strategies or rely heavily on policies of product standardization.)

Global markets. Global markets developed because the demands of customers in many geographic markets became increasingly similar while customer purchasing power rose in many countries.[1] To exploit this revolution, firms reduced differences in products offered to various customers (or in ways that products and services were provided to customers in diverse locations) to gain scale-economy benefits. Each incremental group of customers that accepted international firms' standardized product (or resource) solutions increased the potential cost reductions available to firms through large-scale production.

Standardization versus customization. Firms choose whether to provide superior *value* to customers by adapting products to regional (or industry) idiosyncrasies or achieve superior *cost* performance by standardizing products and selling only to customers who will accept that particular product configuration. Whether firms' domains are regional, national, or international, it is easier to pursue market-share leadership objectives where customer demands are fairly homogeneous. If markets are too segmented—too fragmented—there is a danger that too many customers will want customized (i.e., nonstandardized) product solutions.

When customers grow ever more sophisticated, hence demanding, they become less willing to accept firms' standardized product solutions. When customers demand greater product customization, standardization strategies become less viable because scale economies are lost. Prices must rise to sustain the profit margins that were formerly enjoyed. Because market-share leaders often use lower prices to buy customers away from competitors, they find themselves no longer price-competitive when their markets evolve away from ready acceptance of product standardization (and toward product customization), *unless* they can expand into new geographic markets that will accept their standardized product solutions.

As the endgame progresses, market-share goals become increasingly difficult to attain. Firms that once satisfied the largest market segments find that many of their former customers seek product customization (or switch to new products) as the endgame progresses. Meanwhile, smaller firms that avoided head-to-head competition with market-share leaders by pursuing smaller pockets of demand, have learned to serve fringe customers so well that market-share leaders find it difficult to emulate their successes later, when it becomes clear that the customers that are most lucrative to serve in endgame are those the smaller firms have learned to serve.

Product customization strategies are more successful in very mature industries where different market segments switch to replacement products (or demand deteriorates) at different speeds. They work best where customers will pay a premium for the value added by vendors (including service). If this strategy is implemented well, it raises customers' switching-cost barriers and is tantamount to developing a quasi-integrated relationship with them. Unfortunately, product-customization strategies often incur higher production costs per unit, higher inventory costs, fewer opportunities to enjoy scale economies, and few experience-curve economies. When this occurs, the strategic approach of market-share maximization that was once suitable becomes of questionable value in stagnant industries.

Cost-reduction leadership. In endgame, the lowest-cost producer must squeeze out less efficient producers and oversee the rationalization of excess capacity.[a] Because they often compete on the basis of price and process innovation, cost leaders are likely to become the last icemen of industries where vendors' products cannot be differentiated well (commodities) or diverse market segments have homogeneous needs.

Continued cost-reduction leadership is very expensive. Cost leaders must invest in ways of making continual improvements in operating-cost reductions through long manufacturing runs of products with standardized configurations (to realize scale economies), better access to raw materials, superior productivity (to offset higher labor costs), and the most efficient manufacturing processes, among other tactics. Cost-reduction leaders need superior logistic systems to distinguish between high value-adding tasks (done in-house) and low

---

[a]Excess capacity can be an ambiguous term unless it is placed in the context of manufacturing costs. Plants of a particular technological generation are designed to break even at some minimum volume and operate most efficiently when some proportion of engineered capacity—usually 90 percent—is used. Older plants are considered *obsolete* when the minimum efficient scale of newer technology plants is larger than that of older-generation plants (and the newer plant's operating costs are lower). Capacity is properly called *excess* only when it does not fit its environment. In theory, when capacity does not fit, managers dispose of it, often replacing it with capacity that does fit. In fact, much obsolete, high-cost, and redundant industrial capacity in industrialized economies should have been written down, but companies have not done so (for reasons discussed in chapter 4).

value-adding tasks (for outsourcing), to track costs through firms' operating systems, and to smooth bottlenecks and shortfalls (for efficient plant utilization), among other reasons.

In mature industries, cost-reduction leaders also need superior marketing and selling personnel to persuade customers that their product solution is better than another vendor's customized (but more expensive) product solution. If market segments become more fragmented in their product needs during endgame, competition on price alone may become uneconomic. If customer needs are growing more diverse, cost-reduction leaders that depend on scale- and experience-curve-economies for their competitive advantage in endgame are less likely to be the last icemen.

Summary. Pursuing leadership objectives—technology, market share, and cost-reduction leadership—is expensive. Managers must assess whether continued investments in a particular mature business are warranted and whether they wish to persevere in building the strengths that were once appropriate for competition. It may be more appropriate to build new strengths for endgame competition (discussed below).

There are several ways to profit in mature businesses by managing them intelligently. If firms do not possess the planning infrastructure and managerial skills needed to reach high performance levels (or if analysis suggests that their firms' strategic postures are hopelessly inferior), managers should do all concerned a favor by exiting in a timely and nondisruptive fashion. They should hand over the reins to competent endgame masters by divesting mature businesses.

Creating Strategic Flexibility

Because competitors' actions can shift the balance in mature industries and inhibit firms from adopting economically appropriate strategies, timing is crucial to success in endgame. Because weaker firms have even preempted indecisive, leading firms in some endgames, it is important for managers to begin making improvements to operating systems early. For many firms, time is running out. Shorter product lives and blurring industry boundaries must be fought with new ways of doing things, new ways of conceptualizing markets, and new performance standards. These changes must happen sooner rather than later because the timing advantage to be gained by doing so is substantial.

Some of the strategies outlined in chapter 3 require early execution if they are to succeed because outsiders will buy a finite number of plants from firms that wish to exit. Where reinvestments and repositionings are needed to remain viable, firms must commit their resources to new targets before competitors can maneuver into more advantageous positions. When managers play the endgame successfully, their firms recover investments in mature industries while minimizing pain when plants must be closed. Their firms thrive in adverse environments by preempting other firms that miss opportunities they see.

Timely Information

Successful firms develop superior ways of collecting market and competitor intelligence. Effective scanning systems allow managers to watch the factors that determine demand for their products—acreage that has been planted, customer practices, crop prices, and resource scarcities, for example—to anticipate which actions they should take. They maintain tight internal communications in order to exploit quickly any marketing errors made by competitors. They act on their scanning capabilities by adjusting the timing of their tactics and by developing contingency plans to accommodate the effects of key competitors' actions that they have been able to anticipate.

Competitor-intelligence system. Competitor intelligence, unlike other forms of market intelligence, is used within mature industries to track the milestones that signal the need for divestiture. Briefly, market intelligence concerning competitors is gathered (from the sales force, clipping services, industry analysts, and other sources) and routinely correlated in heuristic programs that create scenarios to forecast conditions that would force firms to exit or take other strategic actions.[b] Adding horizon forecasts to firms' planning processes facilitates creation of contingency plans that identify the competitive factors on which future profitability depends and the responses firms are prepared to undertake to foil competitors' profit-eroding actions.

Horizon forecasts. Horizon forecasting is an explicit discussion of how firms would look if they chose to divest the businesses in question tomorrow. It is a procedure that forces all managers—even those in charge of thriving businesses—to confront the interrelationships of their business units with others within the firm and anticipate their customers' responses. (Narrowly deployed, the planning data are supplied by firms when sales volumes first begin to plateau. A horizon forecast can be developed easily by adding operating details to frequent demand updates from firms' market-research groups. Add to these data, analysis of industry structure factors that may deter exit in order to

---

[b]Corporate strategy determines whether to enter or exit a business, expand capacity (or shrink it), and encourage coordination among diverse business units (or not). Business-unit strategy determines which market segments to serve with which product attributes and technological postures. Business strategy also determines resource allocations and coordination (if any) among geographic sites. Strategic decisions restructure industries when firms raise (or lower) entry or mobility barriers, change the need for vertical integration, change the technological scale needed for lowest-cost operations, or alter other competitive factors that affect industrywide profitability potential.

recognize when to divest, shut down, or change intrafirm coordination.) When horizon forecasts are created, scenarios are generated to estimate the financial effect, asset-usage effect, and manpower effect of divestiture, shutdown, or other strategic actions.

In horizon-forecasting systems, managers are asked to make annual assessments of whether operations should be continued or phased out. Candor is encouraged because all managers are assured that there will be places for them in their firms and that lower-level workers will also be retained and *retrained* for other jobs. In one firm where such planning systems were employed, no plants were sold or closed for as many as six years after business unit managers first began to use this planning format. When it was time to close plants, the details and problems had been anticipated so well that few snags were encountered in implementing the endgame strategy. Top management was kept fully aware of anticipated cash flows, maintenance-investment requirements, and manpower reassignments needed; middle management knew when these requirements exceeded top management's willingness to fund mature businesses. Details were communicated so well that the reorganizations that followed each plant closing were easier as a result of this planning effort.

Closer attentions. As soon as effective information systems are delivering timely information about businesses that have entered endgame, top management should use shorter review intervals to monitor any deterioration of mature businesses. Frequent discussions with endgame masters are needed to sense whether information systems capture important changes in mature industries. Top management must pay special attention to managers and workers within mature businesses to convey to others that their task can be done with dignity. They do this by including endgame masters in interdepartmental memos, seeking their opinions, and sharing ideas with them. Top management should give endgame masters close attention by putting them in the limelight if they are doing well and by talking with them about how to improve if they are not performing well. Whatever happens, excluding them will hurt the viability of mature business units that need longer-term outlooks. Failing to pay attention to their problems fosters images of apparent inattention that may (1) force valued managers to bail out prematurely, (2) kill viable businesses too soon, and (3) generate labor problems that could have been avoided by not pulling any punches with operating managers in discussing corporate plans for mature business units.

Building Strengths

Managers could elect to milk obsolete facilities or convert them (and their work forces) to other uses. But if managers wish to realize the benefits that many firms have enjoyed in endgame industries, it will be necessary to find creative solutions to asset use. Competitive advantage in mature industries can often be better exploited by building strengths in logistics, quality, and service instead of building new facilities; advantages embedded in capital assets are *easier* for competitors to copy than those derived from working practices and management systems.

Operating flexibility in endgame businesses can be enhanced by improving working policies and manufacturing methods. Flexibility is desirable because endgame competition can be so risky. Other firms' imprudent actions can collapse the barriers that protected firms' strategic postures from easy imitation by outsiders, thereby damaging the profitability firms had hoped to enjoy by investing in mature businesses. Operating flexibility makes firms nimble; it allows firms to reach customers that they might not otherwise serve (and prosper from those customers' successes by serving them well). It also allows firms to reduce excessive dependence on risky or dead-end customers.

Three Keys to Operating Flexibility

Flexible vendors are willing to perform unconventional tasks in their quest to serve attractive customers well. Sometimes flexibility means using outsiders to perform tasks that firms once did internally; in other cases flexibility means performing new tasks for valued customers. Vendors retain their flexibility through their willingness to be involved in solving vendors' and customers' productivity problems while making continual improvements in how they perform their own tasks.

Firms sustain competitive advantages in mature businesses through mutually reinforcing strengths in three key areas: logistics, quality, and service. Like credos, or other devices for communicating cultural values throughout organizations, every employee of endgame businesses should know what tradeoffs their firm expects them to make by emphasizing logistics, quality, and service to customers, and should be encouraged to suggest ways to improve working practices further.

Logistics. Logistics is information; it is the backbone and nervous system of implementing endgame strategies. A strong logistical system enhances flexibility by getting information to operating units fast enough to respond to competitive change. Improvements in firms' scanning systems are critical to developing the coordination between information and action that embodies logistical strengths.

Burial caskets. Managers press for improvements in day-to-day logistics by designing ways to get information to employees who must act on it. Hillenbrand Corporation's Batesville Casket Company uses an automated order-picking system in its factories and network of warehouses to maintain inventory levels and load the right pallets onto the right delivery trucks without causing dents or scratches in handling. Inventory costs are low at Batesville Casket factories because sales office and warehouse information is used to schedule each day's manufacturing activities.

Wholesaling. Foremost-McKesson, a leading drug wholesaler, improved its logistics by providing mircocomputer units to drugstores that subscribed to their "Economost" inventorying system. Sales of specific prescription drugs, over-the-counter drugs, and other merchandise were recorded automatically and reordered. Drugstore and wholesaler each reduced their respective inventories because the timely collection of returned merchandise could be indicated by customers and verified by their vendor. Automatic reordering reduced drugstore stockouts.

Food processing. Food processer H.J. Heinz owns farms, orchards, and fisheries for its raw materials, can- and bottle-making plants for its containers, lithographing and label-making plants for its packaging, and packing plants (for the activities for which Heinz is best known). Heinz also has one of the most wide-ranging distribution networks for serving retail grocery outlets—including warehouses, trucks, wholesaling services, and detail sales representatives that may even place its products on shelves in stores where they are sold. Heinz has extremely low processing costs, which it leverages by its involvement in several foods with similar processing requirements—for example, tuna and cat food or a wide range of tomato products like sauce, paste, and catsup.

Textiles. In a reversal of usual runaway plant patterns, Korean textile firms have been building automated plants in the United States. Given the vicissitudes of fashion, they find it more advantageous to win sales by being *near* customers (to produce popular fabrics faster) than to use cheaper, offshore labor but lose sales by being out-of-touch with the rapidly changing fashion industry.

Tailored suits. One of the most successful retailers of men's tailored suits, Hartmarx, buys all its clothing from its own plants and sells them in its own stores. Being close to customers helps Hartmarx to serve consumers better by introducing styling changes faster than its nonintegrated competitors.

Quality. Quality means delivering products with promised configurations and consistency. Quality is the heart of a competitive mature business; managers must keep it healthy. Control of quality means zero defects and no surprises for customers, and it must extend to spare parts, delivery schedules, and other elements of firms' product offerings. Total-quality-control systems ensure consistency in the design process, technical documentation, make-or-buy decisions, manufacturing, inspection, shipping, installation, and after-sale servicing and repair maintenance.

Quality results in better operating-cost structures because fewer defects result in less waste and fewer reworks. Greater operating efficiency results when less time is spent fixing mistakes, and employee morale is higher. Creative changes in sloppy operating systems can reduce costs while improving quality. Quality control relies on excellent logistics to know whether operating systems are in control (or out of control) in delivering products or services of predetermined parameters. Logistics suggest whether expenditures for cost reductions (or operating efficiency) are harming firms' abilities to deliver quality products. The intelligence-gathering network of warehouses and vehicles for distribution helps managers to ensure that customers experience zero defects in delivery services. Quality control also relies on investments in robots, controllers, optical scanners, and other elements of factory automation (where appropriate), as well as dies, jigs, and other devices for ensuring that zero defects are produced. The most important part of quality control systems is astute managers who recognize whether their systems are out of control and how to remedy sick operating systems.

Motorcycles, burial caskets, and home appliances. Japanese motorcycles are encased in styrofoam cocoons for delivery overseas to avoid scratches, dents, or other damage that causes rejected merchandise. Batesville Casket uses special shipping containers and pallets to avoid any denting or scratching of its costly burial coffins. In contrast to this attention to quality, consider that some U.S. home-appliance manufacturers are financing large amounts of inventory that was delivered in damaged condition and never collected for repair, reshipment, and rebilling.

Chain saws. West German chain-saw manufacturer, Stihl, offers highest-quality products. Where competitors' chain saws are made of shabby materials, break easily, and lack a strong dealer network for replacement parts and repairs, Stihl has integrated vertically to control the quality of every component—from chains to engine housings to plastic grips for the starting cords. It builds durable products that a loyal system of dealers can readily service (in the infrequent event that a Stihl chain saw ever fails).

Service. Competing through service means adding value through the tasks and processing steps performed for customers. Service means increasing value-added provided to customers by customizing product configurations, providing design and marketing services, improving delivery services through *kanban*[c] relationships, and other ways of offering more to customers.

---

[c]"Kanban" arrangements employ "just-in-time" systems of inventory management whereby vendors' and customers' total inventorying costs are reduced by coordinating upstream processing activities very closely with those of downstream activities. If inventory needs can be anticipated on a daily (or hourly) basis, customers need accept no larger shipments of components, assemblies, or finished products than they expect to consume in operations during the period covered by the *kanban* arrangement. Customers' inventorying costs are reduced because they do not take legal title to their inventories until they are delivered from suppliers' warehouses (which are frequently located just outside the walls of important customers' plants). Vendors' inventorying costs are reduced because they need not build up buffer stocks of unsold inventories; they produce as per their customers' orders and ship products exactly when customers specify that deliveries should occur.

To provide service effectively, firms rely on quality products, as well as excellent logistics in warehouse networks, distribution vehicles, and other sources of intelligence-gathering. Effective service depends on flexibility to adapt to diverse customer groups with differing product configurations and needs. It requires excellent training systems for field-service representatives to provide consistent corporate images while working independently with customers on trouble-shooting, product-designing, modifying component specifications, and performing other value-adding tasks.

Service strategies work best where customers are willing to pay premium prices for turnkey installations (or extra services) provided by vendors. Frequently the services that vendors add are tasks that customers could not do as well internally or are unwilling to perform in-house due to their high capital-investment requirements. Vendors often have better economics for producing the modules or components that customers desire. When vendors use value-adding strategies to serve customers well, they quasi-integrate to become as close to customers as necessary to anticipate their needs.

Yarn. Firms increase service to customers by offering customized color-dyeing services for yarn. Control over color-dyeing operations eliminates customer complaints of color streaking and product returns. Some vendors hold particular styles and colors for valued customers; others carry complementary products as customer conveniences and are well compensated for the extra value they create.

Tin cans and metal fabrication. Crown, Cork & Seal receives premium prices for its excess capacity when it acts as vendor of last resort by allocating extra personnel for producing tin cans on short notice. Other firms pay for extra personnel to serve on-site at customer facilities, travel to troubleshoot customer problems, or ensure that on-line systems are failsafe. Some metal vendors will roll products for valued customers ahead of schedule to be helpful. Other metal vendors will perform bar-drawing and tube-drawing services if orders are large enough (or if customers will pay price premiums).

Farm machinery. In 1987, Varity Corporation's Massey-Ferguson farm-machinery group introduced seventeen new tractor models, including a family of high-performance, computerized large tractors, three ranges of diesel engines for industrial and construction markets, and new machines for the North American landscaping and municipal markets. That same year, Varity's Perkins diesel engine group won a European award for technological achievement for its "Autotronic" system of computerized tractor controls.

Steel. Although North American steel makers often cut costs across the board when profits fell, Japanese firms believed that expenditures for R&D were critical in times of hardship. While Nippon Steel Corporation, Kawasaki Steel, Nippon Kokan, and Kobe Steel Ltd. were posting losses and cutting jobs in 1987, they were also maintaining research spending. Nippon Kokan, Japan's second-largest steel maker, increased its R&D outlays by 15 percent from 1985 to 1986, to almost $200 million. Kobe Steel kept its respective R&D outlays the same as 1985 spending levels to allow researchers to study steel applications in biotechnology, water processing, and alcohol production. Kawasaki Steel also maintained its previous R&D spending levels. All firms planned to open expensive research laboratories in 1987, while squeezing costs in other areas.

Seeing opportunities to create value. When vendors take the approach of offering high value added, they offer customers opportunities to lower their respective costs for some tasks by letting vendors perform them instead. A well-implemented division of labor—tasks performed internally and those provided by quasi-integrated vendors—allows firms' customers to differentiate their respective product offerings more effectively. As long as tasks are not critical to customers' strategic missions, they are candidates for outsourcing and value-adding services to be performed by vendors.

Burial caskets. In the mortuary business, funeral directors do not maintain their own inventory of burial caskets. Instead, they rely on suppliers to deliver burial caskets in desired styles (and sizes) on short notice. Information from Batesville Casket's automated order-picking system is used by its sales office to respond to emergency orders for large numbers of identical-looking burial caskets in different sizes. The Batesville Casket network locates the very long, large, and infant-sized burial caskets and schedules them for timely shipment with units in commonplace sizes.

Food processing. By 1988, consumers were worried about cholesterol and the high blood pressure that was associated with salt consumption. To cope with stagnant sales, food-processing firms such as Borden were consolidating regional pasta, dairy, and snack food operations to marry scale efficiencies in manufacturing with the marketing nimbleness of a regional operator. As Borden expanded geographically, it centralized production in its most efficient plants to lower costs while using its network of regional companies to take any popular local product into national distribution quickly through a delivery grid that was already in place.

Borden's milk business was among the most profitable in the industry, and Borden charged more for its milk. Consumers bought it instead of other brands because of a well-publicized program of high quality and service standards. Borden reinforced its brand name through extensive use of advertising with a local angle (from its many acquisitions of firms with popular regional brand names) in its product pitches.

Retailing. As the retailing environment became more competitive, firms such as Lord & Taylor were forced to sharpen their operating systems. Where sales receipts were once written by hand and stored in old-fashioned cash drawers, Lord & Taylor (after being acquired by May Department Stores) has replaced cash drawers with computerized registers, added inventory controls, and devised management systems that alert managers to weekly changes in sales trends. The Limited's vertically integrated system allows the specialty apparel chain to respond faster than its competitors to new fashion trends. Retailers are now using bar code scanners to speed up processing times, maintain appropriate inventories, and serve customers more quickly. The Nordstrom retailing chain wins loyal customers by routinely tracking down out-of-stock items in other Nordstrom stores and delivering them to customers' homes.

Grocery retailing. Leading U.S. grocery chains such as Safeway, A&P, Jewel, and others add value by engaging in many processing stages—from contracting with farmers for their crops, to baking their own bread and packing their own vegetables, to maintaining their own fleet of delivery trucks and warehouses for speeding their own products to grocery retail outlets while produce is fresh and before stockouts are incurred. Consumers share in the cost savings of the grocers' vertical-integration strategies because their "house" brands are less costly than heavily advertised national brands of food.

Larger grocery chains balance the use of their vertical chain of activities by purchasing extra supplies at processing stages where owned facilities are fully utilized (and incremental volumes needed do not justify adding another minimum-efficient-scale plant), or by selling excess outputs to other processers where full utilization of a minimum-efficient-scale plant provides slightly more output than their in-house needs can absorb. This swapping of excess products from efficiently utilized plants enables these grocery chains to offer consumers lower prices than nonintegrated grocers could afford to offer. Allocative and technical efficiency goals are served, as well, because capital is used where it earns the best returns—in newest-technology processing plants and logistical systems that yield the lowest operating costs per unit.

Using Assets Effectively

It is critical for top management to recognize the need to change operating systems and working practices in mature businesses. Leaders must be visionaries. Because their middle managers are often reluctant to take the first step, top managers must anticipate when changes will be needed and design operating systems to precipitate necessary changes. (Managers in the trenches are less likely to call attention to systemic changes and are especially unlikely to suggest any downsizings, consolidations, industry restructurings, or other unpleasant changes if they fear losing their jobs.)

Because managerial talent is one of the scarcest of corporate assets, corporate managers should design their operating systems and policies to retain gifted managers and hourly employees until the task of endgame management has been completed. If endgame masters do not receive some indication of their future operating responsibilities and rewards for winning the endgame (assuming that their services will be needed for the duration of endgame competition), their resumes may be circulating before firms have adequately satisfied their obligations to customers and retrieved the value they have invested in mature businesses. If operating systems do not reinforce values conducive to winning the support of every employee, the endgame cannot be won.

Choosing endgame masters. There is no dishonor to managing mature businesses unless top management treats the assignment as a dumping place for burned-out executives and unwanted employees. Top managers must shed the idea that cost-accountant mentalities are the best ones to run mature businesses because supervising the overhaul of endgame operations requires very sophisticated and resourceful managers. Entrepreneurial managers are better at encouraging workers to nurse old assets and jerry-rig machines into running longer. Charismatic managers should be selected for assignments in mature businesses and given free rein to change working policies because such leaders can build the spirit of camaraderie and teamwork needed to get useful ideas to percolate upward. In endgame, every worker is a manager and hourly workers must be won over to the cause of winning the endgame because they know best where the fat is that must be trimmed to be cost effective. Moreover, dedicated cadres work smarter. The most significant experience curve benefits come from the smart and motivated workers who can save troubled plants. In one consumer-goods business, workers suggested that headquarters' advertising campaigns be better coordinated with decentralized manufacturing schedules because they knew that empty shelves wasted advertising dollars. As a result of their suggestions, inventories were built up, distribution pipelines were filled before advertising campaigns were launched, and sales representatives were better able to fill urgent orders for valued customers.

Attentions and overt support from top management motivate the type of swashbuckler needed to inspire heroic actions in endgame situations. Endgame masters can use their charm to introduce cost-saving suggestions that improve employee morale, but their power creates a two-edged sword. Leaders who can inspire confidence and exhort employees to perform heroic deeds that prolong capital assets' lives are often quite concerned with their workers' future treatment at the hands of top management. Not only must endgame masters be assured of new opportunities; their workers must be rewarded if they do their tasks well in endgame.

In an extreme example I studied, one firm had a policy of moving its cadre of business managers to new assignments but had no such policies regarding its *hourly* employees. Yet it encouraged hourly employees to propose methods of making operations more efficient and prospered by their suggestions. When employees became overtly fearful of the consequences of industry maturity and made these fears explicit to the endgame master, he communicated their concerns to management. In a shameful example of double standards, the endgame master discovered that *no* provisions were being made to retrain these spirited workers who had devoted their entire lifetimes to the endgame business. Because no other plants in the firm had expressed a willingness to take these laborers, they appeared to be left high and dry. The endgame master's feelings of guilt on learning that no provisions had been made for his workers was so immense that he jumped ship abruptly. The business's profits spiraled downward quickly without him because he was the kind of gifted leader who knew how to capture the hearts of his workers and get them to work enthusiastically.

Synthetic fibers. In the synthetic fibers endgame, employees at one firm fought to preserve their jobs in the only manner they believed top management could value. As demand plateaued for manmade fibers, corporate staff made a study of the costs of shutting down each of four plants. They estimated the timing of each closing based on milestones of forecasted cash flows and expected business managers to operate on this planned timetable of shutdowns. Both levels of management were surprised, therefore, when employees at the very fibers plant that corporate staff had predicted to be *least* efficient took the initiative in tightening up their operations to become the *most* efficient plant. They did it by finding ways to operate aged equipment productively that included suggestions more spartan than the managers had made. (For example, the shipping dock workers suggested reductions in the number of colors produced because they noticed that a few colors accounted for most of their shipments. Sales representatives suggested that certain heretofore-ignored customers deserved aggressive attention while other, demanding customers be dropped.) News of the first plant's methods for improving productivity spread to the other fiber plants where workers also devised methods to make the very assets that the planning staff considered obsolete become more lucrative than those they had planned to retain.

Based on employee suggestions, ways were found to eliminate redundant operations and low-volume fiber products. Jobs were preserved for over two-thirds of the work force. (Downsizing was achieved through retirements.) The newly streamlined business unit launched an aggressive campaign to serve the customers its sales force believed would offer sustained profitability. Less efficient competitors were forced to close their plants, instead. Divisional management credited the mature business's resurrection to the endgame master's candidness with employees. (A postscript: a newer plant was closed when demand shrank to volumes that necessitated capacity reductions. The oldest and allegedly least efficient facility that fought back was one of the last two plants to close.)

Investing in human assets. Enterprising endgame masters can build a spirit of teamwork to cut costs and maximize productivity. In order to do this, employees' motivation must be high and the firm must win their loyalties. To do so, managers must devise golden handcuffs for the experienced workers who know the little, undocumented tricks that make particular machines more productive. These handcuffs can be inexpensive perquisites that appeal more to camaraderie than material wealth. For example, one firm leased a small lake on the outskirts of town and divided it into campsites. Key employees were permitted to rent the sites for token annual rents of $10. Campers and cabins were quickly erected by the lessees who spent their weekends at their vacation homes talking shop with other workers. (The urban version of this gesture is to purchase blocks of time at local gyms or health clubs where workers and their families can exercise together.) Thoughtful programs for employees are important ways to overcome the labor disputes that damage strategic flexibility by raising exit barriers.

As a prelude to working smarter (instead of laying off workers in mature industries), managers should avoid overstaffing jobs when demand grows rapidly. If downsizing becomes necessary, managers must take steps to make the process as painless as possible by continually retraining the work force and moving work between parallel plants to reduce use of temporary workers and overtime. During periods of slumping demand, managers should have employees take unused vacations and encourage unpaid leaves of absence. Hiring must be curtailed (or frozen) until demand improves and employee requests for transfers to overstaffed plants must be discouraged. To preserve experience-curve advantages, internal transfers to comparable jobs should first be encouraged, then transfers in the same jobs to other sites. As demand deteriorates, workers must be asked to move voluntarily to other facilities—in other, comparable jobs where possible, but sometimes in new jobs at lower grades. As workers are used in new jobs, work that has been subcontracted to outsiders can be brought back into plants. Losses of efficiency from performing subcontracted tasks in-house should be preferred over the option of losing skilled employees. These investments in preserving jobs foster company loyalties at a time when the popularity of using "just-in-time" (or contingent) laborers threatens to erode the creation of a problem-solving skills base.

Turnaround artists. If firms' cultures are so strong that they encourage inertia in endgames, outside help may be needed. The antithesis of investing in smart employees is often the turnaround manager,[2] a well-compensated U.S. folk hero who acts as though nothing motivates surviving employees in mature businesses as much as the sight of colleagues' empty desks. Turnaround managers may be able to release cash that was previously trapped and overcome the ennui that saps the morale of troubled businesses. But the drastic changes that turnaround artists introduce in overcoming implementation barriers are disruptive. Frequently, turnaround managers regain close control over day-to-day activities by rotating complacent workers. Their lieutenants prowl the shop floor or the office bullpen asking questions about the need to perpetuate historic activities. As they scrutinize each activity and compare costs to benefits, they ask whether the activity is necessary rather than fun. They strip firms' activities back to basic operations to restore cash-generating capabilities. Their outlook is short-term; the business must survive before it can think about long-term prosperity.

Sometimes the controversial management style of the turnaround manager is needed to revive mature businesses. In one case, a mature business unit was spun off by a staid corporation because its managers could not make a profit in the dismal endgame environment. A swashbuckling turnaround artist acquired the distressed business and placed almost unattainable demands on its scientists and workers. Given the depressing alternative of no jobs, the work force responded to the charismatic leader's exhortations and, in phoenix-like fashion, revived the company by pushing out a competitor instead. When the turnaround manager took over, industrywide endgame had been running for twenty years. Because of the work force's victory, their firm was expected to enjoy another twenty years of prosperity in the mature industry.

A major drawback in resorting to such shock therapies is the danger that employees will become cynical because they believe that the turnaround manager is draining their business of necessary cash instead of reinvesting cash to build the strengths needed for long-term viability. Some changes in operating systems may be too drastic for unionized workers to accept. Although employees may have surpassed historic production quotas and exceeded other day-to-day performance levels when they accepted the need to do so, the mere promise of keeping plants operating may not be sufficient reward for the concessions employees must make.

Sending a Strong Message

Performance measures should be forged for endgame competition that give operating managers maximum autonomy to manage mature businesses with dignity. If top management takes pains to select appropriate endgame masters and design operating systems that focus managers' attentions on performance measures that are suitable for mature businesses, they will obtain realistic outcomes. If they ask for impossible results, top management loses its credibility while driving away the employees who could save endgame businesses.

When evaluating proposals concerning endgame strategies, different measures are needed to focus managers' attentions on missions selected for maturing businesses (and to remind upper management that the endgame is a different game). Such measures include return on cash utilized, cash contributions to other businesses, capacity utilization, or other operating measures. If aggressive strategies are chosen, top management should devise reward systems that measure how many of the targeted (preferred) customers business units have retained, as well as how profitable operations have been. If the mature businesses must be operated for specified periods regardless of profitability or other performance measures (due to contract obligations that would be too costly to abrogate), cost reductions and improved efficiency should be rewarded.

Subtle messages can be sent by symbolic gestures—scratchy toilet paper in restrooms, nonroutine bonuses (or special bonus pools for long-suffering spouses), running plants seven days per week, wage and salary cuts, and so on. But they should be buttressed by the collection of meaningful data about wage and benefit differences, product-line profitability, and other competitive information that can direct managers' actions. In endgame, managers are coaches; workers follow their leads, rather than call the plays themselves.

Finally, many firms' management systems are archival; managers perpetuate what worked in the past but may no longer be effective in newly competitive industries. Managers of unsuccessful firms are most likely to respond to stagnant demand by favoring their old responses rather than by acting as situations might dictate. In particular, managers in weak firms within unattractive industries tend to hold on to mature businesses too long and ignore what competitors are doing. Most organizations resent the need to change, but they must change to use the endgame strategies effectively.

Notes

1. W. Kiechel III, 1981, "Playing the Global Game," *Fortune,* November 16: 111–126; P.G.P. Walters, 1986, "International Marketing Policy: A Discussion of the Standardization Construct and Its Relevance for Corporate Policy," *Journal of International Business Studies,* vol. 17, no. 2, Summer:55–69; Y.L. Doz, 1987, "International Industries: Fragmentation versus Globalization," in B.R. Guile and H. Brooks (eds.), 1987, *Technology and Global Industry: Companies and Nation in the World Economy,* Washington, D.C.: National Academy Press, pp. 96–118; M.E. Porter, 1987, "Changing Patterns of International Competition," in D.J. Teece (ed.), 1987, *The Competitive Challenge: Strategies for Industrial Innovation and Renewal,* Cambridge, Mass.: Ballinger, pp. 27–58; M.E. Porter, 1987, "Competition in Global Industries: A Conceptual Framework," in M.E. Porter (ed.), 1987, *Competition in Global Industries,* Boston: Harvard Business School Press.

2. See J. Eisenberg (ed.), 1972, *Turnaround Management: A Manual for Profit and Growth,* New York: McGraw-Hill; I. Barmash, 1973, *Great Business Disasters,* New York: Ballantine; M.D. Richards, 1973, "An Exploratory Study of Strategic Failure," *Academy of Management Proceedings:*40–46; A. Robertson, 1973, *The Lessons of Failure,* London: MacDonald; J.E. Ross and M.J. Kami, 1973, *Management in Crisis: Why the Mighty Fall,* Englewood Cliffs, N.J.: Prentice-Hall; T. Levitt, 1975, "Dinosaurs among the Bears and Bulls," *Harvard Business Review,* vol. 53, no. 1, January–February:41–53; T. Levitt, 1975, "Marketing Myopia," *Harvard Business Review,*

vol. 53, no. 5, September–October:26 +; A.C. Cooper and D. Schendel, 1976, "Strategic Responses to Technological Threats," *Business Horizons,* February:61–69; R.G. Hamermesh, 1976, "The Corporate Response to Divisional Profit Crises," Unpublished doctoral dissertation, Boston: Harvard Business School; L.R. Higgins, 1976, *Cost Reduction from A to Z,* New York: McGraw-Hill; M.E. Salverson, 1976, "Business Strategy: Pinning the Blame for Strategic Failures on the CEO," *Planning Review,* vol. 4, no. 5, September:1, 4–7; D.E. Schendel and G.R. Patton, 1976, "Corporate Stagnation and Turnaround," *Journal of Economics and Business,* vol. 28, Spring–Summer:236–241; E.J. Tracey, 1976, "The Loneliness of the Master Turnaround Man," *Fortune,* February:118–122; J. Harris, 1977, "Major Reason Companies Get into Trouble," *Boardroom's Business Secrets,* New York: Boardroom Reports; F.W. Hombrach, Jr., 1977, *Raising Productivity,* New York: McGraw-Hill; D.S. Hopkins, 1977, *Business Strategies for Problem Products,* New York: The Conference Board, Inc., Report No. 714; B. Pearson, 1977, "How to Manage Turnarounds," *Management Today,* April:74–77; R.S. Sloma, 1977, *No Nonsense Management,* New York: Macmillan; J.D. Batten, 1978, *Tough-Minded Management,* New York: AMACOM; M.T. Hannan and J.H. Freeman, 1978, "Internal Politics of Growth and Decline," in Marshall, 1978, *Environments and Organizations,* San Francisco: Jossey-Bass; J.H. Biteman, 1979, "Turnaround Management: An Exploratory Study of Rapid, Total Organizational Change," Unpublished doctoral dissertation, Boston: Harvard Business School; J. Quint, 1979, "Ming the Merciless Loses His Prize: Turnaround Specialist Sandy Sigoloff Brought Daylin out of Bankruptcy But Couldn't Save It from Grace," *Fortune,* May 7:140–142, 146, 148; E.J. Tracey, 1979, "She Has Three Years to Turn Olivetti America Around," *Fortune,* October 22:87–88; P.F. Drucker, 1980, *Managing in Turbulent Times,* New York: Harper & Row; C.W. Hofer, 1980, "Turnaround Strategies," *Journal of Business Strategy,* vol. 1, no. 1, Spring:19–31; D.G. Bibeault, 1982, *Corporate Turnaround: How Managers Turn Losers into Winners,* New York: McGraw-Hill; W.E. Deming, 1982, *Out of the Crisis,* Cambridge, Mass.: Massachusetts Institute of Technology Center for Advanced Engineering Study; S.J. Goodman, 1982, *How to Manage a Turnaround: A Senior Manager's Blueprint for Turning an Ailing Business into a Winner,* New York: Free Press; D.C. Hambrick and S.M. Schecter, 1983, "Turnaround Strategies for Mature Industrial-Product Businesses," *Academy of Management Journal,* vol. 26, no. 2, June:231–248; and J.O. Whitney, 1987, *Taking Charge: Management Guide to Troubled Companies and Turnarounds,* Homewood, Ill.: Dow Jones-Irwin.

6
Illustrative Example—Maturity in Mainframe Computers

This chapter illustrates how firms have adapted to declining demand growth. Mainframe computers eased into the endgame in the early 1980s. Worldwide shipments of mainframe computers (and supercomputers) totaled $17.6 billion in 1987; with their higher prices, mainframe computer sales represented 26.5 percent of worldwide computer revenues. Unit-shipment volumes of mainframe computers peaked in 1973. Five years later, U.S. revenues from sales of personal computers finally surpassed those from mainframe computers. Since 1976, industry observers had been predicting that demand for the general-purpose mainframe computer of the 1960s and the 1970s would gradually fade and be replaced by demand for clusters of highly versatile minicomputers or for high-performance supercomputers. But few industry observers could foresee how dramatically the computer industry would change. By 1988, some industry observers were predicting that the industry would evolve to one of desktop computers and supercomputers—with *no* viable middle ground.

In 1988 the leading vendors of microcomputers, minicomputers, and supercomputers were not the same firms that had dominated sales of mainframe computers. As technological innovations accelerated the shakeouts that signaled an inevitable industrywide restructuring process had begun, weaker vendors of mainframe computers merged or scurried to form joint ventures. Leading mainframe computer vendors downsized themselves.

The Product

The term *mainframe computer* evolved quickly. During the 1950s—when there were no minicomputers or microcomputers—the term referred to any unit that contained the central processor where arithmetic and logic operations were performed. By the mid-1960s, the term *mainframe computer* referred to very large,

---

I am indebted to Thomas W. Aust (Columbia University, M.B.A., 1986) for industry background materials prepared for this chapter.

cumbersome machines that (1) filled entire rooms, (2) required special air-conditioning and climate controls, (3) were installed in rooms with removable subfloors so that wires and cables could be run between different parts of the computer, and (4) needed dedicated staffs of engineers and computer specialists that were constantly on hand to oversee computer operations and program their functions. Mainframe computers were leased, rather than sold outright, and relatively unsophisticated ultimate users communicated their computing needs to the technically trained programmers who operated the mainframe computer. Because of the high capital expense involved in their lease, most mainframe computers were run around the clock with individual work orders (like payroll processing) being performed in one continuous run, or "batch." Unused computing capacity was sold on a "time-sharing" basis to firms that could not afford to lease their own mainframe computers.

Until recently, the guidelines in table 6–1 were adequate to distinguish among the different types of computers.[a] Mainframe computers were distinguished from other computers by (1) main memory size (kilobytes or megabytes), (2) speed of processing (MIPS, or million instructions per second), (3) word length (bytes), and (4) price (thousands or millions of dollars). Even when minicomputers and microcomputers offered speeds, word sizes, and main-memory

---

[a]Industry observers suggested that one rule of thumb for categorizing classes of computers was that if one could push it, the product was a minicomputer, if one could lift it, the product was a microcomputer, if one could throw it. the product was a calculator, and if the product would not move at all, it was a mainframe computer.

Table 6–1
Computer Product Classification Guidelines

	Speed	Memory Size	Word Length	Price
Supercomputer:	20 MIPS or more Vector processing (simultaneous performance of many calculations) as well as scalar processing			$4 to $17 million and above plus operating expenses of $500,000 per year
Mainframe:	2 to 70 MIPS	16 kilobytes to 8 megabytes	8, 16, 32, 48, or 64 bytes	$250,000 to $8 million and above
Minicomputer:	1 to 8 MIPS	16 kilobytes to 5 megabytes	8, 16, 32, or 48 bytes	$20,000 to $800,000
Microcomputer:	.2 to 1 MIPS	8 kilobytes to 2 megabytes	8, 16, or 32 bytes	$1,000 to $20,000

sizes comparable with mainframe computers, the latter could still be distinguished by their physical size, need for climate control, complexity of operating instructions (software), and required level of user-sophistication. By 1988, more than 80 percent of all computer users *purchased* rather than leased their equipment.

Demand for Mainframe Computers

As table 6–2 and figure 6–1 indicate, unit shipments of mainframe computers in the United States peaked in 1973, have been declining since 1981, and are

Table 6–2
U.S. Consumption of Microcomputers, Minicomputers, and Mainframe Computers, 1960–1990
(in units and current million $)

Year	Microcomputers Units	Microcomputers Dollars	Minicomputers Units	Minicomputers Dollars	Mainframes Units	Mainframes Dollars
1960	0	$ 0.0	0	$ 0.0	1,790	$ 590
1961	0	0.0	0	0.0	2,700	880
1962	0	0.0	0	0.0	3,470	1,090
1963	0	0.0	0	0.0	4,200	1,300
1964	0	0.0	0	0.0	5,600	1,670
1965	0	0.0	260	28.6	5,350	1,770
1966	0	0.0	385	40.4	7,250	2,640
1967	0	0.0	720	68.5	11,200	3,900
1968	0	0.0	1,080	100.4	9,100	4,800
1969	0	0.0	1,770	152.2	6,000	4,150
1970	0	0.0	2,620	209.6	5,700	3,600
1971	0	0.0	2,800	218.4	7,600	3,900
1972	0	0.0	3,610	270.7	10,700	5,000
1973	0	0.0	5,270	368.9	14,000	5,400
1974	0	0.0	8,880	577.2	8,600	6,200
1975	5,100	76.5	11,670	641.8	6,700	5,410
1976	25,800	374.1	17,000	816.0	6,750	5,580
1977	58,500	760.5	24,550	1,202.9	8,900	6,600
1978	115,600	1.098.2	29,550	2,595.7	7,500	7,590
1979	160,000	1,488.0	35,130	2,037.5	7,200	7,330
1980	250,500	2,104.2	41,450	2,487.0	9,900	8,840
1981	385,100	2,503.1	44,100	2,699.1	10,700	9.640
1982	735,000	4,190.0	47,820	2,821.3	10,600	10,300
1983	1,260,000	5,300.0	45,420	3,330.0	9.985	10,480
1984	2,100,000	7,750.0	72,130	4,185.0	9.875	10,360
1985	2.992,000	9,858.0	86,426	4,911.0	9,722	10,580
1986E	3,835,000	11,475.0	81,673	5,142.0	9,484	10,938
1987P	5,019,000	13,660.0	93,025	5,641.0	9,313	11,266
1988P	6,943,000	17,261.0	116,746	6,633.0	9,266	11,739
1989P	9,258,000	21,265.0	136,243	7,661.0	9,165	12,173
1990P	11,681,000	25,008.0	143,675	8,463.0	9,027	12,526

Source: Computer and Business Equipment Manufacturers Association (CBEMA).
Note: Shipments are estimated for 1986 and predicted for 1987 through 1990.

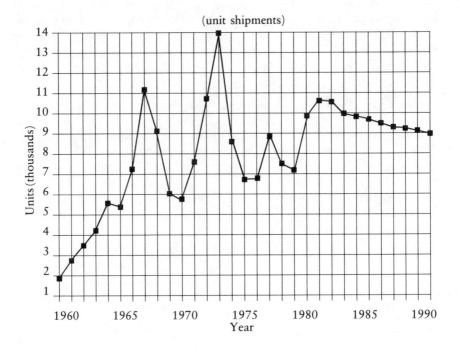

Figure 6–1. U.S. Sales of Mainframe Computers

forecast to decline through 1990.[1] Mainframe computer sales were not expected to increase by more than 4 percent in 1988. Although prices per MIPS (million instructions per second) shown in figure 6–2 were falling in 1988, profit margins remained higher for mainframe computers than for minicomputers or microcomputers.

As figures 6–3 and 6–4 indicate, the proportion of revenues generated by sales of mainframe computers fell dramatically after 1980. In 1980, the Computer and Business Equipment Manufacturers Association (CBEMA) reported that revenues from U.S. shipments of mainframe computers represented 65.8 percent of total computer sales. Five years later, U.S. sales of mainframe computers represented only 41.7 percent of total computer sales. Revenues from shipments of mainframe computers had flattened, and most mainframe computer manufacturers had not participated proportionately in the computer industry's overall explosive growth in demand. Although demand for mainframe computers was increasing more rapidly in Japan than in the United States, shipments of mainframe computers were also plateauing in Japan. In most industrialized economies, demand for minicomputers and microcomputers grew more rapidly than demand for mainframe computers, although they represented a smaller proportion of total computer revenues in 1988.

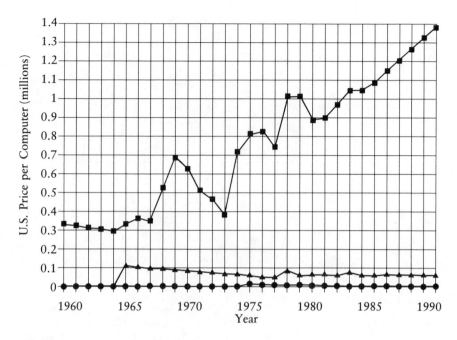

Figure 6–2. Average U.S. Computer Prices

Expectations Concerning Future Demand

Prior to 1988, forecasts had been wildly optimistic about prospects for mainframe computers. In April 1984, *Computerworld* predicted that the mainframe computer industry would experience renewed vigor—despite predictions to the contrary—and attributed its rosy outlook to the proliferation of microcomputers that would seek to access mainframe computers. In 1984, another leading trade journal predicted that demand for mainframe computers would increase exponentially because so much mainframe computer capacity (main memory) had to be expended in running operating systems and database-management software. In March 1985, *Electronics Weekly* reported that worldwide demand for all types of computers was growing by about 18 percent to 19 percent per year (compared with 15 percent growth during the decade 1970 to 1980). It predicted that mainframe computer sales would rise by 15 percent per year (compared with growth rates of 50 percent per year for microcomputers and 25 percent per year for minicomputers). Even when demand cooled during summer 1985 and all computer firms were experiencing a slump in revenues (including IBM), *Electronic Engineering Times* was predicting

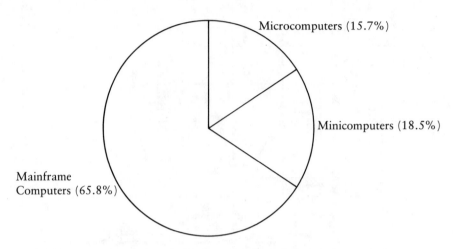

Figure 6–3. Revenue Sources—Computer Sales in 1980

that demand for supercomputers and large mainframe computers would skyrocket during 1987—regardless of what happened to the rest of the economy. Late in November 1987, CBEMA estimated that U.S. mainframe computer sales would climb just 3.3 percent per year for the next decade.

Despite trade magazine bravura concerning a rosy outlook for mainframe computer sales, there was much uncertainty among consumers about future demand by 1988. Controversy was due to technological progress and changes in how customers used computers. Prior to 1988, U.S. computer sales for business applications had grown at an annual rate of 8.5 percent, while sales for technical applications had grown by 27.7 percent. Suddenly in 1987, industry observers were predicting that sales growth in general-purpose mainframe computers would not exceed 2 percent. *Predicasts* noted that unit shipments of general-purpose mainframe computers had declined while revenues increased by only 8.9 percent per year since 1978.

Manufacturers of mainframe computers varied in their willingness to confront these data and act accordingly. Many firms simply ignored all forecasts that were less than optimistic about demand for mainframe computers because it was too unpleasant to accept that fundamental changes in how customers used computers were occurring. In the past, customers had been locked into using a particular family of vendors because software and peripherals for one brand of mainframe computer could not be transferred to another brand. Pretax profit margins on mainframe computers, peripherals, and software often exceeded 70 percent; margins on midsized minicomputers and desktop microcomputers

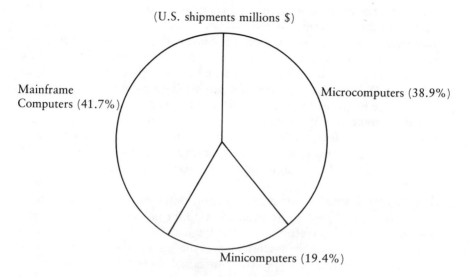

(U.S. shipments millions $)

Mainframe Computers (41.7%)

Microcomputers (38.9%)

Minicomputers (19.4%)

Figure 6–4. Revenue Sources—Computer Sales in 1985

were substantially lower (40 percent to 50 percent), especially where customers began to consider microcomputers as commodities.

Substitutes for Mainframe Computers

In a strict sense, the only substitute for purchasing or leasing a mainframe computer was the use of a computer service bureau. In a broader sense, minicomputers, microcomputers, supercomputers, superminicomputers, and supermicrocomputers were substitutes for mainframe computers in 1988 because they could be programmed to perform tasks that were formerly done by mainframe computers.

Changing Computer Technology

Technological improvements had put vast computing power on managers' desktops. Increasing customer sophistication (due to rising managerial computer-literacy) had decreased the use of central data-processing centers and increased the use of "departmental" computers that managers (or their assistants) could operate themselves. Demand for mainframe computers was slowing because technological improvements gave minicomputers and microcomputers computing speeds so much faster, bit-sizes so much larger, and ease of use so much greater that increasingly sophisticated customers questioned the need to buy a monolithic (and expensive) mainframe computer when a cluster of minicomputers (or desktop-sized microcomputers) could perform as well at a fraction of the mainframe computer's cost. Users found that minicomputers, which were originally created as special-purpose machines to perform engineering applications or control factory processes, performed more efficiently than general-purpose mainframe computers when minicomputers were adapted to perform general-business applications. Users also believed that supercomputers with software for general-business applications offered more computing power while performing as well as general-purpose mainframe computers. (Like subcompact automobiles, smaller computers did not carry the high markups necessary to support the type of intensive marketing efforts that firms like IBM traditionally devoted to high-margin mainframe computers.)

Increasingly sophisticated systems. Improvements in computer technology made many distinctions between the computing power of mainframe computers, minicomputers, and microcomputers meaningless. Each category of computer was capable of imitating the performance of the lower end of the product line in the category above it by 1988. Miniaturization allowed microcomputers to perform more like minicomputers while minicomputers performed more like mainframe computers. For example, a central processing unit (CPU) of thirty-two-bit or sixty-four-bit architecture (or word length) was no longer unique to mainframe computers by 1988. As the cost of computational power dropped steadily, the unit cost for work done on a less expensive small-scale system (a minicomputer or microcomputer) became less than that of the same work done on an expensive, large-scale system (a mainframe computer). Meanwhile, improvements in data communications enabled customers to use clusters of smaller computers to emulate the power of a mainframe computer without providing them with as much special care as mainframe computers typically required.

Less need for special attention. Most mainframe computers had to be located in high-security, specially constructed rooms—often behind cold, distance-creating glass walls. They required special environmental controls, specialized maintenance procedures, and a cadre of programmers (that could not be used readily for other tasks). Many mainframe computers required higher voltages than 120- or 220-volts and were operated in air-conditioned rooms or attached to special plumbing systems (that circulated liquid nitrogen or chilled water to cool their densely packed circuits while operating) in rooms with special subfloors (for routing communications and power cables, cooling systems, and so on). The rooms where mainframe computers operated were free from dust and chemicals that might be emitted from ceiling tiles, wall coverings, or other sources of impurity. Finally, mainframe computers required the services of specialized personnel who performed daily maintenance rituals and wrote software to run desired applications.

By contrast, because minicomputers and microcomputers did not require special environmental systems, they could be placed in virtually any office environment with an electrical outlet that delivered 120- or 220-volts. Because standardized software packages for many applications had become widely available as the installed base of minicomputers and microcomputers mushroomed, a specialized programming staff was not needed. By 1988, minicomputers (and some microcomputers) had the computing power and speed needed to run mainframe computer software, a change that further reduced the need to devote valuable floorspace to mainframe computers. Finally, the combination of greater managerial sophistication about computer capabilities and standardized software enabled managers to eliminate the middleman—the programmer who frequently misunderstood managers' requests or procrastinated in completing jobs for them.

Centralized data processing. The high fixed costs of mainframe computers discouraged the practice of letting them be idle. Twenty-four-hour utilization was necessary to justify their high capital costs. When mainframe computers were first used for business applications, they were centrally located because they handled all data-processing needs for all parts of an organization. Under such centralized data-processing schemes, most often data was physically carried to a "data center" to be left overnight and processed as a "batch" in order to use a mainframe computer's CPU most efficiently. Batch processing involved sequential use of programs that used all or a substantial part of a mainframe computer's power while they ran.

Decentralized departmental data processing. The relative simplicity of minicomputers and microcomputers freed managers from dependence on programming specialists, maintenance personnel, and other computer experts needed in order to use their mainframe computer system while giving them greater involvement and control over their own data-processing needs. Instead of centralized data-processing centers, managers were able to use "departmental computing-centers." (The departmental computing concept—also called "distributed data-processing"—allowed organizational subunits, divisions, regions, local offices, or profit centers to purchase and maintain their own systems and select their own customized programming.)

Customers for Mainframe Computers

By 1988, vendors of mainframe computers were dependent on selling replacement systems to existing customers. Few new buyers could be found. Forecasts of demand for mainframe computers varied by customer group and by geographic region. In 1988, the major customers for mainframe computers included (1) industrial users, (2) government agencies, (3) military organizations,

(4) financial service companies (banks, financial institutions, insurance firms, and business service companies), (5) educational institutions, (6) public utilities (power, fuel, and communications), (7) retailing establishments, (8) transportation firms, (9) health-care organizations, (10) distribution firms, and (11) publishing and printing companies, among others. Table 6–3 indicates that U.S. purchases of mainframe computers were expected to grow most rapidly in the health-care and business-service industries. In Japan, sales were expected to grow most rapidly among retailers. In Western Europe, business service firms were expected to purchase the most mainframe computers.

Industrial users. More computers were used by U.S. assemblers and fabricators of manufactured products in 1988 than by any other U.S. industry, and the value of this installed base accounted for over 30 percent of the total value of all computers in the United States. Large installed bases of mainframe computers were found in assembly-line manufacturing operations (such as automobiles, electronics, and so on) as well as continuous-process operations (chemicals, food-processing, and so on). The role of mainframe computers in factory automation was unclear. Most frequently, mainframe computers were used for administrative applications—computerized accounting, order-processing, purchasing, and inventorying activities. Managerial decision making was supported by computer-generated sales analyses, cost and inventory reports, sales forecasts, sales-driven production-scheduling, and a variety of detailed financial analyses.

Federal, state, and local governments. Many of the tasks that were computerized in business were also found in government agencies that operated manufacturing plants, financial institutions, service operations, hospitals, education facilities, transportation, distribution outlets, and so on. More advanced applications used by the government included information retrieval for weather forecasting and analytical research on a variety of subjects, such as environmental pollution. Government agencies also used computers for administration and accounting, processing and auditing tax returns, maintaining and analyzing census data, order processing, police databanks on criminals and stolen property, emergency response systems, school administration and motor vehicle registration.

Military users. The armed forces and other agencies of federal governments made sophisticated use of mainframe computers for command and control systems for national defense, information retrieval for various functions of intelligence work, and other applications. Although minicomputers and microcomputers were expected to satisfy some of the demand for computing power in these markets, military users were also major customers for supercomputers, a product category that was expected to enjoy sales growth of 45 percent per year.

Table 6-3
Major Markets for Mainframe Computers by Region in 1987

	U.S. Percent Installed Base	U.S. Forecast Growth Rate (%)	U.S. Forecast Revenues $Million	Japan Percent Installed Base	Japan Forecast Growth Rate (%)	Japan Forecast Revenues $Million	Europe Forecast Revenues $Million
Industrial	30%	10%	$ 2,500	19%	9.0%	$ 3,238	$ 1,900
Government	10–11	6	—	13	9.0	624	950
Military	5	—	—	—	—	—	—
Financial services	—	—	2,500	15	—	—	—
Banks, financial institutions	10–11	4	—	—	10.5	3,344	1,900
Insurance	9	—	—	3	9.8	683	—
Business services	7–8	16	3,200	19	9.3	1,009	3,800
Educational	6	15	—	16	7.8	262	—
Public utility	5	12	—	—	11.2	331	1,500
Retail	4	15	1,700	—	16.1	1,282	2,500
Transportation	3–4	—	—	—	6.5	380	—
Health care	2–3	20	—	—	6.8	104	—
Distribution	2–3	11	—	15	—	—	—
Publishing, printing	2	15	—	—	7.1	74	—
Unspecified demand			150,100			669	58,950
Total revenues			$160,000			$12,000	$71,500

Source: Compiled from *Predicasts* and industry trade journals.

Banks and other financial institutions. Banks and other financial institutions were heavy users of mainframe computers because much financial work centers around repetitive operations and transactions, both areas where data-processing power found its greatest utility. Accounts-updating (demand deposits, check-processing, proof and transit operations) was done with mainframe computers, although processing was not done in-house in smaller banks. On-line teller systems and automatic cash dispensers were linked to databases that were maintained in the same mainframe computers used for electronic funds transfers. Mainframe computers assisted banks and financial institutions in investing and controlling the funds essential for efficient operation through decision-making techniques such as portfolio and cash-flow analysis. As they added trading in stocks, futures, and commodities to their product lines, banks and other financial institutions increased their need for the type of computing power that mainframe computers offered. Some banks and financial institutions installed supercomputers instead.

Insurance users. The massive paperwork burden faced by the insurance industry made it an early user of mainframe computers because the volume and task repetition involved in calculating customer premiums and billing policyholders was simplified through computerization. Insurance reserves and actuarial statistics could be readily calculated from the databases that mainframe computers maintained for daily operations. Controlling these data gave insurance firms timing advantages in approving policies, analyzing historical patterns, and predicting future actions from internally generated statistical tables. Insurance firms were also candidates for an early upgrading to supercomputers.

Business and personnel-service users. The business and personnel-services market included computer "service" concerns that provided time-sharing, leasing, or value-added information-processing services, consulting firms, certified public accountants, credit agencies, personnel agencies, and so on. Service bureaus performed many activities that mainframe computers could do well for smaller clients—(1) basic chores like payroll and order processing, preparing tax returns, bookkeeping, and maintaining client records, (2) advanced applications, such as sophisticated econometric models, on-line processing, time sharing, computer-aided design services, and (3) database applications such as legal and medical information retrieval. Although service bureaus had accounted for 7 to 8 percent of mainframe computer use in the past, specialty applications like legal computer systems were expected to grow by 16 percent per year to a market size of $1 billion by 1989.

Educational users. While the instructional market showed strong growth through 1990, stand-alone minicomputers and desktop microcomputers were replacing early educational installations where terminals had been attached to mainframe computers. Schools still used mainframe computers to handle records involving the attendance, grading, and scoring of students, as well as scheduling of administrative tasks similar to those of any business with large numbers of employees. Mainframe computers were used to prepare indexes and databases for library use and keep records for guidance counseling. Mainframe computers were also time-shared by students and faculty for engineering and scientific research and by students of all ages for computer-aided instruction.

Public utility users. Power, fuel, and communications companies used mainframe computers for activities such as customer billing and accounting, automated meter reading, inventory control, and order processing, among others. Telephone companies used mainframe computers to route calls, analyze rate structures, schedule facilities and personnel, simulate service demands, and assess capital requirements for facility maintenance and construction.

Retail users. Wholesalers and retailers had been slow to use mainframe computers initially. Recently, their demand for computing power had increased dramatically—not only for customer-billing, credit acceptance, sales analysis, inventory-reporting, and other administrative tasks, but also for analysis of trends in purchasing habits, advertising effectiveness, and inventorying policies. Mainframe computers enabled retailers to coordinate data gathered from point-of-sale bar-code readers and data-entry stations to trace merchandise through every phase of operations for inventory control, sales analysis, profitability studies, and efficiency studies of distribution and warehousing.

Transportation users. Although transportation companies used mainframe computers for general administrative tasks, cost analysis, calculating tariff rates, scheduling repairs, and vehicle maintenance, their most sophisticated applications included complex reservations-systems, computerized-tracking of shipments, analysis of traffic patterns to optimize routing, and automated tariff-calculation and billing. The transportation industry was struggling to resolve whether decentralized distributed-data-processing systems (like American Airlines' SABRE reservations system) enabled them to deliver better service than centralized systems (like Allegis's reservations system).

Healthcare users. Mainframe computers had become commonplace in hospitals, where they performed administrative jobs, such as patient billing, inventory control of medical instruments and facilities, maintaining patient histories, and producing health-care statistics. The power of mainframe computers was just beginning to be exploited in the health-care market in sophisticated diagnostic tools such as CAT scanners or other instruments that processed digital data to produce an image.

Distribution users. Distributors used mainframe computers to facilitate the flow of material or merchandise from producer to customer—through purchase control, order processing, and inventory and warehouse control. Mainframe computers were also used to operate more efficiently—through vehicle and load-scheduling, forecasting and predicting traffic patterns, and analyzing demographic information for warehouse site selection.

Publishing and printing. Newspapers and publishing houses used mainframe computers for layout operations—to feed typesetting machines directly from newsroom and editorial desks to produce press-ready copy. Computerized production methods facilitated shorter, customized press runs to take advantage of regional distribution patterns or specialized audiences. Demand in parts of the publishing market was expected to grow by 20 percent to 60 percent per year.

Marketing of Mainframe Computers

Like many other high-tech capital goods, mainframe computers were becoming more difficult to sell by 1988 because the identity of key purchase decision makers was changing. If data processing had remained a centralized task, mainframe computer manufacturers with an installed equipment base would have sustained an advantage in selling equipment upgrades to their past customers.[b] But by 1988, management information system (MIS) directors of centralized data-processing centers were deferring to departmental users for some computer purchases. The growing acceptance of departmental computing moved the purchasing decision from middle-level MIS staff managers to senior-level line and departmental managers, especially where capital expenditures for computers were reviewed by corporate-level CIOs (chief information officers) who were themselves more familiar and comfortable with a variety of computers and their uses than previous generations of technically trained managers. Because CIOs had no bias for one manufacturer over another due to the widespread availability of software, they were more likely to select computing equipment based on bottom-line performance and compatibility or connectability with existing equipment, rather than on past relations with a particular vendor. Finally, the buying cycle became especially complex for purchasing mainframe computers that were to be integrated into a network of existing machines.

---

[b]The advantage of manufacturers with an installed equipment base was due to the switching costs involved with certifying new vendors, converting programs and databases, and retraining personnel. These switching costs ("lock-in" costs) had played a major role in deciding the purchase decisions of mainframe-computer customers in the past, and IBM possessed the most substantial advantage in selling equipment upgrades because many data-processing managers gained their first experience with data-processing on IBM equipment and were reluctant to give up the support, prestige, and peace of mind that IBM provided.

Agreement from users who spanned several different departments was needed when tying computers together through a network.

Suppliers to the Mainframe-Computer Manufacturers

Mainframe computers were composed of hardware and software. Hardware components included electrical and electronic parts—including logic- and memory-integrated circuits, circuit boards, display screens, memory devices, cabinets, and so on. Software components included the operating system, applications software, networking software, and other necessary programming.

Hardware components. Because they had commodity-like traits, hardware components for mainframe computers were readily available from a variety of U.S. and foreign sources. Even highly sophisticated logic chips were available on the open market, and state-of-the-art components were often readily available within six to eighteen months after they were first introduced. To cope with their shrinking window of competitive advantage, some computer manufacturers designed proprietary chips—often by forming alliances with semiconductor firms—and refused to license these designs to outsiders. This practice created a dilemma for small suppliers to mainframe computer firms because—as many of them learned during the worldwide recession of demand in 1985—computer firms like IBM that possessed in-house capabilities to make their own components favored their sister divisions as suppliers when times were tough.

Software. During the 1950s, 1960s, and 1970s, template-quality software had been provided by manufacturers of mainframe computers as part of the "package" that vendors offered. Programmers employed at customers' facilities modified this basic software to their firm's precise requirements. By 1987, software had become so important that the value added by sofware often exceeded that of hardware, software was being developed and marketed by specialized software houses, and more standard software could be readily used without modifications. The major exception was operating-system software, which was not standardized in 1988. IBM held a virtual monopoly on operating system software for IBM-compatible mainframe computers that represented 12.6 percent of total sales and yielded pretax margins of 71.4 percent (IBM leased rather than sold its mainframe-computer operating systems.)

Competition in the Worldwide Mainframe-Computer Industry

During the 1970s, sales of computers by United States firms had represented 75 to 80 percent of the worldwide market. By 1988, significant inroads into the worldwide market had been made by Japanese vendors through government-sponsored industrial targeting programs aimed at specialized market segments. In Europe, most production of computers was concentrated into one or two major firms per nation, and national champions usually captured leading market shares (often after IBM) in their home markets due to governments' protectionist policies.

Early Mainframe Computers

Although many historians attribute the invention of the computer to Charles Babbage who developed a hand-cranked, jacquard-like device for computing in 1822, the first electrical computer (the Z1) was designed in West Germany (in 1936, by Konrad Zuse) and the first electronic computer ("Colossus") was designed in the United Kingdom (in 1943, based on a 1936 paper on computer science by English mathematician, Alan M. Turing). The first programming language ("Plankalkul") was designed in West Germany (in 1944, by Konrad Zuse, who was unable to obtain material for hard-wired control circuits for his computer).

Colossus began operations in December 1943 at Bletchly Park (United Kingdom) and was used to decipher secret codes used by the German military. The first general-purpose, automatic digital computer ("Mark I") was developed in 1944 by Harvard Professor Howard Aiken, with the donation of equipment, and engineering and financial assistance from IBM. The Mark I was used to calculate ballistics problems involving ship's guns for the U.S. Navy, and Professor Aiken predicted that six computing machines would satisfy the entire demand for large-scale calculating in the United States. Thomas Watson, Sr. (head of IBM in 1945) saw *no* commercial possibilities from Professor Aiken's work and did not make any plans to add computers to IBM's product line. IBM let other firms pioneer the idea of using computers for general-purpose, business applications and did not manufacture electronic computers until 1952.

During the 1950s technically oriented entrepreneurs who created start-up computer firms found it necessary to merge with larger, established business-products firms. Like firms in many embryonic industries, the entrepreneurial computer ventures lacked the necessary capital to commercialize their products. The well-financed, business-products firms that bought the start-up firms possessed the sales forces and controlled the distribution channels needed to commercialize mainframe computers. Demand for computers was not expected to be large. In 1954, several prominent prognosticators projected that no more than 100 mainframe computers would be needed to handle the computational needs of the entire United States.

In 1950, the Eckert-Mauchly Computer Corporation faced the cancellation of its first contract for the UNIVAC (*UNIV*iversal *A*utomatic *C*omputer) computer due to lack of funds to go forward. In order to obtain financing,

Eckert-Mauchly merged with the Remington Rand Corporation in 1950. The merged company became the UNIVAC division, and in 1951 Eckert and Mauchly delivered the UNIVAC I to the U.S. Census Bureau for tabulating the 1950 census. In 1954, the first nongovernmental installation of an electronic computer was a UNIVAC I at General Electric Company (GE)'s appliance manufacturing plant in Louisville (Kentucky). In 1955, Remington Rand joined Sperry Gyroscope to form Sperry Rand. In 1955, Honeywell bought the Raydac/Raycom computer division of Raytheon Corporation. In 1956, Burroughs Corporation purchased Electro-Data Corporation, an early computer company.

In 1953, Engineering Research Associates merged with Remington Rand, adding to the computer capability introduced by the Eckert-Mauchly group. The Computer Research Corporation sold out to NCR Corporation (then called National Cash Register) in 1953 before delivering its first computer. In 1956, RCA introduced the internally developed BIZMAC computer. (Unlike IBM, which was a leading marketer of business products, RCA was a leading technology firm. Indeed, at that time, RCA was the leading manufacturer of electronic receiving tubes and television receivers. RCA considered itself to be the epitome of an electronics company and considered mainframe computers to be a logical extension of its electronic products line. Similar logic motivated GE's entry into the computer business. GE was a technology firm, not a marketer of business products.)

In 1953, IBM delivered its first computer (the 701) to compete with the UNIVAC I, which was already in use by the U.S. government. IBM introduced its 650 computer (which used punched cards as input devices in 1954 and sold its first commercial computer to Monsanto in 1955. By 1956, IBM shipped 85.2 percent of the value of all new mainframe computer systems in the United States and held a 75.3 percent share of the installed base of computers. Remington Rand followed with 9.7 percent of total computer shipments and an 18.7 percent share of the cumulative installed base of computers. In 1957, William Norris, feeling underutilized, left Remington Rand to form Control Data Corporation (CDC). In 1959, Control Data turned its first profit.

Mainframe Computers in the Transistor Era

Transistorized computers. Bell Labs scientists invented the transistor in 1947. In 1958, Texas Instruments' Jack St. Kilby developed the first working model of the integrated circuit. In August 1958, UNIVAC delivered the first transistorized computer, the Solid State 80 (and in 1966, Sperry Rand's computer operations finally became profitable). RCA also introduced a transistorized computer in 1958 (and in 1964, RCA's computer operations finally became profitable). In late 1958, Philco introduced the first large-scale solid-state system. In July 1959, GE delivered its first transistorized computer, the GE 210. (GE's computer business never became profitable.) IBM introduced its first transistorized computer (the 7090) in 1959 and delivered the highly successful, low-priced 1401 in 1960. In 1960, NCR and Honeywell introduced transistorized computers. (NCR's computer operations finally became profitable in 1973.) After maintaining for three years that its electronic receiving-tube computers were competitive with others' machines, Burroughs hastily converted to transistorized computers in 1961. In 1959, there were approximately 4,000 mainframe computers in use in the United States. They were valued at about $1 billion.

In 1964, RCA decided to mount a direct assault on IBM's System 360 with its Spectra 70 series of IBM-compatible computers, which were designed to outperform the 360. The RCA Spectra was priced about 40 percent less than the comparable IBM product; it offered formats, instructions, and character codes that were identical to the IBM 360. Larger Spectra 70 models pioneered the use of advanced monolithic-integrated circuits, which IBM had feared to use in its 360 series because of the risk of relying on untried technology. RCA licensed its Spectra 70 designs widely throughout the world but did not achieve its goal of wresting away 10 percent of IBM's market. In September 1970, RCA slashed its prices to increase its market share. By August 1971, RCA had lost $63 to $80 million on its formerly profitable computer business. In September 1971, RCA announced that it was leaving the computer business. Sperry Rand purchased what was left of RCA's computer business, including its installed base (1,000 computers, 500 customers), and hired 1,300 RCA customer engineers. Another 8,000 RCA computer employees were laid off.

Supercomputers. In 1958 (while working at Control Data Corporation), Seymour Cray designed the first fully transistorized, large-scale, scientific-oriented computer (the CDC 1604). Its great speed was achieved by replacing its electronic receiving tubes with germanium transistors. The first CDC 1604 was delivered in January 1960. In the next generation CDC 6600, Cray pioneered the use of silicon transistors to increase the speed possible over that of germanium. The first true supercomputer, the CDC 7600, was introduced in 1969, and Control Data dominated this market until 1976 when the Cray-1 supercomputer (which was five times faster than the CDC 7600) was introduced.

Minicomputers. In 1957, Ken Olsen started Digital Equipment Corporation as a mail-order parts business. Digital Equipment delivered its first computer (the transistorized PDP-1) in 1959 and introduced the first minicomputer in 1965. At that time, the installed base of mainframe computers was valued at about $6 billion. IBM had a 65 percent share of the U.S. computer market. Sperry Rand had 12 percent, followed by Control Data with 5 percent, and the next six competitors with 3 to 4 percent each. (Philco had captured 0.7 percent share of the U.S. installed base of mainframe computers by 1965.) By 1967, there were eight major mainframe computer and peripheral equipment firms in the United States: IBM, Burroughs, Sperry Rand, NCR, Control Data, Honeywell, GE, and RCA. There were approximately 50,000 mainframe computers in use in the United States in 1969.

Customers quickly found uses for the minicomputer, which was featured as *Time* magazine's "man of the year" in 1982. During the 1970s, sales of mainframe computers grew about 12 percent per year; minicomputer sales grew by 33 percent during the same period.

The Introduction of Microprocessors

In 1969, the first commercially produced microprocessor chip was introduced by Intel. In 1974, primitive four-bit and eight-bit microcomputers (and do-it-yourself kits) were offered for sale in the United States by obscure firms such as MITS, Altair, and Imsai. Although these early microcomputers were aimed at hobbyists and computer enthusiasts, the microcomputer did not remain a plaything for long. In 1976, Apple Computer began selling the eight-bit Apple II, and VisiCalc software was introduced in 1979. In 1983, Apple Computer introduced a microcomputer (the Lisa) with a thirty-two-bit microprocessor for under $10,000. The price was soon reduced to $7,000, and one year later Apple introduced a thirty-two-bit computer for under $3,000. Customers quickly found uses for their microcomputers when they were capable of processing information in chunks as large as minicomputers and mainframe computers could handle at significantly lower prices.

In 1981, Cray Research announced the Cray-2 supercomputer (for delivery in 1984). The Cray-1 processed 100 million instructions per second (MIPS) and was six feet high by nine feet long. The Cray-2 processed 500 to 1,000 MIPS and was 26 inches high by 38 inches long. In 1983, Cray Research introduced the X-MP supercomputer, which operated three to five times faster than the Cray-1, used Cray-1 software, and employed parallel-processing (or multiprocessing) to operate at increased speeds.

The Shakeout. By 1988, some old-line mainframe computer manufacturers were scurrying to enter joint ventures and OEM agreements or make other arrangements that would help them to supplement their limited (and increasingly obsolete) product lines. Others sought government protection to cope with the challenge of maturing demand for their products. A few firms, like Philips N.V., left the mainframe computer business (or deemphasized it drastically) to recover their investments before other firms acknowledged the endgame had begun. Margins were declining as nervous firms slashed prices to increase volumes. When customers did not respond to pricing tactics as they had in the past, the mainframe computer firms knew—whether they chose to acknowledge the fundamental change or not—that a new competitive era had begun.

Vignettes of Selected Competitors

Amdahl. Amdahl Corporation (a firm co-founded and controlled by Fujitsu) was headquartered in Sunnyvale, California, and had 6,910 employees in 1987. It was engaged in the design, development, manufacture, marketing, and maintenance of large-scale, high-performance, general-purpose computer systems and complementary software, storage, communication, and education products.

Amdahl sold mainframe-computers that were compatible with large-scale IBM products. It claimed that its products performed just as well as IBM products at a better price/performance ratio. Amdahl computers sold at as much as a 30 percent discount to comparable IBM products. In 1985, Amdahl announced three mainframe products that were about 30 percent faster than IBM's products to compete with IBM's 3090 (or Sierra) series. Amdahl distributed Fujitsu's supercomputers.

Control Data. Control Data Corporation (CDC) was headquartered in Minneapolis, Minnesota, and had 38,856 employees in 1987. Control Data designed, developed, manufactured, and marketed large-scale, general-purpose, digital computer systems; it also developed and supported related software. Control Data was at its zenith in 1963 when it introduced the 6600 computer—which was twenty times as powerful as its original Model 1604 and three times more powerful than any computer that IBM had produced up to that time. In 1964 (after IBM announced its System 360/90), orders started dropping off for CDC's 6600 before its first computer was even delivered. Over the following months, CDC had to cut prices on its 6600 computer by $2 million dollars in order to stimulate sales. When demand for all mainframe computers slumped dramatically in 1986, CDC's response was to announce a price cut of 15 to 20 percent and focus its efforts on supercomputer products.

Cray Research. Cray Research was headquartered in Minneapolis, Minnesota, and had 1,500 employees in 1987. It was the leading supercomputer firm and Control Data's major competitor until IBM, Fujitsu, Hitachi, National Advanced Systems, and NEC also entered the supercomputer business in 1983. In 1987, Cray's computer designer, Stephen Chen, left to start his own firm when it was discovered that he was developing a third supercomputer product line instead of creating a follow-up to one of Cray's two existing product lines.

Digital Equipment. Digital Equipment Corporation was headquartered in Maynard, Massachusetts, and had 89,000 employees in 1987. Digital Equipment designed, manufactured, sold, and serviced a wide line of computers—from microcomputers to mainframe computers—and associated peripheral equipment, related software, and supplies. It had dominated the minicomputer market since the mid-1960s. Digital Equipment earned 30 percent of its revenues in the European market where it had a 4 percent market share. Unlike IBM's product line, all of Digital Equipment's computers were compatible with each other. Because of its systems-software compatibility across models and clustering technology, Digital Equipment had expanded its customer base to mainframe-computer users and networking systems. By 1988, Digital Equipment had entered the mainframe-computer market by introducing the "VAX-cluster," a multiprocessing technology that allowed clusters of minicomputers to share a common database run by a mainframe computer. (Clustering allowed users of a common database to add minicomputers and disk drives in configurations yielding computing power similar to very large computer systems.) In March 1988, Digital Equipment introduced a mainframe-computer product line that was plainly designed to penetrate the heart of IBM's most profitable mainframe-computer installations. The war was on, and IBM was forced into a defensive posture.

Fujitsu. Until 1985, Fujitsu manufactured mainframe computers and super-computers for U.S. distribution by Amdahl. By 1988, Fujitsu sold computers under its own brand name in the United States while continuing to supply IBM-compatible computers to its 49 percent–owned Amdahl Corporation. Fujitsu was the leading Japanese computer vendor. Fujitsu's Japanese computer sales first surpassed those of IBM Japan in the 1980s. Computers represented two-thirds of Fujitsu's business, the highest proportion of any of the Japanese computer companies. In 1983, the Japanese government announced a two-pronged plan to help Japanese firms create advanced computer technologies.

In November 1987, Fujitsu settled a copyright dispute with IBM concerning operating systems for mainframe computers. Under their agreement, Fujitsu received access to basic information about the design of IBM software in exchange for payment of substantial fees. The settlement effectively created a new worldwide mainframe computer standard because of the dominance of firms building IBM-compatible mainframe computers. Worldwide price competition in operating-system software products that IBM had virtually dominated was certain to be one result of the settlement.

Hitachi. Hitachi Ltd. was headquartered in Tokyo, Japan, and had 164,951 employees in 1987. Hitachi had original equipment manufacturer (OEM) supply agreements with many U.S. and European firms to provide them with IBM-compatible mainframe computers. Computers accounted for less than 10 percent of Hitachi's overall sales, and computer exports (mostly to the United States) represented only 10 percent of Hitachi's computer business activity. In 1987, Hitachi entered the race to produce the fastest supercomputer by introducing its S-820/80 model.

The Honeywell-NEC-Bull joint venture. In 1986, Honeywell announced that it had negotiated the combination of its computer operations with those of

NEC Corporation and the Groupe Bull of France. The Honeywell-NEC-Bull combination produced an entity with sales of $7.5 billion, behind IBM at $48 billion and Unisys at $9.4 billion. The venture closed a Phoenix (Arizona) plant in November 1987 in an attempt to improve manufacturing efficiency. Elsewhere, the venture consolidated operations.

Honeywell Inc. was headquartered in Minneapolis, Minnesota, and had 94,022 employees in 1986. It marketed a wide product line from minicomputers to mainframe computers. Honeywell's Information Systems Division designed, manufactured, marketed, and serviced computers and computer-related products for business, government, and industrial applications. After Honeywell revealed that its second quarter net income fell by 31 percent, it announced a September 1986 cost-cutting move that eliminated about 4,000 jobs or 4.3 percent of its work force. At first Honeywell denied rumors that it was ripe for takeover. Two weeks later Honeywell formed a joint venture with NEC and the Groupe Bull of France.

NEC Corporation (formerly Nippon Electric Corp.) was headquartered in Tokyo, Japan, and had 90,102 employees in 1986. NEC purchased Honeywell's Japanese subsidiary in 1985. Computers accounted for 25 percent of NEC's revenues until 1986 but because NEC's mainframe computers were not IBM-compatible, it had played a limited role outside the Japanese market before the joint venture with Honeywell and Bull. Until late 1987, NEC's SX-2 model supercomputer was the fastest machine designed and built in Japan. The SX-2 was marketed worldwide through Honeywell-NEC Supercomputers Inc., a 50 percent–50 percent joint venture of Honeywell and NEC.

In 1988, Honeywell indicated that it might leave Honeywell Bull Inc., the joint venture between Groupe Bull, NEC Corp., and Honeywell by selling its 42.5 percent stake to Bull. The joint venture planned to eliminate $40 million in manufacturing costs in 1988 by consolidating all U.S. production in one site and cutting employment by 10 percent. NEC's role in the venture appeared to be primarily that of supplying mainframe computers for resale to customers that Honeywell Bull was best suited to serve—government and manufacturing users. The partners' computers shared common Honeywell designs licensed to NEC and Bull during the 1960s. Differences in their subsequent designs were being eliminated in 1988 to make their respective computers compatible with each other.

ICL. ICL was a combination of International Computers and Tabulators, Ferranti, Elliot Automation, and the English Electric-Leo-Marconi Company. It received financial backing from Plessey. ICL had its headquarters in London, United Kingdom. It was partially owned by the British government (which provided ICL with emergency loans and blocked foreign purchase of ICL on several occasions). ICL was the largest European computer manufacturer and was one of the few firms that was not dependent on U.S. computer firm technology in the 1970s. (Japan's Fujitsu was the other major independent developer of non-U.S.

computer technology.) European sales represented 14 percent of ICL's 1987 revenues. ICL had facilities in twenty-five countries around the world and the largest non-U.S. software organization in the world. It held a 25 to 30 percent market share in the U.K. market (as compared to IBM's 50 percent to 60 percent share in the U.K. market in 1986) and had a technology transfer agreement with Fujitsu (as well as OEM supply agreements) for the supercomputer end of its computer product line. In 1983, ICL established a joint research center with Bull and Siemens to study computer applications.

IBM. IBM was headquartered in Armonk, New York, and had 405,535 employees in 1987. IBM manufactured data-processing equipment and systems in the information-handling field, encompassing information-handling systems, equipment, and services to solve the increasingly complex problems of business, government, science, space exploration, defense, education, medicine, and many other areas of human activity. It earned 27 percent of its revenues in Europe on a 28 percent market share.

IBM was the largest industry competitor in 1988. It made or marketed a full line of computer products from microcomputers to supercomputers, although its large computer systems offered the highest profit margins. In 1986, mainframe computers accounted for 45 percent of IBM's sales, but 65 percent of its profits. In 1988, IBM still derived most of its revenues from mainframe computers. It had long controlled about 70 percent of the mainframe-computer business, and the sheer weight of its market presence tended to establish its products' engineering standards as industry norms. Nevertheless, IBM's earnings had been deteriorating since 1986. It suffered because generations of IBM mainframe computers—and other products—were not compatible with each other as competitors' products were.

IBM had restructured its marketing function in October 1986 to reflect the growing role of lower-priced computers as well as that of the independent dealers ("value-added resellers") who resold its computers after adding customized software or other specialized features. IBM also reorganized its system for distributing products in Europe to cut costs and increase efficiency. Analysts noted that IBM's reorganizations reflected the market threats it faced from microcomputers and minicomputers. (They also noted that more of IBM's revenues were derived from lower-margin product sales, rather than from higher-margin *rentals*.) Not only had IBM's share of the microcomputer market fallen from 84 percent in 1984 to 34 percent in 1986, but IBM's pretax margins on microcomputers had fallen to about 43 percent—far below IBM's customary 70 percent pretax margins on mainframe computers. To avoid across-the-board price reductions while investing more heavily in the lower-priced (lower-margin) minicomputer market, IBM introduced seemingly different products like the 9370 "superminimainframe computer" and the "midrange computer" with prices closer to mainframe computers.

Sales of the 3090 series of mainframe computers (the new-generation product line that IBM introduced in 1985) started slowly in 1986 because customers said the new computers were not powerful enough to justify prices that were higher than the earlier-generation 3080 product line. (IBM's February 1986 cut in upgrade charges encouraged customers to add enhancements to their installed 3080 machines instead of buying the new 3090.) Sales of the 3090 were still stalled in 1987. Customer complaints that IBM's product cycles were too long and did not offer enough performance improvements for their higher prices did not prompt IBM to change, but three years of losses and falling stock prices did ignite changes at IBM at last.

In 1985, IBM had launched a downsizing program in which no involuntary separations occurred. Using early retirements to eliminate jobs that were no longer needed, IBM cut 16,200 employees and retrained 9,400 others. Then it retrained 45,000 employees to fill vacancies created by transfers and relocations. Early in 1988, IBM reorganized the top management structure of its U.S. operations to change from a structure with highly centralized, shared activities into five decentralized product divisions—each empowered to do everything from their own product development to marketing. Products from each division adopted compatible technical standards (IBM's "Systems Applications Architecture"). In February 1988, IBM announced software enhancements (MVS/ESA) designed to revitalize its 3090 mainframe computer product line by making it run 12 percent faster. Under the reorganization, IBM's troubled new 9370 superminimainframe computer product line was placed in the mainframe computer division instead of the minicomputer division. At the upper end of the mainframe computer line, IBM agreed to back the development of a new supercomputer designed by a former Cray Research employee, Stephen Chen.

National Semiconductor. National Semiconductor Corporation was headquartered in Santa Clara, California, and had 37,000 employees in 1987. National Semiconductor's computer division, National Advanced Systems, marketed IBM-compatible mainframe computers manufactured by Hitachi Ltd. (Japan). National Advanced Systems had introduced several new peripheral and mainframe-computer products in 1985 (known collectively as the Alliance Generation of products) that were considered by many industry observers to be the most advanced of their kind. National Advanced Systems expected these products to provide a strong foundation for continued growth and expansion while enhancing its position as the leading "IBM-compatible mainframe" vendor.

NCR. NCR Corporation was headquartered in Dayton, Ohio, and had 62,000 employees in 1987. NCR developed, manufactured, marketed, installed, and serviced total business information processing systems for worldwide markets. NCR's strategy was to concentrate on two segments of the large computer market—transaction processing and office automation. NCR saw transaction processing systems as building on their traditional base of retail and financial systems. Office automation was viewed as a new area for NCR. In 1986, NCR introduced its new mainframe-computer product line. In 1988, NCR was de-emphasizing its large mainframe-computer products and focusing efforts on serving its loyal customers well.

Nixdorf Computer. Nixdorf Computer A.G. developed, manufactured, and marketed electronic data-processing systems. It was headquartered in Pader-dorn, West Germany, specialized in smaller mainframe computers, and had a 22 percent market share in the West German market in 1981.

Siemens. Siemens A.G. was headquartered in Munich, West Germany, and had once sold RCA computers under an OEM supply agreement. Siemens used the process control competence of Zuse, a pioneering German computer firm, in its first- and second-generation computers. Siemens occupied a position within the West German economy like that of the General Electric Company in the United States. Siemens emphasized larger mainframe computers and had a 21 percent share of the West German market in 1981. It had a marketing link with Fujitsu Ltd. until IBM sued Fujitsu for copyright infringement. Then Siemens linked up with Hitachi (the other Japanese vendor of IBM-compatible computers) to challenge IBM in office computers. In October 1986, Siemens A.G. and BASF A.G. linked their computer businesses in a joint venture, thereby becoming the second-largest IBM-compatible mainframe-computer vendor in Europe after Amdahl.

Unisys. In June 1987, Burroughs and Sperry announced their merger to create "Unisys," the second largest U.S. computer manufacturer. Their announcement came as all mainframe-computer manufacturers were experiencing an in-dustrywide slump in revenues and profits. The merger created a company with revenues of $9.4 billion.

Burroughs Corporation was headquartered in Detroit, Michigan, and had 40,700 employees before the merger. Burroughs made or marketed a full line of computer products from microcomputers to mainframe computers for sale or lease. It had the second largest installed base of mainframe computers, a market share of about 8 percent. In 1985, Burroughs undertook restructuring actions to rationalize facility utilization and reshape its manufacturing and marketing organizations into better strategic focus. It consolidated its product development and marketing functions to reduce manpower requirements, im-prove Burroughs' cost structure, and lower its breakeven point. In 1986, Bur-roughs had earned about 56 percent of its revenues from sales of computer and information systems.

Sperry Corporation (formerly Sperry Rand UNIVAC) was headquartered in New York City before it combined with Burroughs to form Unisys, and it had 65,932 employees in 1987. Sperry had a broad line of computers, although it was generally seen as a mainframe-computer manufacturer. Sperry's sales comprised 7 to 8 percent of the U.S. market; its installed base of computers was slightly larger, and 46 percent of Sperry's revenues were from sales of computer systems. Sperry's Computer Systems and Equipment Segment sold electronic data-processing systems and services for commercial, defense, aerospace, and marine applications. Because Sperry's smaller computers did not carry the higher markups that it typically enjoyed in its other product lines, Sperry (like IBM) introduced seemingly different computer products to avoid outright entry into the lower-priced (lower-margin) minicomputer market. It also began to market Mitsubishi's small and medium-sized mainframe computers. In November 1986, Sperry announced a small, inexpensive, and easy-to-use product with all of the features of a mainframe computer (the 2200/200 midframe computer). It ran the same software that programmed Sperry's Series 1100 mainframe computers and could be connected with a wide range of computers made by several other vendors.

The Mainframe-Computer Endgame

In 1988, the entire computer industry was in the doldrums. Most U.S. customers for mainframe computers were replacing existing machines, rather than buying their first computer. The markets that had been thought to be most promising, the office-automation and smart-building markets, were not growing as rapidly as had been expected. Demand in the financial services and manufacturing markets was also depressed. Only the government market appeared to be healthy, but many of its purchases went for desktop microcomputers, standardized (and easily portable) software, and networking systems, rather than for mainframe-computer systems.

With computer power increasing and prices per MIPS falling for substitute products, the mainframe-computer industry was due for a downsizing and shakeout in which fewer firms remained to compete for pieces of a shrinking pie. Some firms focused their efforts on other computer products. For example, mainframe-computer firms tried to develop supercomputers—a very risky strategy, when governments became active in the race to build ever-faster supercomputers. Other mainframe-computer firms offered minicomputers and microcomputers—and tried to change how customers used their products, by emphasizing a system solution that assumed product-connectability and -compatibility in the office and factory.

The need for model- and brand-compatibility was expected to drive other changes in the mainframe-computer industry. Although mainframe computers were still the best tool for processing large databases in 1988, high volume sales of mainframe computers were expected to depend on the use of microcomputers for networking with other work stations ("distributed data processing"). Decentralized data processing was expected to increase demand for mainframe computers to serve as the network's hub, communications center, and database for rapidly changing information.

Industry observers expected only a few large mainframe-computer vendors to survive. Underdog competitors merged—like Burroughs and Sperry—to attain the critical mass needed to realize scale economies. Others formed strategic alliances—like the Honeywell-NEC-Bull venture—to offer diverse and sophisticated product lines that matched those of larger competitors. Some vendors used OEM supply arrangements to fill out gaps in existing product lines. Others left early—like Philips N.V. The drive to attain scale economies while also offering compatibility and connectability was expected to result in acquisitions of minicomputer firms (like Data General and Wang Laboratories), communications firms, and remaining mainframe-computer firms. Acquiring firms were expected to be European or Japanese—possibly BASF, Siemens, Nixdorf, ICL, Bull, NEC, Hitachi, Toshiba, Fujitsu, Philips, or other firms offering patient capital.

Note

1. The sharp increase in average U.S. mainframe computer prices shown in figure 6–2 reflects the greater proportion of supercomputers included in that product class.

7
Implications for Governments

Tis chapter reviews findings concerning strategies for mature businesses and discusses their public policy implications. To that end, points raised in earlier chapters must be reviewed in the context of public-policy concerns. Assumptions concerning corporate strategy and performance must also be reviewed and contrasted with the socioeconomic objectives of governments.

Earlier chapters have noted that competitive environments associated with slowing, stagnant, and declining sales growth differ across industries, and different strategies were used successfully by firms to cope with the problems of mature demand and excess capacity. Differences in firms' endgame strategies were attributable, in part, to their differing positions of strength as their respective industries entered the endgame and to the diverse types of corporate strategies that various firms were pursuing. Differences in firms' strategies were also attributable, in part, to the public policies governments pursued with respect to each troubled industry.

Corporate Strategy and Performance

Managers are responsible for creating wealth for their firms' owners through the actions they take. In addition to this *primary* objective, managers are judged by other stakeholders on performance criteria as diverse as allocative-efficiency, technical-efficiency, and the maximization of consumer welfare. Managers are expected to ensure fair prices to customers and guarantee them a choice of vendors. They are expected to find funds for innovation, make improvements in productivity, and ultimately improve cost efficiency. Managers are expected to invest in cutting-edge technologies in their firms' plants—in automated factories, if necessary—while also providing meaningful jobs for employees. Because such a large portion of employees' waking hours are spent at work, managers are charged with disseminating cultural values that are consistent with national development goals, such as equal employment opportunity, continuing education, and the sanctity of private property. Managers are even asked to contribute to fundamental economic goals, such as income redistribution, full employment, increasing the gross national product, maintaining acceptable levels of inflation, and maintaining a favorable balance of payments. It is in the interest of managers to attend to these sometimes-contradictory goals because if managers do not take responsibility for performing these socio-economic tasks, governmental agencies possessing the power to intervene in managers' strategic decisions will do so instead. The legitimacy of business and government is tested when endgame strategies are formulated and implemented. Governments, like managers, seek to remain in power and risk defeat if their shareholders are not satisfied.

Managers' Resource-Allocation Decisions

Managers make resource-allocation decisions to engage in the best combinations of wealth-creating activities possible, within the constraints of their firms' accumulated skills and other assets—both capital and intangibles. If managers are competent, they are free to reinvest any excess cash generated from mature businesses in appropriate wealth-producing projects—while being ever aware of the differing utilities that diverse types of owners assign to the receipt of differently timed cash flows.[a]

Allocative-efficiency. Competent managers are assumed to allocate the reources of their firms to the best possible uses, and governments use tests of allocative efficiency as one dimension for assessing an industry's performance. Managers often allot more cash to growing industries than such lines of business generate because they assume that the benefits of investments in developing market share and sources of competitive advantage can later be recovered successfully. Managers hope that competition in endgames will be without disastrous incidents that prevent them from retrieving funds previously invested in mature industries. Or they hope that they will be able to sell mature businesses to outsiders before competitive conditions sour and no buyers will pay the prices that managers are demanding.

---

[a]Briefly, some owners seek instant gratification. They use the compressed information contained in stock prices (and variability of stock prices) to judge management's performance because they hold utilities that value receipt of a dollar *now* more highly than receipt of a dollar a year later and value cash flows generated beyond a decade near zero. These owners also believe that the future earnings potential of managers' investment decisions is reflected in firms' stock prices. Many of these owners are "twenty-minute share-holders" who sell their equity holdings in particular firms when their computer programs advise that the value of stocks held in companies that compete in particular industries has grown to be greater than the portfolio-percentage chosen under investors' (or their money managers') predetermined allocative-efficiency decision rules. If owners held utilities that valued long-term survival, they would not use analyses based on discounted cash flows to evaluate reindustrialization investments.

Antitakeover laws and allocative efficiency. Earlier chapters have suggested practical ways to realize hopes of value retrieval by restructuring mature industries. Governments must ponder whether antitakeover laws and other policies that support status quo managers help or harm consumer welfare. Some antitakeover-protection legislation seems to be motivated by desires to avoid plant closings (and protect blue-collar jobs) rather than by desires to improve allocative efficiency. In cases where takeovers are led by financial speculators who intend to liquidate acquired firms by breaking them up and selling their component parts, governments may be justified in creating impediments for raiders. But protection against unwanted change is unwarranted where managers have become complacent, and it raises incorrect expectations in workers. Managers that do nothing to improve the competitiveness of mature businesses deserve to be replaced by acquiring firms, but it may be appropriate to allow endgame strategy investments extra time to show the results of new working practices and other changes to internal operating systems.

Belief in the sanctity of private property and market economies suggests decisions that maximize allocative efficiency should not be in the bailiwick of government. The wisdom of managers' endgame strategies (and risk preferences of acquiring firms) will determine whether resources will be allocated to mature businesses—or whether those businesses will be sold. Antitakeover protection interferes with interstate commerce and the market for corporate control. It also prevents managers from allocating resources efficiently. Because capitalism is by nature a form of change and never is (never can be) stationary, it may be necessary to close some plants, transfer some employees, and offer early retirement to others that operate in mature industries.

The Need for Anticipating Industry Maturity

Preemptive investment decisions can influence how competition within industry endgames will evolve. Managers that make early and efficacious investments to improve asset deployment and cost effectiveness place their firms in stronger competitive positions for weathering later, inevitable industry shakeouts. Managers that are not committed to continued competition in endgame environments can realize higher selling prices for their firms by divesting unwanted lines of business early—before the problems of maturity are widely recognized.

New ballgame. Managers that can anticipate how competition in endgame differs from that in growing industries will be better able to cope with rival firms that engage in behaviors that disrupt the profitability potential of mature industries. In particular, managers should recognize that competitors with excess capacity will look for new customers and that sluggish growth will thrust their own firms into competition against new players—firms that once served different market segments, different geographic regions, or engaged in different value-adding steps. Initial confusion regarding how to compete against the new players could become devastating for subsequent industry attractiveness if wrong actions are taken. Firms that are not accustomed to competing against specific rivals will be more likely to use destructive price wars to fill their plants because they have no history of nonprice ways to compete. The result of these price wars will be lower profit margins (or losses) for all involved firms, as the examples of the cigar and electric-percolator coffee-maker industries have shown.[1] In extreme cases, surviving firms will not be able to invest in the new technologies necessary for producing next-generation products to serve loyal customers.

Rayon fibers. Misunderstandings concerning competitors' strategic posturings have resulted in poorly timed exits, unremunerative asset disposals, and otherwise disruptive and painful adaptations to declining demand. In extreme examples like FMC's disposal of its Avtex Fibers division, failure to provide for continuity in suppliers resulted in market entry by offshore vendors and subsequent litigation concerning the dumping of their excess capacity in domestic markets. Forethought may avoid such problems in other mature industries.

Food-processing. In 1986, consumers favored established brand names over generic brands. Frequently this shift resulted in a concentration in the number of brands carried in grocery stores. Rather than try to build market share, many firms bought it by acquiring the dairy products of firms like Beatrice Companies (Borden), Drake Bakeries (Ralston Purina's Continental Baking division acquired Drake from Borden), and others.

In 1986, most European food-and-drink firms were medium-sized and poorly equipped to cope with the market power of increasingly demanding retailing chains. Many of them chose to grow by acquisition instead of geographic expansion, and 1986 and was one of the heaviest years for food-related mergers in Western Europe. The restructuring continued in 1987, when Jaquet (France's leading producer of sliced bread) acquired Rugenberger (West Germany's leading baker of processed bread). The shakeout in the European food and drink business continued in 1988 as firms scurried to internationalize. Ferruzzi (the Italian sugar-based conglomerate) acquired Lesieur (the French vegetable-oils firm) and held controlling interest in Beghin-Say (the leading French sugar firm). Seagrams (of Canada) acquired Martell.

Anticipation of the effects of the 1992 Single European Act[b] accelerated the frenzy to restructure mature industries in Western Europe where the shakeout

---

[b]The end of internal tariffs and nontariff trade barriers within the European Economic Community (EEC) is scheduled for 1992. When trade liberalization occurs, price equalization across national borders for identical products is expected to occur. After government policies that have protected weak local firms are removed, managers will be forced to take necessary actions that they have long postponed if their firms are to survive. (Many coddled firms will not survive.) If the 1992 Single European Act does facilitate the free movement of goods across EEC borders, it is highly likely that the free movement of capital will follow.

was expected to accelerate the polarization of manufacturing industries into two groups—the very large, international players at one extreme and the small, niche players at the other. The global firms will be best suited to offer standardized, often branded quality products at popular prices. The niche players will have to be more flexible if they are to develop more specialized products at healthy margins. The markets served by niche players will be limited, unless niche players are extremely successful at their task.

Uncontrollable Events

Results indicate that certain external events could be particularly catastrophic for the viability of mature industries because investments made there may not be easily recovered. These events include legislation concerning effluent standards, pollution controls, employee-health work rules, import tariffs, export quotas, and a variety of other public policies that are imposed on firms because managers did not attend to their nonfinancial responsibilities. Opportunistic managers will see ways for such events to benefit their firms. For example, if managers wished to ease other firms out of mature industries, they might make investments in anticipation of onerous pieces of legislation being enacted. Once their firms are in compliance with new regulatory standards, managers can encourage such laws to be enacted.

Because many of the uncontrollable events that destroyed entire industries (like leather tanning and synthetic soda ash) are created by government policies, it is essential for managers to monitor regulatory agencies closely. They should prepare factual forecasts of likely economic impacts of proposed policy or legislation changes on communities where firms operate to draw attention to losses of jobs, tax revenues, and other benefits that firms' demises would cause. Such analyses should include internal and external forecasts of exit costs in order to facilitate informed decision making. In addition, it may be appropriate for managers that have performed such analyses to provide copies of their findings to the salient public policymakers and affected residents of communities where their firms operate. Employees should be fully informed of controversies that require governments to make socioeconomic tradeoffs.

Changes in Public Policy

Public policymakers who wish to encourage resource reallocation from low-return to high-return industries should recognize the stultifying impact of exit barriers on the ease of resource movements. Governmental policies themselves may actually discourage timely exits. Although it is possible that some government programs (such as plant-closing allowances as compensation for import competition) could help firms to exit in an orderly fashion, other interventions (such as subsidies and antitakeover-protection legislation) harm the profitability of firms by keeping inefficient competitors in business longer than free and unfettered markets might encourage them to remain. In the long run, such policies harm consumer welfare more than enhance it.

Maximization of Consumer Welfare

Economic regulation through antitrust laws uses maximization of consumer welfare as its primary assessment of industry performance. The principal measures used to infer consumer welfare are price levels, number and size distribution of competitors serving a market (detected through concentration ratios and Herfindahl-Hirschman indices), and ease of industry entry. These performance measures were chosen during an era of economic history when demand for the products of most industries were growing. In the endgame, however, the special economic and competitive problems firms encounter suggest that use of these measures should be modified to satisfy other public policy goals, such as maximization of technical efficiency and the replenishment of problem-solving skills bases.

Technical-efficiency. Managers must address two issues in serving technical-efficiency objectives: making continual improvements in productivity while also satisfying loyal customers. Technical efficiency is often attained by substituting capital assets for labor or by training human resources to work in new ways. West German firms have tended to invest in new technology rather than add new jobs because health insurance and pension costs add 50 percent or more to their already high wage bills. In the West German case, continual substitutions of capital for labor has been consistent with reputations for product quality and innovation. Public policy accepts that jobs are eliminated (or that new jobs are not created). In the British automotive plants where new working practices were used, productivity improvements were substantial but came at a cost.

Automobiles. For example, British workers at Ford in Dagenham (a thriving section of east London) went on strike in early 1988 because they were unwilling to accept changes in working practices that managers believed would improve productivity. The practices they resented were closely identified with leading Japanese automotive firms and teamwork values. The flexible work practices in question broke down strict demarcation lines in workers' roles and undermined their class consciousness. In particular, the Ford employees resented the suggestion that skilled workers (who had long since graduated from working on production lines) who had finished their tasks should help less skilled workers on the production line, instead of taking breaks. Although Ford had made the greatest progress among U.S. automotive firms in 1987 by improving its productivity and working practices, Ford's ability to realize further improvements was limited by its managers' abilities to persuade Ford employees to work (and think) differently by accepting new cultural values. Nissan automotive workers in depressed northeast England accepted the new working practices more readily.

Managers and labor unions have revitalized former rust-bowl industrial areas in southeast Michigan by building on the region's local strengths: schools with a tradition of training technicians and engineers, generations of experience in working to a thousandth of an inch, suppliers able to serve factories with an hour's notice, local services able to solve the special problems of engineering firms, and imaginative local bankers and investors. The modernization of Michigan's automotive industry built on the region's nine graduate engineering schools, 500 R&D centers, 2,000 machining shops, and $18 billion per year business of producing precision parts. Technical-efficiency objectives were served by investing in conducive industrial sites with flexible work forces.

Technical-efficiency objectives imply that firms that do not continually innovate in capital investments, asset deployments, and working practice improvements suffer in comparisons of productivity and cost effectiveness. But mature industries often suffer from shortages of the capital needed to invest in operating quality, better logistics, and service creation because providers of capital pursue allocative-efficiency objectives. Managers of mature businesses (or their corporate managers) must find the necessary capital to pursue technical-efficiency in endgame or surrender their mature businesses to others with different performance criteria who are willing to invest in them.

Blue-collar workers can alter the timing of plant closings by changing their economics. Such appeals to allocative efficiency require workers to make sizable concessions on wages and working practices. These concessions cannot prevent managers from selling revitalized plants to new owners who may value subsequent use of capital and human assets differently than previous owners (and their managers) did. Realization of operating synergies often requires human assets to make changes in working practices that they may not accept readily.

While managers pursue technical efficiency by adopting the best available technologies, loyal customers must not be unduly inconvenienced if they are satisfied with existing products. The need to encourage technological progress does not necessarily mean that older products are doomed to extinction, provided that technological laggards and other customers who do not wish to convert to substitute products are willing to pay the higher prices necessary to indemnify surviving producers of obsolescing products. What is inevitable in endgame is exits by marginal competitors, as well as higher prices for customers.

Fair prices to customers. The competition laws of many Western nations were developed to cope with industries that were growing. They understandably did not anticipate the adjustments that would be necessary to serve public interest when demand matured (or declined). New rules apply to mature industries.

Antitrust policy is based on assumptions that free-market economies favor *many* competitors and encourage the *lower* prices that accompany volatile competition in endgame (even if lower prices mean that several plants are operating at less efficient capacities instead of a few plants operating at fully loaded levels of capacity utilization). Antitrust policy does not see that volatile competition is inimical to technical-efficiency goals. Briefly, if customers capture all of the profit margins available from mature products, nothing remains for managers to reinvest in technical-efficiency objectives. Moreover, owners have no incentives to keep their firms invested in industries that are not experiencing growth if profits are competed away. Manufacturers must be rewarded for continuing to provide mature products if customers hope to enjoy their availability.

It has been many years since the Japanese economy could be considered to be a newly industrializing one that could justify stringent protection of its native industries and local producers. Yet these import barriers persist. Moreover, Japanese consumers absorb the cost of subsidizing exported products (to obtain foreign currency) by paying higher prices for their products, thereby allowing exporters to undercut the fair prices of non-Japanese competitors in their home markets.

Although Japanese consumers are reputed to possess an almost infinite capacity for pain, there is evidence that their subsidization of exported products may not last much longer. Briefly, affluent middle-class Japanese have been astonished to discover cheaper prices overseas for products manufactured in Japan, until recently. Now when they travel abroad, Japanese consumers load up on consumer products and *reexport* them back into their homeland.

Japanese consumers may also be more loyal to local producers than European consumers. When the 1992 Single European Act is in force, it is difficult to believe that European retailers and consumers will buy goods only from noncompetitive European vendors.

In successful endgame environments, prices to customers will be *higher* over time. This is a reasonable expectation (especially if workers receive wage increases) because fair prices in mature industries must contain reasonable markups to provide surviving firms with profit margins that are sufficient to encourage them to remain in operation, even if they must carry some excess capacity. When plants are underutilized, unit costs rise because fixed costs must be absorbed by the smaller volumes produced. If customers are willing to pay higher prices for obsolescing products, one or more vendors will provide them. Retailers extract higher margins from carrying mature products (because they must be remunerated for the convenience they provide by using shelf space occupied by slowly moving products). Vendors must do so as well.

Choice of vendors. Modern interpretations of U.S. antitrust policy have often protected competitors for the sake of providing customers with two or more vendors. This preference is also contrary to the realities of competition in mature industries. As long as consumers can choose among brands of products, they are served better than if no choice existed at all. Moreover, the public interest is served well where only three major and global firms—Unilever, Procter & Gamble, and Colgate-Palmolive—account for the bulk of all sales of laundry soap, shampoo, deodorant, household cleansers, and other personal care products as long as prices remain fair and unemployment levels remain high.

Managers in charge of mature businesses prefer rational patterns of exits over the chaos and wastefully volatile price cutting that enforcement of traditional antitrust laws fosters. Such policies drive all producers out of an industry without regard for firms' operating efficiencies. In mature industries suffering from excess capacity, a rational scheme of retreat has greater intuitive appeal than the irrational events that actually occurred in many of the industries I studied. A by-product of orderly industry restructurings will be fewer surviving vendors.

The restructuring investments that best serve the public interest are those that retain consumer choice by strengthening a few survivors instead of forcing all vendors to languish near death while their inefficiencies cause prices to rise and shortages of desired products to persist. It is critical for policies to be embraced that lower firms' exit barriers in mature industries. The public goals of employment, choice, and living standards are not inconsistent with the business goals of viable industries. During an era when many investors are reluctant to commit funding to mature and troubled industries, managers that lobby for opportunities to make restructuring investments should be regarded as heroes, rather than treated with suspicion.

Business is society's best engine for change. Governments attract investment by making prudent policies that enhance their business environment while also serving the public interest.[c] Firms will be willing to renovate facilities, improve products and distribution systems, offer better products, and devote continual efforts to cost reductions only if they can reasonably expect fair returns for their efforts.

Carbon black. The Federal Trade Commission (FTC) tried to prevent the inevitable rationalization of the carbon-black industry in 1984 when it opposed the acquisition of Ashland Oil Inc.'s carbon-black division by Bass Brothers Enterprises Inc. and the acquisition of Conoco's Continental Carbon Company by Columbian Chemicals Company. The FTC noted that combining the Bass Brothers affiliate, Sid Richardson Carbon & Gasoline Company, with

---

[c]Despite its financial problems, Brazil can scarcely be considered a newly industrializing economy. Yet government policies regarding business have made it highly unattractive as a site for investment by local businesses. The wealth of its population has given a vote of "no confidence" to government. The continual outflow of personal savings and corporate funds (through every imaginable form of subterfuge) has weakened Brazil's financial system further while penalizing the living standards of its people. Only through significant working practice concessions has Brazil's government been able to woo foreign investors to undertake the capital formation tasks that local interests were unwilling to embrace.

the Ashland division would create a firm with a resulting carbon black market share of 21 percent (third largest in the U.S. market). As a result of this decision, Ashland Oil could not exit because the only firms interested in its carbon-black assets were competitors. The FTC believed that consumer welfare was maximized by ensuring that there were many ailing vendors, instead of fewer (but healthier) U.S. carbon-black producers. Unfortunately for U.S. competitiveness, carbon black proved to be a global industry like its major customer industry (tires), and soon Ashland Oil was not the only troubled U.S. firm that wanted to sell its carbon-black assets.

The major public-policy justifications for preserving inefficient firms when demand is declining include a desire to (1) protect industries with national-defense content against import competition, (2) provide relief against massive unemployment in depressed industrial regions, and (3) preserve critical manufacturing and technology-creation skills. The income-guarantee policies of some European governments have made them willing to subsidize the losses of firms that employ their local laborers for other economic reasons. Governments' logic in this policy suggests that it is *less* costly to subsidize a plant that lost money (but made some contributions to employees' wages) than for government to bear the full cost of welfare payments for unemployment. As a result of these policies, some European firms that should have closed uncompetitive facilities or made other capacity adjustments to bring supply in line with demand have not done so.

The advent of the 1992 Single European Act suggests that individual governments within the EEC will no longer be permitted the luxury of coddling inefficient producers through trade barriers that discriminate against their more efficient international or European competitors. Unless the European consumer is as loyal as the Japanese consumers discussed herein, it is doubtful that retailers and consumers will purchase only European goods indefinitely when better products are available from other vendors at lower prices.

Concerns about job protection and desires to preserve a lifestyle based on an economy of shopkeepers are surely high among the tradeoffs that must be balanced against the naturally destructive forces of capitalism when technical efficiency is maximized. Similar political dilemmas exist in the midwestern United States where the small family farm is rapidly becoming an anachronism. As much as U.S. farmers long for the subsidies that allowed Mom-and-Pop farms to survive, however, they prefer to pay the lower retail prices afforded by larger-scale and vertically integrated farming corporations (which are currently the only form of farming that earns fair profits on their investments in the United States) when farmers purchase foodstuffs that their own farms do not produce.[d]

---

[d] In Japan, by contrast, farmers are subsidized heavily by urban dwellers (who vastly outnumber the rural population) through extremely high foodstuff prices. Moreover, scarce land continues to be allocated to the less-efficient Japanese farming industry due to outdated national defense concerns. The Japanese people continue to accept the need to sacrifice their personal living standards for the sake of other national goals.

The public interest is better served by allowing industry structures to evolve naturally and creatively, rather than impeding them. Innovations that change the required skills mix serve both technical efficiency and the public interest by creating jobs that increase a nation's ability to engage in high-value-adding activities that cannot be as readily undercut by competitors from nations that are willing to sacrifice their populations' living standards for the sake of advantages in international trade. Policies that allow competition to take its natural course would be consistent with others that serve the public interest well by requiring firms to stand on their own feet in the national and international competitive arena.

New Perspectives on Corporate Strategies

U.S. antitrust policy has no provision for a "failing industry," as does the spirit of European antitrust decisions that permit resource-sharing. Not only are policies needed that facilitate rational decisions regarding which firms should exit and at what time, but as endgames progress, antitrust policies should be modified to recognize that cost-efficient use of productive assets may involve competitors engaging in co-production alliances whereby one firm produces products and both firms sell them (as in the example of Pet and Carnation sharing a condensed milk plant where neither firms' sales of condensed milk were sufficient to utilize an entire processing plant alone).

Rising concentration. There can be but one "last iceman." As demand growth slows, concentration will increase because fewer firms will find endgame environments attractive enough to remain invested. Given the decreased attractiveness of endgame businesses, exiting firms are most likely to sell their abandoned productive capacity to surviving firms who, in turn, will retire obsolete assets and fortify those that they continue to operate. Tables 7–1 through 7–3 illustrate how concentration *rises* as industries enter maturity and *decreases* as demand declines. The tables were compiled by using *Census of Manufactures* data for U.S. industries with large shipment revenues. (Industries were defined by the Department of Commerce using four-digit Standard Industrial Classification codes.) Results suggest that the absolute number of firms decreased from 1947 (or the earliest available date) to 1982 in twenty-three of the forty-five major U.S. industries listed in table 7–1. In 1982, fewer U.S. firms shipped products in the mature food, textile, and paper-related industries than in 1947. The number of firms shipping products increased substantially in the revitalized synthetic rubber, valves and pipe fittings, semiconductor, and electronic computing-equipment industries from 1947 to 1982, in part, due to entry by overseas firms.

Concentration of shipments made by industries' four largest firms increased (or did not change) in twenty-four of the forty-five industries examined in table 7–2, and the proportion of shipments made by industries' eight largest firms increased in twenty-two of the forty-five industries examined in table 7–3.

Table 7-1
Number of Firms in Major U.S. Industries

Standard Industrial Classification Code	Industry	1947	1954	1958	1963	1967	1972	1977	1982	Percentage of Change in Number of Firms	Herfindahl-Hirschman Index for Fifty Largest Firms 1982
2011	Meat packing	1,999	2,228	2,646	2,833	2,529	2,291	2,404	1,659	−17%	325
2026	Milk	NA	NA	5,008	4,030	2,988	2,025	1,516	854	−83	151
2041	Flour	1,084	692	703	510	438	340	301	251	−77	551
2046	Corn wet milling	47	54	53	49	32	26	24	25	−47	1491
2051	Bread, cake	5,985	5,470	5,305	4,339	3,445	2,800	2,549	1,869	−69	410
2065	Confectionery	1,620	1,388	1,301	1,142	1,091	917	867	718	−56	584
2075	Soybean oil	105	55	66	68	60	54	65	34	−68	1204
2082	Malt beverages	404	263	211	171	125	108	81	67	−83	2089
2085	Distilled liquors	144	98	88	70	70	76	64	71	−51	741
2086	Soft drink bottling	5,169	4,334	3,989	3,569	3,057	2,273	1,758	1,236	−76	109
2111	Cigarettes	19	12	12	7	8	7	8	8	−58	2623
2121	Cigars	765	375	247	164	126	113	94	54	−93	1085
2221	Weaving mills	432	396	328	277	272	256	267	340	−21	510
2311	Men's suits, coats	1,761	1,255	1,275	1,031	904	721	619	443	−75	261
2396	Trimmings, automotive	NA	NA	NA	746	762	644	686	801	7	1734
2621	Paper mills	NA	NA	NA	186	203	194	171	136	−27	311
2643	Paper bags	NA	NA	NA	495	466	466	462	448	−9	272
2647	Sanitary paper goods	NA	NA	NA	97	91	72	72	84	−13	1328
2711	Newspapers	8,115	8,445	7,947	7,982	7,589	7,461	7,821	7,520	−7	193
2822	Synthetic rubber	5	13	13	16	33	50	56	63	1160	935
2834	Pharmaceuticals	1,123	1,128	1,064	944	791	680	655	584	−48	318
2844	Toilet preparations	692	693	721	673	628	593	644	596	−14	469
2911	Petroleum refining	277	253	289	266	276	152	192	283	2	380
3011	Tires	NA	NA	NA	105	119	136	121	108	3	1591
3111	Leather tanning	500	525	520	482	474	468	428	342	−32	206
3221	Glass containers	41	38	42	40	39	27	31	41	0	966

3291	Abrasives	236	290	318	340	320	335	353	326	38	1688
3312	Steel mills	NA	NA	148	161	200	241	395	219	43	650
3321	Iron foundries	1,554	1,321	1,199	1,062	969	893	865	800	-49	348
3334	Aluminum	3	3	6	6	10	12	12	15	400	1704
3411	Metal cans	102	109	84	99	96	134	153	168	65	790
3494	Valves, fittings	436	523	535	580	575	643	741	945	117	92
3511	Turbines, generators	NA	NA	NA	17	20	59	68	77	353	2602
3531	Construction machinery	NA	NA	NA	561	578	644	807	815	45	838
3573	Electronic computers	NA	NA	NA	NA	134	518	808	1520	1034	793
3621	Motors and generators	224	266	317	316	320	325	343	348	55	476
3633	Laundry appliances	59	48	34	31	25	20	21	15	-75	NA
3651	Radio and television receivers	NA	NA	NA	322	303	343	546	435	35	751
3674	Semiconductors	NA	NA	NA	86	141	289	499	685	697	597
3694	Engine electrical	100	154	147	163	239	266	372	393	293	1122
3711	Motor vehicles, bodies	NA	NA	NA	NA	107	165	254	284	165	NA
3724	Aircraft engines	54	202	186	194	205	189	226	279	417	1778
3751	Motorcycles, bicycles	75	44	49	85	87	219	343	269	259	1077
3811	Instruments	NA	NA	NA	571	642	703	740	738	29	353
3861	Photographic equipment	346	NA	450	499	505	555	702	723	109	2157

Source: U.S. Department of Commerce, "Concentration Ratios in Manufacturing," *1982 Census of Manufactures.*
Note: I am indebted to Rocki-Lee DeWitt for her assistance in compiling this table.

Table 7–2
Proportion of Industry Shipments Made by Four Largest Firms in Major U.S. Industries

Standard Industrial Classification Code	Industry	1947	1954	1958	1963	1967	1972	1977	1982	Percentage of Change in Four-Firm Concentration
2011	Meat packing	41	39	34	31	26	22	19	29	-29%
2026	Milk	NA	22	23	23	22	18	18	16	-30
2041	Flour	29	40	38	35	30	30	33	40	38
2046	Corn wet milling	77	75	73	71	68	63	63	74	-4
2051	Bread, cake	16	20	22	23	26	29	33	34	113
2065	Confectionery	17	19	18	15	25	32	38	40	135
2075	Soybean oil	44	41	40	50	55	54	54	61	39
2082	Malt beverages	21	27	28	34	40	52	64	77	267
2085	Distilled liquors	75	64	60	58	54	47	52	46	-39
2086	Soft drink bottling	10	10	11	12	13	14	15	14	40
2111	Cigarettes	90	82	79	80	81	NA	NA	NA	-10
2121	Cigars	41	44	54	59	59	56	56	60	46
2221	Weaving mills	31	30	34	39	46	39	42	40	29
2311	Men's suits, coats	9	11	11	14	17	19	21	25	178
2396	Trimmings, automotive	NA	NA	NA	58	57	67	71	NA	22
2621	Paper mills	NA	NA	NA	26	26	24	23	22	-15
2643	Paper bags	NA	NA	NA	22	23	25	26	25	14
2647	Sanitary paper goods	NA	NA	17	62	63	63	65	62	0
2711	Newspapers	21	18	17	15	16	17	19	22	5
2822	Synthetic rubber	NA	53	60	57	61	62	60	49	-8
2834	Pharmaceuticals	28	25	27	22	24	26	24	26	-7
2844	Toilet preparations	24	25	29	38	38	38	40	34	42
2911	Petroleum refining	37	33	32	34	33	31	30	28	-24
3011	Tires	NA	NA	NA	70	70	73	70	66	-6
3111	Leather tanning	27	18	18	18	20	17	17	18	-33
3221	Glass containers	63	63	58	55	60	55	54	50	-21
3291	Abrasives	49	50	58	58	48	59	58	63	29
3312	Steel mills	50	55	53	48	48	45	45	42	-21

SIC										
3321	Iron foundries	16	26	28	28	27	34	34	29	81
3334	Aluminum	100	100	NA	NA	NA	79	76	64	−36
3411	Metal cans	78	80	80	74	73	66	59	50	−36
3494	Valves, fittings	24	17	17	13	14	11	13	13	−46
3511	Turbines, generators	NA	NA	NA	93	76	90	86	84	−10
3531	Construction machinery	NA	NA	NA	42	41	43	47	42	0
3621	Motors and generators	59	50	47	50	48	47	42	36	−39
3633	Laundry appliances	40	68	71	78	78	83	89	91	128
3651	Radio and television receivers	NA	NA	NA	41	49	49	51	49	20
3674	Semiconductors	NA	NA	NA	46	47	57	42	40	−13
3694	Engine electrical	67	62	66	69	68	65	62	52	−22
3711	Motor vehicles, bodies	NA	NA	NA	NA	92	93	93	92	0
3724	Aircraft engines	72	62	56	57	64	77	74	72	0
3751	Motorcycles, bicycles	42	50	58	56	57	65	66	59	40
3811	Instruments	NA	NA	NA	29	28	22	25	31	7
3861	Photographic equipment	61	NA	65	63	69	74	72	74	21

Source: U.S. Department of Commerce, "Concentration Ratios in Manufacturing," 1982 *Census of Manufactures*.
Note: I am indebted to Rocki-Lee DeWitt for her assistance in compiling this table.

Table 7–3
Proportion of Industry Shipments Made by Eight Largest Firms in Major U.S. Industries

Standard Industrial Classification Code	Industry	1947	1954	1958	1963	1967	1972	1977	1982	Percentage of Change in Eight-Firm Concentration
2011	Meat packing	54	51	46	42	38	37	37	43	-20
2026	Milk	NA	28	29	30	30	26	28	27	-7
2041	Flour	41	52	51	50	46	53	54	60	46
2046	Corn wet milling	95	93	92	93	89	86	89	94	-1
2051	Bread, cake	26	31	33	35	38	39	40	47	81
2065	Confectionery	25	27	27	25	35	42	49	53	112
2075	Soybean oil	63	64	63	70	76	69	73	83	32
2082	Malt beverages	30	41	44	52	59	70	83	94	213
2085	Distilled liquors	86	79	77	74	71	73	71	68	-21
2086	Soft drink bottling	14	14	15	17	20	21	22	23	64
2111	Cigarettes	99	99	99	100	100	NA	NA	NA	1
2121	Cigars	57	64	75	81	83	81	79	82	44
2221	Weaving mills	39	39	44	48	54	54	58	43	36
2311	Men's suits, coats	15	18	19	23	27	31	32	37	147
2396	Trimmings, automotive	NA	NA	NA	63	63	74	77	70	11
2621	Paper mills	NA	NA	NA	42	43	40	42	40	-5
2643	Paper bags	NA	NA	NA	36	38	41	40	38	6
2647	Sanitary paper goods	NA	NA	NA	76	79	82	84	81	7
2711	Newspapers	26	24	24	22	25	28	31	34	31
2822	Synthetic rubber	100	81	86	80	82	81	83	74	-26
2834	Pharmaceuticals	44	44	45	38	40	44	43	42	-5
2844	Toilet preparations	38	40	45	52	52	53	56	49	29
2911	Petroleum refining	59	56	55	56	57	56	53	48	-19
3011	Tires	NA	NA	NA	89	88	90	88	86	-3
3111	Leather tanning	39	28	30	30	31	28	28	31	-21
3221	Glass containers	79	78	75	72	75	76	75	73	-8
3291	Abrasives	56	58	68	67	47	60	65	71	27
3312	Steel mills	66	71	70	67	66	65	65	64	-9

3321	Iron foundries	24	34	33	37	36	45	44	37	54
3334	Aluminum	100	100	NA	NA	NA	92	93	88	-12
3411	Metal cans	86	86	89	85	84	79	74	68	-21
3494	Valves, fittings	32	27	27	23	23	21	21	21	-34
3511	Turbines, generators	NA	NA	NA	98	82	96	97	92	-6
3531	Construction machinery	NA	NA	NA	53	53	54	59	52	-2
3621	Motors and generators	66	59	56	59	60	59	55	50	-24
3633	Laundry appliances	65	85	90	95	95	98	NA	NA	51
3651	Radio and television receivers	NA	NA	NA	62	69	71	65	70	13
3674	Semiconductors	NA	NA	NA	65	66	70	62	57	-12
3694	Engine electrical	81	83	78	79	77	78	75	67	-17
3711	Motor vehicles, bodies	NA	NA	NA	NA	98	99	99	97	-1
3724	Aircraft engines	88	81	77	79	81	87	86	83	-6
3751	Motorcycles, bicycles	68	77	81	77	76	78	81	79	16
3811	Instruments	NA	NA	NA	40	38	33	37	43	8
3861	Photographic equipment	70	NA	74	76	81	85	86	86	23

Source: U.S. Department of Commerce, "Concentration Ratios in Manufacturing," 1982 *Census of Manufactures*.
Note: I am indebted to Rocki-Lee DeWitt for her assistance in compiling this table.

Concentration increased most substantially among the four and eight largest firms in the maturing U.S. bread and cake, confectionery product, malt beverage, tailored suit and coat, and laundry home-appliance industries. Concentration of shipments decreased most substantially among the four and eight largest firms in the U.S. valve and pipe-fitting, motor and generator, distilled liquor, aluminum, metal can, leather-tanning, petroleum-refining, fluid milk, and meat-packing industries, in part, due to entry by overseas firms. The proportion of industrywide shipments made by industries' largest four firms declined, also in part, due to the greater use of leveraged buyouts (by manager and investor groups) and spinoffs of unwanted plants (by diversified firms).

The Herfindahl-Hirschman indices in table 7–1 suggest that the greatest concentrations of 1982 shipments made by industries' fifty largest firms occurred in the mature turbine and power generator, cigarette, and malt beverage industries. The Herfindahl-Hirschman Index is calculated by summing the squares of the individual firm's market share ratios across the largest fifty companies (or the complete universe, whichever is lower) to a cumulative total. The index is used to predict when rationalizing and unifying acquisitions will be challenged by antitrust enforcement agencies. Strategic restructurings have not been permitted within industries where resulting Herfindahl-Hirschman indices would exceed scores of 1,000. Yet the longitudinal data regarding changes in concentration ratios suggest that policies prohibiting restructuring may not be realistic, especially in stagnant (or declining demand) industries where technical-efficiencies are also being pursued.

If customers deem it desirable to keep at least one local manufacturer of declining products in operation (to supply needed components for costly machinery, for example), changes in public policies regarding industry structure and market behavior may be necessary. In particular, anticompetitive costs due to rising concentration after production facilities have been rationalized must be weighed against expected benefits to customers that are gratified by obtaining continuing supplies of obsolescing products.

Cooperation and cartels. Results suggest that formal pooling or sourcing arrangements among producers that go far beyond tacit coordination are needed in endgame. Despite objections from some antitrust policymakers who view maturing and declining-demand industries in the same way they view competition in growing industries, cooperative strategies in mature industries are likely to yield the most efficient cost structures if managers are given necessary freedoms to sort through pooled assets and make necessary capacity retirements. It should be regarded as a positive development when managers use joint ventures to enable their firms to retrench and consolidate operations when industrywide demand for products slows. Cooperation allows managers to make more effective use of surviving facilities. As the examples of Honeywell-Bull-NEC in mainframe computers and Hercules and Montedison in polypropylene have suggested, the most effective use of strategic alliances in endgame industries has resulted in the retirement of less efficient facilities and stronger surviving entities.[2]

In the British case, industrywide capacity rationalizations were needed when demand for locally produced goods declined unexpectedly in the fibers, bulk steel, petrochemicals, and steel-castings industries. The British experience in textile cartels suggests that pointed government assistance is especially needed in coordinating cartel schemes to coax inefficient capacity out of mature industries. Studies of this problem have revealed that the most efficient producers tend to exit from endgames in industries *first,* leaving least efficient firms' assets in operation.[3]

Bower's conclusion in his 1986 study of European petrochemicals that there are too many countries in the European Economic Community[4] rings true because each sovereign nation wants its own "token" factory. The result of this policy is a hodgepodge of facilities that may not be of the most economic size. Moreover, the resulting patchwork quilt of plant locations is not likely to be conveniently located for cooperative schemes of coordination and efficient transshipment. Without the constraints of national borders and atomistic public policies, European managers could integrate forward to rationalize their firms' fragmented distribution systems, unify checkered sales territories, and lower operating costs. Managers could swap redundant facilities for those of competitors or take other steps to forge vertically integrated survivors that are well-suited to cope with the challenges of liberalized commerce within the Common Market in 1992 as well as global competition from outsiders.

Steel. In the Brussels steel-cartel scheme, which was created by EEC members in 1980 to end the subsidy races among national governments and controls 60 percent of the European steel industry's output, steel-making capacity was reduced by 31 million tons to 140 million tons—20 million tons of which were not utilized in 1988. Difficulties arose within the cartel scheme because some steel makers were more efficient than others, yet all were expected to contribute *equally* to capacity reductions. The rigid quota system penalized efficient steel producers, discouraged technological innovation, and perpetuated a fragmented industry structure where a rationalized (hence concentrated) industry of efficient survivors would better serve socioeconomic objectives. (Meanwhile, governments of several EEC member countries continued to pump money into failing local steel firms despite formal agreements to stop subsidies. Since the excess capacity crisis began in the late 1970s, over $40 billion in subsidies has been spent to stave off or absorb the social costs of European steel industry restructurings.)

Vertical integration. Modern interpretations of U.S. antitrust policy have often argued that vertical integration gives firms market power and results in increased industry concentration. This argument reflects a static and ethnocentric viewpoint. Results suggest that market power is intransitive and temporary. Vertical bargaining power, like market power, is also temporary.[5] Successful firms *adjust* their vertical-integration strategies to the mix of processing stages, degree of intrafirm transactions, and ways of organizing interrelated activities that are most suitable for competitive conditions. Because well-adjusted uses of vertical integration can give firms listening posts in several industries, it can make firms more competitive. Accelerated exchanges of information and improved coordination of resources through effective vertical-integration strategies can foster opportunities for more rapid technological changes and faster responses to changing customer preferences. Cross-subsidization of international networks of vertically integrated activities may be the only way that some firms can retain competitive standing against maverick competitors.

Firms need not own their suppliers or distributors if they possess bargaining power, and quasi-integrated relationships can provide sufficient vertical control for firms with market power.[6] But in slumping industries, firms find it especially difficult to extend their competitive strengths from one stage of processing to another, especially if downstream industries are more fragmented than upstream industries. Stagnating sales reduce upstream firms' bargaining power, rather than increase it. That is why firms seek to increase their degree of internal transfers when their market power diminishes in endgame.

Petroleum refining. Although the vertically integrated oil firms possessed the world's most efficient system for moving petroleum products, they were not allowed to use their expertise in the United States during the oil crisis of the 1970s. Instead, government policies that sought to preserve the survival of *all* refiners—regardless of their operating efficiency—created a crude oil allocation scheme that dramatically increased the costs borne by U.S. consumers.

Future Public-Policy Dilemmas

Managers are asked to produce growth in excess of growth in gross national product, but few industries in mature economies enjoy significantly increasing unit sales. Antitrust policies threaten to erode the rewards of endgame successes because if obsolete plants are not retired when excess capacity depresses industrywide price levels, surviving firms are robbed of profit margins that could be used to invest in new processes for making mature products more efficiently. Surviving firms also forgo funds for innovation in new lines of business when they are trapped in destructive price wars, thereby raising more public-policy issues that governments may wish to act on.

Short-term performance goals. Managers that want to face the risks of endgame competition need patient suppliers of capital. It is difficult for managers to do long-term strategic planning when strong-minded providers of capital can direct their attentions to short-term measures of performance. Investors have a right to seek high margins and profits, but they forget that the development of new businesses involves breakevens, on average, of seven years. Moreover, investments in new and rapidly growing industries are often risky. Venture capitalists that take equity in fledgling firms risk losing their investments.

How very different are the behaviors of takeover and turnaround artists— the new venture capitalists of the 1980s. Their pressures to satisfy short-term performance objectives cause managers to cut corners in ways that destroy their firms' investments in customer goodwill and market image.

Baby foods. In 1973 (during the baby-foods endgame), Squibb sold its nearly bankrupt Beech-Nut Foods subsidiary to a lawyer-entrepreneur in a leveraged buyout. From 1973 to 1977, demand for baby foods did not stop falling and rival firms, Gerber Products and H.J. Heinz, were locked in a vicious baby-food price war that destroyed industrywide profit margins. As Beech-Nut managers were turning around their baby-foods business by differentiating their brand as being the one containing no artificial ingredients, they began buying inexpensive apple concentrate from a new supplier. Despite protests from their R&D scientists that their supplier's cheap apple concentrate was adulterated, Beech-Nut managers continued to purchase raw materials that were later found to be largely synthetic because the troubled firm could not afford to dismiss its low-priced supplier. Even after the Food and Drug Administration warned Beech-Nut managers that samples of its apple juice were adulterated, its managers continued to sell baby apple juice at deep discounts until Beech-Nut and its top managers were indicted for fraud in 1986.

Eroding capital base. Although returns on investment (long-term debt and equity) rose in 1987 after fifteen years of decline, the profitability of U.S. manufacturing businesses (as measured by returns on capital assets) was not yet high enough in 1988 for corporate managers to support major rounds of factory modernization. Even after all of the investments in plant closings, layoffs, wage reductions, working-practice concessions, and other cost-cutting measures that restructured many U.S. industries during the 1980s, paybacks were not high enough for beleaguered managers to justify further investments in much-needed factory modernizations when using financial performance criteria based on current "value-based" thinking about allocative efficiency.

Loss of manufacturing base. The short-term orientations of many U.S. providers of capital makes investments in long-term competitiveness undertaken by firms that seek to become the "last iceman" of their industry seem riskier than taking actions that promise less-risky, short-term payoffs. Thus, abdicating (by selling assets employed in industries facing endgame) is valued *more highly* than making investments that promise longer-term payoffs but will ultimately improve firms' capabilities for delivering customized products of better quality to customers faster.

Biases in favor of short-term paybacks inevitably lead to losses of the know-how needed to innovate next-generation products. Failure to develop new skills internally prevents firms from replenishing their abilities to create value for customers.[e] Although acquiring businesses (or licenses and products) from outsiders seems less risky to investors than growing them from within, firms that lose their problem-solving edge are ripe for losing their manufacturing base, as well. Skills (like the ability to operate sewing machines) are being lost forever when lower-wage overseas workers are more efficient to use than investments in capital assets.

Changing work force. The blue-collar worker is entering endgame in industrialized economies. Managers are creating jobs for technicians, professionals, specialists, and more managers as their firms create new jobs that require more training—often formal degrees in technical fields. Managers are not creating as many of the jobs that unionized laborers can readily fill as they are destroying. The loss of blue-collar jobs follows the loss of labor-intensive industries to overseas competitors, and it leaves governments of industrialized nations with militant unemployed (or soon-to-be-redundant) populations that need significant retrofitting to fit the jobs that managers have created. European firms have found the retrofitting especially difficult to achieve. Skilled workers, especially technicians, have been in short supply due to welfare systems that sap worker incentives. European compulsory military service, lack of university space, and courses ill adapted to work-place needs have also been blamed for shortages of skilled workers.

International commerce. Problems of excess capacity can escalate beyond the competitive arena and into the political arena where governments use international commerce as a tool of domestic economic development. As each newly industrializing economy develops its own plants to make chemicals, steel, and other basic products, the problem of international excess capacity is exacerbated. This occurs because demand within industrializing countries is initially insufficient to absorb the full outputs of economic-sized plants that operate

---

[e]As chapter 5 has noted, *value creation* refers to ways of adding value to products sold to customers by customizing product configurations, providing design and/or marketing services, improving delivery services through *kanban* relationships, and other ways of offering more to customers. Proponents of "value-based planning," however, see the "value" of businesses as being the value of its expected future cash flows discounted back to their present value using the business's cost of capital as the discount rate. They believe that business decisions create value as long as the returns from business activities exceed their costs of capital. For more information see W. Kiechel III, 1988, "Corporate Strategy for the 1990s," *Fortune,* February 29:34–42.

near engineered capacity—especially if the physical assets employed are of newest vintages. (New technologies often feature larger minimum efficient scales—and higher breakeven volumes—than older generations of productive assets.)

Managers of multinational firms are likely to be whipsawed by conflicting loyalties—to nations and to the well-being of their firms. This conflict is inevitable because of firms' needs for activities and suppliers that are increasingly global. Few firms can afford to limit their activities to single countries any longer while also hoping to fend off international competitors successfully. Yet global firms are enjoying fewer choices about their global make-or-buy decisions. Components that were formerly imported must now be purchased locally (or offsetting purchases of local goods are required to aid local development objectives). The problems of strategic flexibility are especially acute in mature industries where local governments impose offsetting purchases and co-production requirements while competitive realities call for global sourcing policies.

Similar difficulties are emerging downstream. Many foreign direct investments made by multinational firms within newly industrializing nations take the form of joint ventures with competitors. This arrangement is intended to avoid creating capacity in excess of volumes that can be sold locally or in neighboring countries. By contrast, governments that seek foreign currency for their socioeconomic programs encourage exporting ventures. Neither extreme is best for firms with global outlooks that must utilize a system of well-coordinated transshipments. Global strategies work only so long as trade barriers are not overly restrictive and trade incentives are not skewed to produce short-sighted results at the cost of domestic welfare.

In Hong Kong, managers paid redundant Chinese laborers $5 per day to live in company-provided houses until their firms again needed these trained employees. As this example suggests, some governments have traded their peoples' current living standards for the promise of future rewards for so long that trade balances have become unduly skewed. Other governments have been lax in pushing their people to become more productive, thereby justifying tolerance of worker demands by citing studies that found employees in workaholic nations suffered problems from rising alcoholism, emotional breakdowns, suicide, broken marriages, and lack of physical fitness.

Changing cultural values. Pursuit of global strategies assumes that customers' wants and needs are similar enough across national borders that some product configurations can be standardized to realize scale and experience curve economies. Global strategies also assume that working practices can be standardized among interchangeable operating centers located at geographically diverse, cost-effective sites. As the example of Ford's British automotive employees suggests, standardization of working practices and managerial operating systems assumes that employee values in diverse operating sites are similar enough that the same procedures can be used across the globe. Inflexible human resources prevent managers from realizing the benefits of continual improvements in managerial operating systems, especially if the working practices violate cultural values of the work force.

Summary

Market maturity and excess capacity are inevitable problems that governments of industrialized nations and managers of firms operating within them must confront. Managers must generate proactive solutions to the need for industry restructuring to minimize the pain imposed by redeploying human and capital assets. Governments must ensure that their own short-sighted policies do not obstruct managers' programs for achieving allocative, technical, and operating efficiency.

When managers confront the strategic challenge of endgame, they must acknowledge that some businesses will be less profitable than others (even if their firms hold leading market shares) because competitive differentials have faded and will be revived with difficulty. When governments confront the challenge of endgame, they must acknowledge that some nations' living standards are being sacrificed for capital formation while others rise. Managers pursue allocative-efficiency objectives by withholding funds from unpromising lines of business and unpromising plant sites. Activities must be competitive if they are to be continued. Governments must justify their policies regarding mature businesses using similar, well-understood criteria.

Notes

1. See K.R. Harrigan, 1980, *Strategies for Declining Businesses,* Lexington, Mass.: Lexington Books, chapters 7–8, pp. 202–228, 247–271.

2. See K.R. Harrigan, 1985, *Strategies for Joint Ventures,* Lexington, Mass.: Lexington Books, chapters 11 and 16.

3. See C.W.F. Baden Fuller (ed.), 1988, *Management of Excess Capacity in the European Environment,* London: Basil Blackwell, especially the following articles: C.W.F. Baden Fuller, "Corporate and Industry Factors Influencing Closure Decisions"; C.W.F. Baden Fuller, "Cartels, Government Intervention, and Firm Decision Making in Declining European Industries"; P. Bianchi and G. Volpato, "Excess Capacity from Rigidity to Flexibility: The Case of the Automobile Industry"; J.L. Bower, "The Management Challenge to Restructuring Industry"; H. Daems, "Industry and Country Exit: Reflections on Country Differences"; F. Forutan, "Rationalization Schemes and the European Steel Industry"; P. Ghemawat and B. Nalebuff, "Excess Capacity, Efficiency, and Industrial Policy"; P. Ghemawat and B. Nalebuff, "The Devolution of Declining Industries"; R.M. Grant, "Capacity Adjustment through the Market Mechanism:

Exit and Rationalization in the British Cutlery Industry, 1974–1984"; P. Lorange and R.T. Nelson, "Organizational Momentum: Key to Long-Term Strategic Success"; and R. Shaw and P. Simpson, "Rationalization within an International Oligopoly: The Case of the West European Synthetic Fibres Industry."

4. J.L. Bower, 1986, *When Markets Quake: The Management Challenge of Restructuring Industry,* Boston: Harvard Business School Press.

5. See K.R. Harrigan, 1983, *Strategies for Vertical Integration,* Lexington, Mass.: Lexington Books, chapters 4–8, and 13.

6. See K.J. Blois, 1972, "Vertical Quasi-Integration," *Journal of Industrial Economics,* vol. 20, no. 4, July:253–272; K.J. Blois, 1975, "Supply Contracts in the Galbraithian Planning System," *Journal of Industrial Economics,* vol. 24, no. 1, September:29–39; J. D'Cruz, 1979, "Quasi Integration in Raw Materials Markets: The Overseas Procurement of Coking Coal," Unpublished doctoral dissertation, Harvard Business School; K.J. Blois, 1980, "Quasi-Integration as a Mechanism for Controlling External Dependencies," *Management Decision* (UK), vol. 18, no. 1:55–63; D.J. Teece, 1980, "Economies of Scope and the Scope of the Enterprise," *Journal of Economic Behavior and Organization,* vol. 1:233–247; R. Eccles, 1981, "The Quasi Firm in the Construction Industry," *Journal of Economic Behavior and Organization,* vol. 2:00–00; K. Monteverde and D.J. Teece, 1982, "Appropriable Rents and Quasi Integration," *Journal of Law and Economics,* October; D.J. Teece, 1982, "Towards an Economic Theory of the Multiproduct Firm," *Journal of Economic Behavior and Organization,* vol. 3:39–63; K.R. Harrigan, 1983, *Strategies for Vertical Integration,* Lexington, Mass.: Lexington Books; J.A. Stuckey, 1983, *Vertical Integration and Joint Ventures in the Aluminum Industry,* Cambridge, Mass.: Harvard University Press; K.R. Harrigan, 1986, "Quick Change Strategies for Vertical Integration," *Planning Review,* vol. 14, no. 5, September:32–37; D.J. Teece, 1986, "Firm Boundaries, Technological Innovation, and Strategic Management," in L.G. Thomas III (ed.), *Economics of Strategic Planning,* Lexington, Mass.: Lexington Books; H.B. Thorelli, 1986, "Networks: Between Markets and Hierarchies," *Strategic Management Journal,* vol. 7:37–51.

Bibliography

Abernathy, W.J., Clark, K., and Kantrow, A. 1983. *Industrial Renaissance: Producing a Competitive Future for America*. New York: Basic Books.

Adams, F.G., and Klein, L.R. (eds.). 1983. *1983 Industrial Policies for Growth and Competitiveness*. Lexington, Mass.: Lexington Books.

Adams, W.J., and Stoffaes, C. (eds.). 1986. *French Industrial Policy*. Washington, D.C.: The Brookings Institution.

Alexander, R.S. 1964. "The Death and Burial of 'Sick' Products," *Journal of Marketing*. 28:1–7.

"American Divestment: Back to Basics." 1981. *The Economist*. May 2:74.

Ariga, M. 1973. *International Conference on International Economy and Competition Policy*. Tokyo: Japanese Institute of International Business.

"Asset Redeployment, Everything Is for Sale Now." 1981. *Business Week*. August 24:68–74.

Baden Fuller, C. 1984. "Industry Strategies for Alleviating Excess Capacity: The Case of the Lazard Scheme for UK Steel Castings." Working paper, London School of Business.

———. 1988. "Cartels, Government Intervention and Firm Decision Making in Declining European Industries." In C. Baden Fuller (ed.), *Management of Excess Capacity in the European Environment*. London: Basil Blackwell.

——— (ed.), 1988. *Management of Excess Capacity in the European Environment*. London: Basil Blackwell.

Bhagwati, J.N. (ed.). 1982. *Import Competition and Response*. Washington, D.C.: National Bureau of Economic Research.

Baumol, W.J., and McLennan, K. (eds.). 1985. *Productivity Growth and U.S. Competitiveness*. New York: Oxford University Press.

Berenson, C. 1963. "Pruning the Product Line," *Business Horizons*. 6:63–70.

Bettauer, A. 1967. "A Strategy for Divestments," *Harvard Business Review*. March–April:116–124.

Bianchi, P., and Volpato, G. 1986. "Excess Capacity from Rigidity to Flexibility: The Case of the Automobile Industry." In C. Baden Fuller (ed.), *Management of Excess Capacity in the European Environment*. London: Basil Blackwell.

Bing, G. 1978. *Corporate Divestment*. Houston: Gulf.

Biteman, J.H. 1979. "Turnaround Management: An Exploratory Study of Rapid, Total Organizational Change." Unpublished doctoral dissertation, Harvard Business School.

Bock, B. 1977. "The Lizzie Borden Solution," *Across the Board.* 14(3):46–53.

Boddewyn, J.J., and Torneden, R. 1973. "U.S. Foreign Divestment: A Preliminary Survey," *Columbia Journal of World Business.* Summer:25–29.

Bower, J.L. 1986. *When Markets Quake: The Management Challenge of Restructuring Industry.* Boston: Harvard Business School Press.

———. 1986. "The Management Challenge to Restructuring Industry." In C. Baden Fuller (ed.), *Management of Excess Capacity in the European Environment.* London: Basil Blackwell.

Browne, L.E. 1985. "Structural Change and Dislocated Workers," *New England Economic Review.* January–February.

Burch, J.G., Jr., Strater, F.R., and Grudnitski, G., 1979. *Information Systems: Theory and Practice.* New York: John Wiley.

Bylinsky, G. 1983. "The Race to the Automatic Factory," *Fortune.* February:21, 52–64.

Cable, V., and Weale, M. 1983. "Economic Costs of Sectoral Protection in Britain," *The World Economy* 6(4), December.

Caves, R.E., and Porter, M.E. 1976. "Barriers to Exit." In R.T. Masson and P.D. Qualls (eds.), *Essays on Industrial Organization.* Cambridge, Mass.: Ballinger.

Clark, K. 1987. "Investment in New Technology and Competitive Advantage." In D.J. Teece (ed.), 1987, *The Competitive Challenge: Strategies for Industrial Innovation and Renewal.* Cambridge, Mass.: Ballinger.

Cohen, S.S., Galbraith, J., and Zysman, J. 1982. "Rehabbing the Labyrinth: The Financial System and Industrial Policy in France." In S. Cohen and P.A. Gourevitch (eds.), 1982, *France in the Troubled World Economy.* London: Butterworth.

Cohen, S., and Gourevitch, P.A. (eds.). 1982. *France in the Troubled World Economy.* London: Butterworth.

Cohen, S.S., and Zysman, J. 1987. *Manufacturing Matters: The Myth of the Post Industrial Society.* New York: Basic Books.

Cooper, A.C., and Schendel, D. 1976. "Strategic Responses to Technological Threats," *Business Horizons.* February:61–69.

Crosby, P.B. 1979. *Quality Is Free: The Art of Making Quality Certain.* New York: Mentor.

Daems, H. 1986. "Industry and Country Exit: Reflections on Country Differences." Draft outline.

Davenport, M. 1983. "Industrial Policy in the United Kingdom." In F.G. Adams and L.R. Klein (eds.), 1983, *Industrial Policies for Growth and Competitiveness.* Lexington, Mass.: Lexington Books.

Davis, J.W. 1974. "The Strategic Divestment Decision," *Long Range Planning.* February.

Davis, L. 1965. "Corporate Separations," *The Journal of Accountancy.* September: 35–42.

Deming, W.E. 1982. *Out of the Crisis.* Cambridge, Mass.: MIT, Center for Advanced Engineering Study.

Dore, R. 1986. *Flexible Rigidities: Industrial Policies and Structural Adjustment in the Japanese Economy 1970–1980.* Stanford, Calif.: Stanford University Press.

Doz, Y.L. 1978. "Managing Manufacturing Rationalization within Multinational Companies," *The Columbia Journal of World Business.* Fall 13(3):82–94.

———. 1980. "Strategic Management in Multinational Companies," *Sloan Management Review.* 21(2):27–46.

———. 1985. *Strategic Management in Multinational Companies.* Oxford: Pergamon Press.

———. 1987. "International Industries: Fragmentation versus Globalization." In B.R. Guile and H. Brooks (eds.), 1987, *Technology and Global Industry: Companies and Nations in the World Economy,* Washington, D.C.: National Academy Press, 96–118.

Drucker, P.F. 1980. *Managing in Turbulent Times.* New York: Harper & Row.

Duhaime, I.M. 1981. "Influences on the Divestment Decisions of Large Diversified Firms." Unpublished doctoral dissertation, University of Pittsburgh.

Duhaime, I.M., and Grant, J.H. 1984. "Factors Influencing Divestment Decision-Making: Evidence from a Field Study," *Strategic Management Journal.* 5(4): 301–318.

Duhaime, I.M., and Schwenk, C.R. 1985. "Conjectures on Cognitive Simplification in Acquisition and Divestment Decision Making, *Academy of Management Review.* 10(2):287–295.

Duncan, N.E. 1986. "U.S. Industry: Restructuring? Yes. Declining? No," Staff Memo: Shell Oil Inc., Houston, July.

Dymsza, W.A. 1972. *Multinational Business Strategy.* New York: McGraw-Hill.

Eads, G.C. 1987. "Government Policy Towards Industry." Manuscript prepared for H. Patrick (ed.), 1987, *Workshop on the Political Economy of Adjustment in Troubled Industries,* Columbia University, May 1.

Easton, A. 1976. *Managing for Negative Growth: A Handbook for Practitioners.* Reston, Va.: Reston.

Fierman, J. 1986. "How to Make Money in Mature Markets," *Fortune.* November 25:46–53.

Flaherty, M.T. 1987. "Coordinating International Manufacturing and Technology." In M.E. Porter (ed.), 1987, *Competition in Global Industries.* Boston: Harvard Business School Press.

Ford, J.D. 1980. "The Administrative Component in Growing and Declining Industry: A Longitudinal Analysis," *Academy of Management Journal.* 23(4):615–630.

Foroutan, F. 1986. "Rationalization Schemes and the European Steel Industry." In C. Baden Fuller (ed.), 1986, *Management of Excess Capacity in the European Environment.* London: Basil Blackwell.

Franko, L.G. 1971. "Joint Venture Divorce in the Multinational Company," *Columbia Journal of World Business.* May–June:13–22.

———. 1971. *Joint Venture Survival in Multinational Corporations.* New York: Praeger.

Freeman, J., and Hannan, M.T., 1975. "Growth and Decline Processes in Organizations," *American Sociological Review.* 40:215–228.

Geneen, H.S. 1984. "The Strategy of Diversification." In R. Lamb, 1984, *Competitive Strategic Management.* Englewood Cliffs, N.J.: Prentice-Hall.

Ghemawat, P., and Nalebuff, B. 1988. "The Devolution of Declining Industries." In C. Baden Fuller (ed.), 1988, *Management of Excess Capacity in the European Environment.* London: Basil Blackwell.

———. 1988. "Excess Capacity, Efficiency, and Industrial Policy." In C. Baden Fuller (ed.), 1988, *Management of Excess Capacity in the European Environment.* London: Basil Blackwell.

Gilmour, S.C. 1973. "The Divestment Decision Process." Unpublished doctoral dissertation, Harvard University.

Gluck, F. 1983. "Global Competition in the 1980s," *Journal of Business Strategy*. Spring, 3(4):22–27.

Hall, W.K. 1980. "Survival Strategies in a Hostile Environment," *Harvard Business Review*. 58(5):75–85.

Hambrick, D.C., and Schecter, S.M. 1983. "Turnaround Strategies for Mature Industrial-Product Businesses," *Academy of Management Journal*. 26(2):231–248.

Hamermesh, R.G. 1976. "The Corporate Response to Divisional Profit Crises." Unpublished doctoral dissertation, Harvard University.

Hannan, M.T., and Freeman, J.H. 1978. "Internal Politics of Growth and Decline." In Marshall (ed.), 1978, *Environments and Organizations*. San Francisco: Jossey-Bass.

Harrigan, K.R. 1979. "Strategies for Declining Businesses." Unpublished doctoral dissertation, Harvard University.

———. 1980. "The Effect of Exit Barriers upon Strategic Flexibility." *Strategic Management Journal*. 1(2):165–176.

———. 1980. "Strategies for Declining Businesses," *Journal of Business Strategy*. 1(2):20–34.

———. 1980. *Strategies for Declining Businesses*. Lexington, Mass.: Lexington Books.

———. 1980. "Strategy Formulation in Declining Industries," *Academy of Management Review*. 5(4):599–604.

———. 1981. "Deterrents to Divestiture," *Academy of Management Journal*. 24(2):306–323.

———. 1982. "Exit Decisions in Mature Industries," *Academy of Management Journal*. 25(4):707–732.

———. 1984. "Innovation within Overseas Subsidiaries,"*Journal of Business Strategy*. Spring, 5(1):47–55.

———. 1984. "Managing Declining Businesses," *Journal of Business Strategy*. 3(4):74–78.

———. 1984. "The Strategic Exit Decision: Additional Evidence." In R. Lamb, 1984, *Competitive Strategic Management*. Englewood Cliffs, N.J.: Prentice-Hall.

———. 1985. *Strategic Flexibility: A Management Guide for Changing Times*. Lexington, Mass.: Lexington Books.

———. 1986. "The Cost of Bailing Out," *Strategic Direction*. May:5–7.

———. 1986. "Strategic Approaches to Failing Businesses," *Strategic Direction*. April:5–7.

———. 1987. "Anticipating Crises: Recognizing and Acting to Resolve Business Problems." In F. Corno, 1987, *Prevenzione e Terapia della Crisi d'Impresa*. Valmadrera (Lecco), Italy: Centro Studi d'Impresa. Originally prepared for CIS Conference, May 15–16, 1987.

———. 1988. "Implementing Endgame Strategies for Declining Industries." In C. Baden Fuller (ed.), 1988, *Management of Excess Capacity in the European Environment*. London: Basil Blackwell.

———. 1988. *Managing Maturing Businesses*. Lexington, Mass.: Lexington Books.

Harrigan, K.R., and Porter, M.E. 1978. "A Framework for Looking at Endgame Strategies." Paper presented at the National Meetings of the Academy of Management, San Francisco.

———. 1986. "Endgame Strategies for Declining Industries." In *Harvard Business Review* (ed.), 1986, *Strategic Planning Comes of Age*. Boston: Harvard Business Review Press.

Hayes, R.H. 1969. "Optimal Strategies for Divestiture," *Operations Research*. March–April:292–310.

———. 1972. "New Emphasis on Divestment Opportunities," *Harvard Business Review*. July–August:55–64.

Hayes, R.H., and Wheelwright, S.C. 1984. *Restoring Our Competitive Edge: Competing through Manufacturing*. New York: Wiley.

Hilton, P. 1972. "Divestiture: The Strategic Move on the Corporate Chessboard," *Management Review*. March:16–19.

Hofer, C.W. 1980. "Turnaround Strategies," *Journal of Business Strategy*. 1(1):19–31.

Hopkins, D.S. 1977. "Business Strategies for Problem Products," *The Conference Board, Inc.* Report No. 714.

Hufbauer, G., and Elliot, K. 1987. "The Political Economy of Adjustment in Troubled Industries: The Role of Industrial and Trade Policies." Manuscript prepared for H. Patrick (ed.), 1987, *Workshop on the Political Economy of Adjustment in Troubled Industries,* Columbia University, May 1.

Hutchinson, A.C. 1971. "Planned Euthanasia for Old Products," *Long Range Planning*. December.

Jacques, L.L. 1986. "Oligopolistic Pricing and Asymmetric Currency Pass Through: Econometric Evidence from Japanese Exports." Unpublished manuscript, Philadelphia: Wharton School.

Johnson, C. 1982. *MITI and the Japanese Miracle*. Stanford, Calif.: Stanford University Press.

——— (ed.), 1984. *The Industrial Policy Debate*. San Francisco: Institute for Contemporary Studies.

Johnson, M.L. 1975. "End of the Line for Weak Products?," *Industry Week*. September:25–29.

———. 1976. "Pruning Products to Pad Profits," *Industry Week*. May 31:37–40.

Kantrow, A.M. 1983. "Political Realities of Industrial Policy," *Harvard Business Review*. 61(5):79–86.

Keegan, W.J. 1979. "The Future of the Multinational Manufacturing Corporation: Five Scenarios," *Journal of International Business Studies*. 10(1):98–104.

Kiechel, W., III. 1981. "Playing the Global Game," *Fortune*. November 16:111–126.

Kikkawa, M. 1983. "Shipbuilding, Motor Cars and Semiconductors: The Diminishing Role of Industrial Policy in Japan." In G. Shepherd (ed.), 1983, *Europe's Industries: Public and Private Strategies for Change*. London: Frances Pinter.

Kogut, B. 1984. "Normative Observations on the International Value-Added Chain and Strategic Groups," *Journal of International Business Studies*. Fall, 15(2): 151–167.

Kotler, P. 1965. "Phasing Out Weak Products," *Harvard Business Review*. March–April:107–118.

Kotler, P., and Fahey, L. 1982. "The World's Champion Marketers: The Japanese," *Journal of Business Strategy,* Summer, 3(1):3–13.

Krugman, P.R. 1983. "Targeted Industrial Policies: Theory and Evidence." In Federal Reserve Bank of Kansas City, 1983, *Industrial Change and Public Policy*. Kansas City: Federal Reserve Bank.

Krugman, P.R. (ed.). 1986. *Strategic Trade Policy and the New International Economics.* Cambridge, Mass.: MIT Press.

Labor-Industry Coalition for International Trade. 1983. *International Trade, Industrial Policies, and the Future of American Industry.* Washington, D.C.: Labor-Industry Coalition for International Trade.

Lawrence, P.R. 1987. "Competition: A Renewed Focus for Industrial Policy." In D.J. Teece (ed.), 1987, *The Competitive Challenge: Strategies for Industrial Innovation and Renewal.* Cambridge, Mass.: Ballinger.

Lawrence, R.Z. 1986. *Can America Compete?* Washington, D.C.: The Brookings Institution.

———. 1987. "Troubled Industries and Industrial Policies." Manuscript prepared for H. Patrick (ed.), 1987. *Workshop on the Political Economy of Adjustment in Troubled Industries,* Columbia University, May 1.

Leavitt, T. 1975. "Dinosaurs among the Bears and Bulls," *Harvard Business Review.* 53(1):41–53.

———. 1975. "Marketing Myopia," *Harvard Business Review.* 53(5) September–October:26 + .

Lehnerd, A.P. 1987. "Revitalizing the Manufacture and Design of Mature Global Products." In B.R. Guile and H. Brooks (eds.), 1987, *Technology and Global Industry: Companies and Nations in the World Economy.* Washington, D.C.: National Academy Press.

Leontiades, J.C. 1985. *Multinational Corporate Strategy: Planning for World Markets.* Lexington, Mass.: Lexington Books.

Lorange, P., and Nelson, R. 1986. "Managing Organizational Momentum: Managing Denial and Complacency Factors." In C. Baden Fuller (ed.), 1986, *Management of Excess Capacity in the European Environment.* London: Basil Blackwell.

Lovejoy, F. 1971. *Divestment for Profit.* New York: Financial Executives Research Foundation.

Lucas, H.C., Jr. 1973. *Computer Based Information Systems in Organizations.* Chicago: Science Research Associates.

———. 1974. *Toward Creative Systems Design.* New York: Columbia University Press.

———. 1975. *Why Information Systems Fail.* New York: Columbia University Press.

Magaziner, I.C., and Reich, R.B. 1982. "International Strategies." *Minding America's Business.* New York: Harcourt Brace Jovanovich.

Magiera, F.T., and Grunewald, A.E. 1978. "The Effect of Divestiture Motives on Shareholder Risk and Return." Paper at Western Finance Association Meeting, Kona, Hawaii.

Mascarenhas, B. 1984. "The Coordination of Manufacturing Interdependence in Multinational Companies." *Journal of International Business Studies.* Winter, 13(2):91–106.

Matthews, W., and Boucher, W.I. 1977. "Planned Entry–Planned Exit: A Concept and an Approach," *California Management Review.* 20(2):36–44.

Meeker, G.B. 1971. "Fade Out Joint Venture: Can It Work for Latin America?," *Inter-American Affairs.* 24:25–42.

Mehta, N.T. 1978. "Policy Formation in a Declining Industry: The Case of the Canadian Dissolving Pulp Industry." Unpublished doctoral dissertation, Harvard Business School.

Michael, G.C. 1971. "Product Petrification: A New Stage in the Life Cycle Theory," *California Mangement Review.* Fall:81–94.

Montgomery, C.A., Thomas, A.R., and Kamath, R. 1984. "Divestiture, Market Valuation, and Strategy," *Academy of Management Journal.* 27(4):830–840.

Morrison, J.R., and Neushcel, R. 1962. "The Second Squeeze on Profits," *Harvard Business Review.* July–August:49–66.

Nees, D. 1979. "The Divestment Decision Process in Large and Medium-Sized Companies: A Description," *International Studies of Management and Organizations.* Winter 78–79:35–67.

———. 1981. "Increase Your Divestment Effectiveness," *Strategic Management Journal.* 2(2):119–130.

Ohmae, K. 1985. *Triad Power: The Coming Shape of Global Competition.* New York: Free Press.

Patrick, H. 1987. *Japanese High Technology Industries: Lessons and Limitations of Industrial Policy.* Seattle: University of Washington Press.

———. 1987. "Reflections on U.S. Industrial Policy for Troubled Industries, in Light of Japanese Experience." Manuscript prepared for H. Patrick (ed.), 1987, *Workshop on the Political Economy of Adjustment in Troubled Industries,* Columbia University, May 1.

Patton, G.R., and Duhaime, I.M. 1978. "Divestment as a Strategic Option: An Empirical Study." Paper presented at the National Meetings of the Academy of Management, San Francisco.

Peck, M.J. 1987. "The Political Economy of Adjustment in Troubled Industries." Manuscript prepared for H. Patrick (ed.), 1987, *Workshop on the Political Economy of Adjustment in Troubled Industries,* Columbia University, May 1.

Pickering, J.F. 1978. "The Abandonment of Major Mergers in the UK, 1965–75," *Journal of Industrial Economics.* 27(2):123–131.

Pinder, J. (ed.). 1982. *National Industrial Strategies and the World Economy.* London: Allanheld, Osmun.

Porter, M.E. 1976. "Please Note Location of Nearest Exit: Exit Barriers, Strategy and Organizational Planning." *California Management Review.* 19(2):21–33.

———. 1987. *Changing Patterns of International Competition.* In D.J. Teece (ed.), 1987, *The Competitive Challenge: Strategies for Industrial Innovation and Renewal.* Cambridge, Mass.: Ballinger.

Porteus, E.L. 1977. "On Optimal Dividend, Reinvestment, and Liquidation Policies for the Firm," *Operations Research.* 25(5):818–834.

Predicasts. 1983. *Factory of the Future.* Cleveland: Predicasts.

Pugel, T.A. 1984. "Japan's Industrial Policy: Instruments, Trends, and Effects," *Journal of Comparative Economics.* December:420–435.

——— (ed.). *Fragile Interdependence: Economic Issues in U.S.-Japanese Trade and Investment.* Lexington, Mass.: Lexington Books.

Richards, M.D. 1973. "An Exploratory Study of Strategic Failure," *Academy of Management Proceedings.* August.

Robichek, A., and Van Horne, J.C. 1967. "Abandonment Value and Capital Budgeting," *Journal of Finance.* December:577–589.

Root, F.R. 1987. *Entry Strategies for International Markets.* Lexington, Mass.: Lexington Books.

Rothe, J.T. 1970. "The Product Elimination Decision," *MSU Business Topics.* 18:45–52.

Rugman, A.M. 1981. *Inside the Multinationals: The Economics of Internal Markets.* London: Croom Helm.

Salancik, G.R., Staw, B.M., and Pondy, L.R. 1980. "Administrative Turnover as a Response to Unmanaged Organizational Independence," *Academy of Management Journal.* 23(3):422–437.

Salverson, M.E. 1976. "Business Strategy: Pinning the Blame for Strategic Failures on the CEO," *Planning Review.* 4(5):1–7.

Schendel, D.E., Patten, R., and Riggs, J. 1975. "Corporate Turnaround Strategies." Working Paper 486, Krannert School.

Schwartz, K.B., and Menon, K. 1985. "Executive Succession in Failing Firms," *Academy of Management Journal.* 28(3):680–685.

Scott, B.R. and Lodge, G.C. (eds.). 1985. *U.S. Competitiveness in the World Economy.* Boston: Harvard Business School Press.

Shaw, R., and Simpson, P. 1986. "Rationalization within an International Oligopoly: The Case of the West European Synthetic Fibers Industry." In C. Baden Fuller (ed.), 1986, *Management of Excess Capacity in the European Environment.* London: Basil Blackwell.

Shillinglow, G. 1959. "Profit Analysis for Abandonment Decisions." In Ezra Solomon (ed.), 1959, *Management of Corporate Capital.* Glencoe, Ill.: Glencoe Press.

Siegel, S. 1966. "When Corporations Divide: A Statutory and Financial Analysis," *Harvard Law Review.* 79:534–570.

Skinner, W. 1985. *Manufacturing: The Formidable Competitive Weapon.* New York: Wiley.

Speiser, M.M. 1969. "Corporate Divestitures: How to Sell Off a Subsidiary," *Management Review.* April:2–8.

Starbuck, W.H., and Hedberg, B.L.T. 1977. "Saving an Organization from a Stagnating Environment." In H. Thorelli (ed.), 1977, *Strategy and Structure Performance.* Bloomington, Ind.: University of Indiana Press.

Stobaugh, R., and Telesio, P. 1983. "Match Manufacturing Policies and Product Strategy," *Harvard Business Review.* March–April, 61(2):113–120.

Talley, W.J., Jr. 1964. "Profiting from Declining Product," *Business Horizons.* 7:77–84.

Teece, D.J. 1976. *Vertical Integration and Vertical Divestiture in the U.S. Oil Industry.* Stanford, Calif.: Stanford University, Institute for Energy.

———. 1987. "Capturing Value from Technological Innovation: Integration, Strategic Partnering, and Licensing Decisions." In. B.R. Guile and H. Brooks (eds.), 1987, *Technology and Global Industry: Companies and Nations in the World Economy.* Washington, D.C.: National Academy Press.

———. 1987. *The Competitive Challenge: Strategies for Industrial Innovation and Renewal.* Cambridge, Mass.: Ballinger.

Thackray, J. 1972. "Spin-Off—A New Lease on Corporate Life," *European Business.* Winter.

———. 1976. "Disinvestment: How to Shrink and Profit," *European Business.* Spring.

Thurow, L. 1985. "The Case for Industrial Policies in America." In T. Shishido and R. Sato (eds.), 1985, *Economic Policy and Development: New Perspectives.* Dover, Mass.: Auburn.

Torredon, R.L., and Boddewyn, J.J. 1974. "Foreign Divestments: Too Many Mistakes," *Columbia Journal of World Business*. Fall:87–94.

Trezise, P.H. 1983. "Industrial Policy Is Not the Major Reason for Japan's Success," *The Brookings Review*. 1(3):13–18.

"Trustbusting in Japan: Cartels and Government-Business Cooperation," *Harvard Law Review*. 94:1064.

Tsuruta, T. 1983. "A Criticism of Cartels in Ailing Industries," *Economic Eye*. June: 7–9.

Tyson, L., and Zysman, J. (eds.). 1983. *American Industry in International Competition*. Ithaca, N.Y.: Cornell University Press.

United States Department of Commerce, 1983. *Japan Industrial Policies and the Development of High Technology Industries: Computers and Aircraft*. Washington, D.C.: Department of Commerce.

United States Congress. 1983. *Industrial Policy, Economic Growth and the Competitiveness of U.S. Industry*. Hearings before the Joint Economic Committee, June 1983. Washington, D.C.: U.S. Government Printing Office.

———. 1986. *Impact of Trade Policy on the American Worker*. Hearing before the Committee on Government Operations, House of Representatives, October 3, 1985. Washington, D.C.: U.S. Government Printing Office.

Uttal, B. 1987. "Speeding New Ideas to Market," *Fortune*. March 2:62–66.

Utterback, J.M. 1987. "Innovation and Industrial Evolution in Manufacturing Industries." In B.R. Guile and H. Brooks (eds.), 1987, *Technology and Global Industry: Companies and Nations in the World Economy*. Washington, D.C.: National Academy Press.

Vernon, R. 1979. *The Product Cycle Hypothesis in a New International Environment*. Oxford Bulletin of Economics and Statistics. November, 41(4):255–267.

Vignola, L. 1974. *Strategic Divestment*. New York: AMACOM.

Wallender, H. 1973. "A Planned Approach to Divestment," *Columbia Journal of World Business*. Spring:33–37.

Walters, P.G.P. 1986. "International Marketing Policy: A Discussion of the Standardization Construct and its Relevance for Corporate Policy." *Journal of International Business Studies*. Summer, 17(2):55–69.

Wasson, C.R. 1974. *Dynamic Competitive Strategy and Product Life Cycles*. St. Charles, Ill.: Challenge Books.

Wheelwright, S.C. 1987. "Restoring Competitiveness in U.S. Manufacturing." In D.J. Teece (ed.), 1987, *The Competitive Challenge: Strategies for Industrial Innovation and Renewal*. Cambridge, Mass.: Ballinger.

Whitney, J.O. 1987. *Taking Charge: Management Guide to Troubled Companies and Turnarounds*. Homewood, Ill.: Dow Jones-Irwin.

Wilks, S., and Wright, M. (eds.). 1987. *Comparative Government-Industry Relations: Western Europe, the United States, and Japan*. Oxford: Oxford University Press.

Willoughby, J. 1987. "Endgame Strategy," *Forbes*. July 13:181–182.

———. 1987. "The Last Iceman," *Forbes*. July 13:183–204.

———. 1987. "Leaning against the Wind," *Forbes*. July 13:206–210.

Wilson, B.D. 1979. "The Disinvestment of Foreign Subsidiaries by US Multinational Companies." Unpublished doctoral dissertation, Harvard Business School.

Winter, S.G. 1987. "Knowledge and Competence as Strategic Assets." In D.J. Teece (ed.), 1987, *The Competitive Challenge: Strategies for Industrial Innovation and Renewal*. Cambridge, Mass.: Ballinger.

Yamamura, K. 1982. "Success That Soured: Administrative Guidance and Cartels in Japan." In K. Yamamura (ed.), 1982, *Policy and Trade Issues of the Japanese Economy: American and Japanese Perspectives*. Seattle: University of Washington Press.

Young, M. 1986. "Comment on Japanese Antitrust Policy Formulation and Development." In T. Pugel (ed.), 1986, *Fragile Interdependence: Economic Issues in U.S.-Japanese Trade and Investment*. Lexington, Mass.: Lexington Books.

Zysman, J. 1983. *Governments, Markets and Growth: Financial Systems and the Politics of Industrial Change*. Ithaca, N.Y.: Cornell University Press.

Index

Page numbers followed by n indicate material in footnotes.

About the Author

Kathryn Rudie Harrigan (D.B.A., Harvard; M.B.A., Texas; B.A., Macalester) is professor of strategic management and director of the Strategy Research Center at Columbia University in New York City. Her research interests include industry restructuring, mature (and declining) businesses, strategic alliances, internal venturing, diversification, turnaround strategies, make-or-buy strategy, industry and competitor analysis, global strategies, and strategic planning. Her books include three research studies—*Strategies for Declining Businesses* (1980), *Strategies for Vertical Integration* (1983), and *Strategies for Joint Ventures* (1985)—and two managerial books—*Strategic Flexibility: A Management Guide for Changing Times* (1985) and *Managing for Joint Venture Success* (1986), all published by Lexington Books.

In 1980, Professor Harrigan received the General Electric Award for Outstanding Research in Strategic Management (presented by the Business Policy and Planning Division of the National Academy of Management) for her research on declining businesses, and their Best Paper Award in 1983 for her research on vertical integration (or make-or-buy decisions). She also received the Columbia Business School's Schoenheimer Award for Research Excellence in 1986 for her research on strategic alliances, an IBM Research Fellowship in Business Administration, and a Division of Research Fellowship from Harvard Business School (during her doctoral studies), and she received the Dean's Excellence Award and Texas Competitive Scholarship from the University of Texas at Austin (during her M.B.A. studies).

Professor Harrigan is a founding member of the Strategic Management Society and appears on their international programs. She served as their Corporate Strategy track chairperson in 1987 and Rationalization/Restructuring track chairperson in 1988. She has taught in several executive development programs for Columbia Business School, for Management Centre Europe (London), for Frost & Sullivan (London and Frankfurt), and *Business Week* Executive Programs (Amsterdam and several U.S. cities). Professor Harrigan has been a featured speaker at the Oslo Marketing Symposium (Norway), Top Management Center (Belgium), the St. Gallen International Management

Symposium (Switzerland), Centro Studi d'Impresa (Valmadrera), the Planning Forum's annual meetings, the Conference Board's annual conference on corporate strategy (New York), and several in-house programs on competitive strategy. Her clients include firms located in Europe and Australia, as well as the United States, seeking help on strategic alliances, internal ventures, synergies from make-or-buy (or interbusiness unit) relationships, and mature (or declining) industries. She has also been an entrepreneur; Professor Harrigan has founded and managed four ventures, including the North Suburban Young People's Theatre in Minneapolis.

Professor Harrigan has served on the board of governors of the Academy of Management and the advisory board of Ronin Development Corporation. She writes for and is consulting editor of the *Academy of Management Review* and serves on the board of editors of the *Strategic Management Journal*. She has served on the editorial boards of and contributes to the *Academy of Management Journal*, the *Columbia Journal of World Business, Academy of Management Executives,* and the *Journal of Business Strategy.* She also contributes to *Harvard Business Review, Issues: The Journal for Management,* the *Euro-Asia Business Review, Management International Review, Long Range Planning, Management Review, Planning Review, Strategic Direction, Working Woman,* the *Boardroom Reports,* and the *Best Paper Proceedings* of the National and Regional Meetings of the Academy of Management in the United States.